PREJUDICE

Japanese-Americans:
Symbol of Racial Intolerance

BOOKS BY
CAREY McWILLIAMS

Factories in the Field

Ill Fares the Land

Brothers Under the Skin

Prejudice
Japanese-Americans: Symbol of Racial Intolerance

PREJUDICE

Japanese-Americans:
Symbol of Racial Intolerance

by

CAREY McWILLIAMS

Of all the vulgar modes of escaping from the consideration of the effect of social and moral influences on the human mind, the most vulgar is that of attributing the diversities of conduct and character to inherent natural differences.

— J. S. MILL

LITTLE, BROWN AND COMPANY · BOSTON

1944

FIRST EDITION

Published October 1944

Dedicated
to
IRIS McWILLIAMS

Acknowledgments

In preparing this volume, I have become indebted to a number of individuals for invaluable and generous assistance which they have provided. I should like, first of all, to acknowledge my indebtedness to the staff of the War Relocation Authority, both in the Washington office and in the various relocation centers. Likewise, I am deeply indebted to the Reverend Fred Fertig and to Miss Emily Lehan, both of Los Angeles, for such generously offered help and assistance. Dr. Jesse Steiner, Dr. Bruno Lasker, Dr. Kenneth Scott Latourette, Dr. John Rademaker, Mr. John Collier, and Mr. George LaFrabraque have also been most helpful. I am greatly indebted to many Nisei friends who have sent me letters, documents, and clippings. Since they number over a hundred individuals, I find it impossible to list their names. Finally, as always, I owe a great debt to my friend Ross Wills for his brutal comments, caustic observations, and vigorous criticism. Needless to say, none of these individuals is in any manner responsible for any statement of fact or opinion in this volume.

This study was prepared at the request of the American Council of the Institute of Pacific Relations and was made possible by grants from the Institute and a fellowship which I received from the John Simon Guggenheim Foundation. Although this book is issued under the auspices of the Institute, the author alone is responsible for statements of fact and opinion contained in it. A short article entitled "The Nisei in Japan," taken from this book, appeared in *Far Eastern Survey* for April 19, 1944.

I have not included a bibliography for the reason that adequate bibliographies, both on the relocation program and on the West Coast Japanese, have been prepared in mimeographed form by the War Relocation Authority and can be obtained upon request.

C. McW.

Contents

Contents

PREJUDICE

Japanese-Americans: Symbol of Racial Intolerance

Introduction

IN THE spring of 1942, the government of the United States placed approximately 100,000 men, women, and children of Japanese ancestry, residing on the West Coast, in protective custody. Two thirds of these people were citizens of the United States. Within three months after evacuation had been decreed, the entire group had been lodged in assembly centers, under military guard, awaiting removal from the area. In the excitement of these months, the evacuation of the Japanese seemed merely a minor incident of the war. But as we proceeded with their removal, and as we got used to the idea of being at war, the nation began to focus a measure of its attention upon this seemingly insignificant "episode." It was really *after* these people had been placed in protective custody that the nation began to be interested in them. In part, the growing national interest in the problem itself is to be accounted for in terms of a rather extraordinary occurrence, the significance of which is not yet fully appreciated.

For after evacuation had been effected, the nation noted, rather to its amazement, that agitation against persons of Japanese ancestry on the West Coast noticeably increased. Instead of total mass evacuation resulting in a measure of greater calm and a more vigorous concentration on the war, the opposite happened. What had been a small flame of race prejudice became a raging fire. Agitation on the West Coast for the removal of the Japanese was as nothing compared to the agitation that developed, after their removal, to prevent their return. As the danger of an invasion of the West Coast receded, measures were taken against this minority which no one had advocated prior to their removal. Internment, for example, had not been originally contemplated by the authorities; yet internment was ordered. Evacuation was seized upon as ostensible justification for still more drastic measures, some of which were clearly acts of reprisal, savoring of vengeance and vindictiveness. Already prejudiced persons construed the government's action in ordering removal as an implied endorsement of their views and as vindication of their suspicions. As the government proceeded with the removal program, each step began to involve increasingly important, and in some cases perhaps irreversible, consequences — consequences which were never originally contemplated or anticipated.

Why were these people removed from the West Coast?

How does it happen that their removal has stimulated further aggressions against them?

What effect has their removal had upon the racial mores of the West Coast?

Just what is back of the current renewal of agitation against this particular minority on the West Coast?

What has happened to these 100,000 men, women, and children?

Are the measures which have been taken against them actually related to the reasons which were advanced for their removal?

Just what implications are involved in the mass evacuation of this minority in response to West Coast pressure?

These questions raise basic and urgent issues of national importance. The welfare of the evacuees themselves actually becomes of minor importance when measured against these larger issues. A precedent of the gravest possible significance has been established in ordering the removal and internment of this one racial minority. This precedent has been established not by a locality or state or region, but by the government of the United States. That the federal government was pressured, or perhaps more accurately "stampeded," into the adoption of this unfortunate precedent by the noisy clamor of certain individuals, groups, and organizations in the three West Coast states does not minimize the seriousness of the precedent itself. For perhaps the first time in our national history, the federal government has singled out for particularly harsh treatment a section of our population and has based the discrimination solely on racial grounds

4

(more accurately, perhaps, on the grounds of ancestry). "It is doubtful," writes Dr. Robert Redfield, "if any deprivation of civil rights so sweeping and categoric as this has ever been performed under the war powers and justified by our courts." The very core of the problem, as he points out, "lies in the fact that the evacuation and confinement were done on a racial basis." War makes for harsh measures; but, unfortunately, we cannot justify the evacuation of the West Coast Japanese even as a war measure.

For we are at war with Germany and we were at war with Italy. No such measure was taken against German or Italian nationals, either on the West Coast or elsewhere. Citizens of Japanese ancestry have been subjected to measures which were deemed unnecessary even in the case of German and Italian nationals; and these measures have been imposed without charges, hearings, or due process of law. That German and Italian aliens belong to the same racial stock as a majority of the people of this country would merely indicate, on its face, that they occupied a better position to commit acts of sabotage or espionage than did either aliens or citizens of Japanese ancestry. The consequences of this precedent are not merely national in scope, for the real consequences, as Dr. Redfield has noted, "lie in the effects of what we have done on the conduct of the war and on the making of a world after the war." These consequences lie outside the United States — in Asia, in the Pacific, throughout the vast area around the rim of the Pacific Basin where a new world is emerging from this war.

Our relations with this small group of 70,000 American citizens may well prove to be the key to the complex problem of our relations with the peoples of a postwar Japan as well as with the other peoples of the Far East. Most of the issues of the war, in fact, are bound up in the ten relocation centers which we have established from California to Arkansas, in which most of the evacuees are to be found today. By the same token, the test of our ability to cope with the whole complex of postwar problems in the Far East — vital problems of rehabilitation and reconstruction — is likewise involved in this seemingly insignificant domestic "episode." For, as John Embree has said, "if administrative prob-

5

lems involving a hundred thousand people can not be intelligently and democratically solved, how are we to solve the complex postwar problems of, say, Southeast Asia with its mixed population of a hundred million?" There is scarcely a single problem involved in administering the affairs of an occupied area that is not to be found in each of these ten relocation centers.[1]

Actually what is involved in the relocation program is the whole question of what has been happening around the rim of the Pacific Basin for the last several decades and what is likely to happen in the future. "What is taking place around the Pacific," wrote Dr. Robert E. Park in 1926, "is what took place some centuries ago around the Atlantic. A new civilization is coming into existence. The present ferment in Asia and the racial conflicts on the Pacific Coast of America are but different manifestations of what is, broadly speaking, a single process; a process which we may expect to continue until some sort of permanent equilibrium has been established between the races and peoples on both sides of the Pacific." It is quite important that the nation realize that our policy toward this process is being made today in the relocation centers and on the West Coast.

Just as we are in danger of altogether failing to recognize the importance of what is involved in the relocation program, so, for somewhat the same reasons, we failed to recognize, in the long years of anti-Japanese agitation on the West Coast before the war, the portent of things to come. We insisted on regarding this agitation as a manifestation of provincial prejudice unrelated to what was happening in the Far East and throughout the Pacific Basin. We seemed incapable of visualizing this area as a world region of which our West Coast was an integral part. Astute foreign observers were never under any illusion about the significance of anti-Oriental agitation in the Pacific Coast states. In their eyes this agitation involved far more than the question, for example, of who was to operate strawberry farms in Sacramento County. Some of these observers were quick to relate happenings on the western rim of the Pacific to happenings throughout the entire

[1] See comments of Lieutenant Alexander H. Leighton, *Public Opinion Quarterly*, Winter, 1943, pp. 652–668.

6

area. They at least had the wit to see what the geographers had long known — namely, that California was a part of this emerging Pacific world. They recognized that the echo of racial and cultural conflict which the nation heard from time to time in California had to be related to similar echoes in New Zealand and Australia, the China coast and Japan itself.

Failing to correlate the different aspects of what was essentially a single process, we blindly ignored its varied manifestations. We could see no connection between the development of "yellow peril" agitations on the West Coast and the rise of "white peril" movements in Japan; between our treatment of resident Chinese and the outbreak of the Boxer Rebellion; between the changes taking place in the Japanese settlements on the Coast and the changes taking place inside Japan; between the passage of the Immigration Act of 1924 and the ascendancy of the military in Japan. We had, as Walter B. Pitkin once said, but three habits of thinking about Japan: the missionary habit, the California habit, and the foreign-trade habit. We marveled at the extraordinary facility with which the Japanese people were adopting Western industrial arts and techniques in Japan, yet, at the same time, we strenuously insisted that the Japanese on the West Coast were "incapable of assimilation."

When, as happened on occasion, the "Japanese problem in California" was related to larger issues in the Pacific world, it was usually done in a misleading and inaccurate manner. The charge was frequently raised in California, for example, that Japan was attempting a "bloodless conquest" of the West Coast and the absorption of Hawaii by "seepage." The evidence indicates, however, that the initial immigration of Japanese to Hawaii and the West Coast was not planned or instigated by Japan. For it was after and not before this movement had reached important proportions that Japan began to use the issues involved to her own advantage. It was our reaction to these immigrants that Japan was exploiting, rather than the immigrants themselves. Had Japan really intended the conquest of California by colonization, she must have pursued altogether different tactics. She would, for example, have sought to minimize friction in California. Actually

7

she always sought to exploit the question and never seemed genuinely interested in a final solution.

It was after this immigration had reached sizable proportions that Japan discovered that anti-Oriental agitation on the West Coast could be used for a variety of purposes: as a smoke screen for Japanese aggression in Asia; as a means of inflaming Japanese public opinion against America; as the excuse for ever-increasing military and naval appropriations; as an excellent issue to exploit for domestic political purposes inside Japan; as a *quid pro quo* in dealings with the United States; and as a means of diverting widespread social discontent in Japan into chauvinistic channels. These considerations were of far greater importance to ruling factions in Japan than the issue of who was to operate strawberry farms in Florin, California; more important, by far, than the well-being of 100,000 people of Japanese ancestry living in America.

It is part of my purpose, in this volume, to show that military cliques in Japan began, nearly fifty years ago, to lay the foundation for the acceptance, by the Japanese people, of the idea of an eventual war against the United States; that it was necessary to build this campaign gradually, incident by incident, because of the long-standing friendship that had prevailed and because of the friendly manner in which the Japanese people were inclined to regard this country. It will be shown that Japan was consistently aided in this campaign by jingoists and racists in this country and that many of these same individuals are still — I am sure unwittingly — playing the Japanese game. It will be noted that the moment we admitted a large number of Japanese immigrants as permanent residents, while refusing to make it possible for them to become citizens, we had in effect created a situation which Japan could exploit to great effect for the purposes indicated. In exploiting the West Coast situation, Japan succeeded in heightening racial consciousness throughout America which she in turn exploited in the Orient. First a single state, then a region, and finally the nation developed a racial ideology which Japan discovered she could use to further her own dynastic ambitions. During all these years, the manipulators of this campaign in Japan were not only poisoning the minds of the Japanese people and delaying the initiation of long-needed social reforms in Japan, but they were practising a kind of "psychological warfare," making use of such dynamic myths as "the yellow peril," and provoking racial antipathy. When these elements discovered that, owing to peculiar historical, social, and economic circumstances, California was the "nerve center" of anti-Oriental feeling, they became skilled in the art of baiting the Californians.

These same cliques in Japan were not interested in racial equality: they were at all times interested in imperialistic aggrandizement. They used the issue on the West Coast to make us appear, in the eyes of all Orientals, as race bigots and hypocrites. The impression of the United States that these elements succeeded in creating, at least in the mind of their own people, was essentially a false impression. Since our federal government came to feel that it was virtually powerless to deal with the conditioned reflexes that had developed in California, Japan was able to spread the impression that the entire nation was victimized by these same reflexes. Our government did not control the press of the nation. It could not manipulate opinion as the Japanese militarists were able to do in Japan. Actually Japan had no grievance against the United States, for the federal government had gone out of its way, over a long period of years, to adopt a conciliatory policy toward Japan. That we did so, however, only encouraged Japan to "work on" the situation in California with renewed vigor whenever it suited her interests to do so. It will also be shown that our other enemy, Germany, has made use of these same conditioned reflexes in California, both during the First World War and during the present war.

It would be highly misleading, however, to suggest that Japanese military cliques created an issue when none existed in the minds of the Japanese people. The fact that wide sections of the Japanese public were fully aware of the discrimination being practised on the West Coast, and that they deeply resented this discrimination, gave the militarists an issue which they could manipulate. In other words, they manipulated an already existing issue; they did not create the issue itself. Their attitude toward

9

this issue and the uses they made of it were purely opportunistic. This qualification must be kept in mind, therefore, in reviewing the entire controversy; otherwise, the interpretation that I have placed on certain aspects of the matter might well be characterized as an oversimplification of a highly complex situation.

It is against this background and in relation to this frame of reference that the story of what has happened to the Japanese in the United States since December 7, 1941, must be told. It is a story which must necessarily be related to their entire experience in America, for evacuation and relocation are merely the latest — the current — chapter in the history of their troubled residence in this country. While I have not sought to rewrite this complex history in detail, I have sought to discuss its essentials in realistic terms. It would be impossible to describe what has happened on the West Coast since the removal of the Japanese without going into this background. For "today is yesterday's effect and tomorrow's cause, and not merely yesterday's future and tomorrow's history."

In recounting the experience of the Japanese on the West Coast, I have also sought to indicate how racial ideologies come into existence. In the case of most racial ideologies, the factual background is so complex as to make such a demonstration difficult if not impossible. In the case of the West Coast Japanese, however, a number of peculiar factors make it possible to chart, in broad outline at least, the evolution of a particular racial ideology. For one thing, the problem of the West Coast Japanese is of comparatively recent origin: it has a history of only about forty years. It also happens to be isolated in space, for up to December 7, 1941, the problem was essentially confined to the three West Coast states and pretty largely restricted to California. In a newly formed state such as California, the development of a racial ideology can be traced — and the various factors involved can be isolated — with a clarity that is not possible, for example, in the case of the Negro in the Deep South. Unlike the Negroes in the Deep South, the Japanese on the Coast were, from the outset, not only represented by articulate spokesmen but they were compactly organized, so that it becomes possible to follow the polemics of the controversy from its inception. Since the traditional culture of Japan contrasted so sharply with the culture of Western America, it also becomes possible, in the case of the West Coast Japanese, to show how cultural traits mistakenly become identified as racial traits, and with what consequences.

It is, therefore, my hope that this study will throw some light upon the whole problem of racial ideologies. Some of the conclusions drawn are doubtless not applicable to other racial minority problems; but some of them, I believe, do have a wide applicability. A comparison of the racial creed of the West Coast on the Japanese with the racial orthodoxy of the Deep South will reveal the existence of the same fallacies, stereotypes, and myths. It will show how what is called "the race question" can be exploited and manipulated. It will also show, I hope, how persistent and vicious these myths and stereotypes can become once they are implanted, through a process of conflict and controversy, in the mores of a particular region.

I also propose to show the alarming extent to which the foreign policy of the government of the United States toward "colored" races and nations has been determined by the provincial prejudices of a particular region; more precisely, of a particular state. The extent to which local aspects of "the race question" have influenced our foreign policy is a question which, of necessity, will loom much larger in the future than it has in the past. As a nation, we shall discover that we are unable to implement a sound postwar foreign policy until we formulate and rigorously apply a comprehensive *national* policy on racial minorities in our midst. In the absence of such a federal policy, we shall be constantly embarrassed in the conduct of our foreign affairs, if not completely frustrated, by the strident insistence of some state or region that its official attitude toward a particular race must, per se, be the attitude of the United States. In default of a national policy and program on racial minorities, local attitudes are likely not only to prevail in particular situations, but to become national attitudes.

A dramatic recognition of precisely this danger is found in a recent editorial of the *Washington Post* in which it was suggested that South Carolina arrange now to send Senator Ellison Smith as its delegate to the next peace conference. After considering a resolution of the South Carolina legislature reasserting the antediluvian nonsense of "White Supremacy," the *Post* properly stated that, if this resolution really represented the thinking of the people of South Carolina, then it was painfully apparent that South Carolina did not share the stated war aims of the federal government. As long as we continued to pursue a policy of isolationism in foreign affairs, we could, with a certain amount of reason, say that it was no other nation's business how we treated racial minorities in the United States. But the abandonment of isolationism in the field of foreign policy necessarily involves an abandonment of the same principle so far as our domestic racial minorities are concerned. We have too long permitted the Deep South to characterize the Negro problem as its "peculiar problem"; the Southwest to deal with Mexicans as it saw fit; and the West Coast to refer to Orientals as a "regional problem." In the secular society of our times, as Dr. Robert Redfield has so cogently observed, racial cleavages or differences may well become more important as divisive factors than national, religious, or cultural differences have been in the past.

I also propose to show that the main reason the federal government permitted the West Coast to dictate important aspects of our Far Eastern policy was that, as a nation, we had not yet concluded the unfinished business of the Civil War. Theodore Roosevelt, William Howard Taft, Woodrow Wilson, and Calvin Coolidge were all forced to recognize a connection between the Oriental problem on the Pacific Coast and the Negro problem in the Deep South. Since the federal government had capitulated to the South on the Negro question, it found itself powerless to cope with race bigotry on the Pacific Coast. Whenever the West Coast racial creed was seriously challenged in Congress, or when the spokesmen for this creed were proposing new aggressions, representatives from the Deep South quickly rallied to their defense. It may, at first blush, sound farfetched to contend that we cannot formulate an intelligent Far Eastern policy until we have recognized that the Negro problem is a responsibility of the federal government and have undertaken to discharge this responsibility, but such, I believe, is the case. The relocation program, therefore, directly and indirectly involves the whole question of racial minorities in the United States.

Throughout the following pages, I am constantly compelled, by the nature of the inquiry, to refer to racial attitudes on the West Coast. I have sought throughout to preserve a distinction between the people of the region and those individuals and organizations that have so consistently cultivated misunderstanding and prejudice. It is quite likely that, in a few passages, I have neglected to maintain, or have not sufficiently emphasized, this distinction. It would hardly seem necessary for me to say that the residents of the Pacific Coast are no more inclined to racial bigotry than are the residents of other sections of the United States. They represent, in fact, a good cross section of American opinion since so many of them were either born in other states or formerly resided in other sections. It is certainly not my intention to indict a region, a state, or a locality; nor am I seeking to castigate *all of the members* of the various organizations that have so consistently manufactured prejudicial attitudes in California. Members of an organization are not always aware of all of its policies and practices. The people of a region often acquiesce, or appear to acquiesce, in doctrines that have acquired, by whatever process, an official or semiofficial status for reasons that do not necessarily imply an unqualified endorsement, such as uncertainty, indifference, laziness, or timidity. In fact, it is a basic contention of this book that prejudice is not an "instinctive" expression of deep-seated aversion but is manufactured out of conflicts, the real nature of which is frequently misunderstood.

CHAPTER II

The California-Japanese War (1900-1941)

"No QUESTION of our time," wrote Frederick McCormick in 1917 in *The Menace of Japan*, "can vie in importance with that of the contact of alien races and systems on the Pacific Slope. It is, more than anything else, an indication of the swift development of the Pacific." The principal area in which these alien races and cultural systems came in contact was California. The meeting that took place in mid-Pacific, in Hawaii, was of a different character. There people came together but systems did not collide; races met but competition was minimized. The tensions that developed in California, on the other hand, represented sharp and basic conflicts: racial and cultural, economic and political. What happened in California determined the course of events in Oregon and Washington, in Alaska and Peru. It unquestionably influenced the course of events between the United States and Japan.

Anti-Oriental agitation in California, in addition to being one of the most important, is also one of the most curious phenomena of our time. In expressing their dislike of Japanese, West Coast residents seldom stress a particular factor but are satisfied with the repetition of a generalized statement. After a thorough investigation of anti-Oriental feeling on the West Coast, Ruth Fowler concluded that "group values and opinions are more influential than direct personal experience based on primary contacts. Immediate influences alone do not produce the opinions of the moment, but rather all the accumulated influences both present and past play a part in its creation. Thus changes in individual opinion do not greatly change the total group reaction." [1] Paradoxically, the Japanese were warmly regarded in California, on

[1] "Some Aspects of Public Opinion Concerning the Japanese in Santa Clara County," unpublished dissertation, Stanford University, June, 1934.

14

an individual-to-individual basis, but personal friendship for a particular Japanese seldom changed the attitude toward the group as a whole. Leaders of the anti-Oriental agitation in California will tell you that "some of my best friends" are Japanese.

The basis for this apparently inconsistent attitude is to be found in the distinction which Dr. Robert E. Park has made between public opinion and racial ideologies. "Public opinion," he states, "is the public mind in unstable equilibrium. It is concerned with what is in process and therefore problematic and debatable." Racial ideologies, on the other hand, "are rooted in the memories, the tradition, and the mores of the particular community . . . they are not mere logical artifacts, formulas, or general conceptions; they are rather the historical products of long-continued conflict and controversy." [2] The historical product of fifty years of conflict and controversy, anti-Oriental feeling has become deeply imbedded in the mores of the West Coast as a region. During brief intervals or "lulls," anti-Oriental feeling has remained dormant; but, given a new stimulant or crisis, it quickly reappears. To understand how this peculiar ideology came into being, it is necessary to review the protracted California-Japanese conflict as it developed over the years from 1900 to 1941.

For nearly fifty years prior to December 7, 1941, a state of undeclared war existed between California and Japan. During these years, as Dr. Thomas A. Bailey has noted, "the general controversy lay not between the United States and Japan but between Japan and California, with the federal government seeking to secure justice for the aggrieved foreign power and at the same time endeavoring to convince the state of its obligation to the rest of the union." [3] "Every man, woman and child in Japan," wrote Louis Seibold, "knows a great deal more about California than he does about the United States. . . . California is anathema to the average Japanese, and when he talks of war against the United States, he really means California." [4] On at least one occa-

[2] *American Society in Wartime*, 1943, pp. 165–184.
[3] *Theodore Roosevelt and the Japanese-American Crisis*, 1934.
[4] *Japan: Her Vast Undertakings and World Expansion*, 1921.

sion, Japan even threatened to take action against California "a
an independent nation." [5]

1. The Opening of Hostilities

Japanese immigrants had been arriving in California at th
rate of about 1000 a year from 1890 to 1900; but, following th
annexation of Hawaii, some 12,000 arrived in 1900. This sudde
increase in the number of immigrants occasioned an immediat
protest in California. As a result of a thirty-years' agitatio
against the Chinese, Californians had been conditioned to re
spond quickly and stormily whenever the "Oriental Question
was raised. Although Chinese immigration had been suspende
since 1882, this earlier anti-Chinese feeling was very much aliv
in 1900. While anti-Oriental agitation gradually became synony
mous with anti-Japanese agitation, as the Chinese and Korean
were tacitly excepted from the category, popular opposition i
1900 embraced all Oriental groups.

The first overt act, so to speak, in the California-Japanese Wa
occurred in March, 1900, when Mayor James D. Phelan of Sa
Francisco, using some idle gossip about an alleged "buboni
plague" as an excuse, quarantined both the Chinese and the Japa
nese sections of the city. The local Japanese immediately pro
tested, claiming that the order was motivated by politica
considerations and that its effect was to put them out of busi
ness. To protect their interests, they proceeded to form th
"Japanese Association of America." As a result of this flurry o
excitement, the first anti-Japanese mass meeting was called i
San Francisco on May 7, 1900. The meeting was sponsored by
the San Francisco Labor Council; the chief speaker was Dr
Edward Alsworth Ross, professor of sociology at Stanford Uni
versity. Repeating the stock arguments that had been develope
against the Chinese, Dr. Ross found the Japanese objectionabl
on four counts: —

[5] See *Japan Inside Out* by S. Rhee.

16

1. They were unassimilable.
2. They worked for low wages and thereby undermined the existing labor standards of American workmen.
3. Their standards of living were much lower than those of American workmen.
4. They lacked a proper political feeling for American democratic institutions.

In the *San Francisco Call* of May 8, 1900, Dr. Ross was quoted as having said that "should the worst come to the worst it would be better for us to turn our guns on every vessel bringing Japanese to our shores rather than to permit them to land." From these views, Dr. Ross never wholly departed.[6]

At this mass meeting a resolution was passed urging the extension of the Chinese Exclusion Act to the Japanese. In the same year, the State Labor Commissioner referred to the sudden increase in Japanese laborers and Governor Henry T. Gage, in a message to the legislature on January 8, 1901, called attention to the existence of "a Japanese problem." Taking note of this incipient agitation in California, the Japanese government in July, 1900, announced that no further passports would be issued to contract laborers seeking to enter the United States (the first Gentlemen's Agreement); and, as a result, the number of Japanese arrivals declined 50 per cent in 1901.

This conciliatory action, however, failed to abate popular feeling in California. At the 1901 convention of the Chinese Exclusion League and at the 1904 convention of the American Federation of Labor, resolutions were passed asking Congress to exclude further Japanese immigration. At both of these conventions, Japanese distributed leaflets asking that they be distinguished from the Chinese! During this early agitation, from 1900 to 1905, no mention was made of the menace of Japan as a foreign power; and, at this time, the incidents occurring in California occasioned no counter-demonstration in Japan.

The "golden age" of Japanese-American friendship still pre-

[6] See, for example, his autobiography: *Seventy Years of It*.

vailed in 1900, although it was rapidly drawing to a close. After 1900 both Japan and America emerged as world powers and, more particularly, as great powers in the Pacific. In 1894 Japan had fought a victorious war against China. In 1898 we had annexed the Hawaiian Islands, which were 40 per cent Japanese in population, and had acquired the Philippines. Despite the fact that Japan had noted its objection to our annexation of Hawaii, these parallel developments momentarily served to draw the two countries closer together. As late as 1900 it was generally felt that the interests of Japan and America were not antagonistic, but rather that they tended to be complementary. Tupper and McReynolds, in their interesting volume *Japan in American Public Opinion* (1937), quote an American naval officer who (in 1900) referred to the Japanese as a "kindly, generous, large-hearted, good-mannered, honest and loyal people." [7]

Even during the Russo-Japanese War, American public opinion (including West Coast opinion) was strongly pro-Japanese. Our preference was indicated not by a slight trend, but by the great preponderance of opinion. In the West as in the East, each Japanese victory was hailed with delight. As the war drew to a close, however, West Coast opinion began to shift, and by the time the delegates met for the peace conference in Portsmouth, national opinion had likewise changed. As a nation we did not turn from Japanophilism to Japanophobia overnight, but a gradual change occurred, first in California, and later throughout the nation. At the same time, notes Dr. Bailey, public opinion in Japan "regarding the United States was undergoing a marked change as a result of recent disturbances in California." [8] It was this shift in public opinion toward Japan that set the stage for the next outburst of anti-Japanese feeling in California.

The campaign was launched on February 23, 1905 — just before the siege of Mukden — by a series of sensational and highly inflammatory articles in the *San Francisco Chronicle*. Some of the captions on these articles were: CRIME AND POVERTY GO HAND IN HAND WITH ASIATIC LABOR; BROWN MEN ARE AN EVIL

[7] Page 5.
[8] *Ibid.*, p. 21.

IN THE PUBLIC SCHOOLS; JAPANESE A MENACE TO AMERICAN WOMEN; BROWN ASIATICS STEAL BRAINS OF WHITES. "Every one of these immigrants," said the *Chronicle*, "so far as his service is desired, is a Japanese spy." Just why the *Chronicle* should have launched this attack has never been determined. But the owner of the *Chronicle*, M. H. DeYoung, had been a candidate for the United States Senate a few years previously and some observers construed these vicious articles as a renewal of his candidacy. The series ran throughout February and March, 1905, and was most effective in whipping up popular feeling against the resident Japanese. It should be noted, however, that this feeling was not restricted to California. All America had suddenly become apprehensive of Japan. The chairman of the House Committee on Military Affairs had declared that if Japan won the war with Russia, she would "fight a bloody war with the United States over the Philippines"; and Senator Selvage had discovered in Japan "a serious menace, not only to California, but to the nation."

Following the appearance of the *Chronicle* articles, the California legislature, on March 1, 1905, by a vote of twenty-eight to nothing in the Senate and seventy to nothing in the Assembly, passed a resolution urging Congress to exclude the Japanese. Two months later, the Japanese and Korean Exclusion League was formed in San Francisco. Within a year, this organization had a membership of 78,500 (three fourths of its membership being located in the San Francisco Bay area). By 1905 the fight had been narrowed down to the Japanese. "The Chinese," the *Chronicle* observed, "are faithful laborers and do not buy land. The Japanese are unfaithful laborers and do buy land." At this time, however, California was, as David Starr Jordan pointed out, "by no means a unit on the question of the immigration of Japanese laborers. The fruit growers openly welcome it. Business men generally, quietly, favor it; and, outside of San Francisco and the labor unions, it is not clear that a majority of the people are opposed to the free admission of Japanese laborers or even of Chinese." [9] The southern part of the state and the rural areas

[9] *Out West*, March, 1907.

generally were not favorable to the agitation. Furthermore, the whole movement received a definite setback in President Theodore Roosevelt's message to Congress of December 1, 1905, in which he spoke out most emphatically in favor of a nondiscriminatory policy.

2. The Irish and the Native Sons

From 1870 to 1920, anti-Oriental agitation in California was fomented, directed, and financed by the powerful trade-union movement that, from the earliest days, had centered in San Francisco. It is, indeed, remarkable that in a pioneer nonindustrial state a labor movement of such strength had developed that by 1879 it was able, through the Workingmen's Party, to seize control of the state and enact a new, and in some respects quite radical, constitution. The secret of the success of this early movement lay in the fact that Irish immigrants constituted one fourth of the large foreign-born element in the state. Furthermore, virtually all of the Irish were concentrated in San Francisco. "The Sons of Ireland," as Janzo Sasamori observed, "are fond of politicianing." [10]

Most of the leaders of the anti-Oriental movement, in its early phases, were Irish and they were also the leaders of the San Francisco labor movement. Dennis Kearney, Walter MacArthur, P. H. McCarthy, and many other labor leaders fall within this category. These leaders had been quick to realize the possibilities of uniting their notoriously clannish fellow countrymen around a negative issue, namely, "The Chinese Must Go!" It was the political, rather than the economic aspects, of Oriental immigration that interested these clever and resourceful leaders. Scientific evidence has always been lacking to prove that Oriental immigrants ever actually *displaced* American workmen in California or that they ever constituted a permanent threat to labor standards in the state. But, given the chaotic state of affairs in California in the seventies, no shrewder slogan could have been devised than "The Chinese Must Go!" At this time, more-

[10] *Facts About the Japanese in America.*

20

er, Irish immigrants were being assaulted and abused in Eastern dustrial areas. Their aggressions against Orientals on the West oast tended to compensate for these attacks. The fact that pan had an alliance with Great Britain merely gave them an additional reason for being opposed to Oriental immigration.

During the long depression years of the nineties, the Workgmen's Party had disintegrated. But, with the turn of the ntury, the annexation of Hawaii and the discovery of gold in laska had brought boom times to California. With the formaon of the State Federation of Labor in January, 1901, the San rancisco labor movement began to revive. As an aftermath to great teamsters' strike in July, 1901, the Union Labor Party cceeded in electing Eugene E. Schmitz as mayor of San Fransco. In campaigning against Mayor James D. Phelan, Schmitz ad forced such antilabor publications as the *San Francisco hronical* and *Call* to compete for the "anti-Oriental" vote. Thus e violently prolabor and the violently antilabor forces both ught to exploit anti-Oriental sentiment. Formerly a bassoon layer in a San Francisco orchestra, Schmitz was the henchman f Abe Ruef, an exceedingly able and notoriously corrupt polician. In the years following the victory of the Union Labor arty, San Francisco wallowed in corruption. Raymond Leslie uell has said that, during these years, the political corruption at existed in San Francisco would "make the blackest deeds of oss Tweed look as harmless as politics in a woman's club." [11] he history of these lawless and tumultuous years in San Fransco has been carefully recorded (see, for example, Fremont lder's autobiography *My Own Story*, 1919; and Franklin litchborn's interesting document, *The System*, 1915). Alough he had been re-elected as Mayor of San Francisco, chmitz was facing indictment in 1906 for his many crimes. lard-pressed for an effective diversionary issue, Schmitz and uef saw an opportunity to save themselves by whipping up a apanese pogrom.

At about this time, other groups in California began to use he tactics so successfully employed by the Irish labor leaders

[11] *Political Science Quarterly*, December, 1922.

to develop a strong in-group feeling and to create solid politic organizations. Foremost among these organizations was the N: tive Sons of the Golden West. Created in 1875, this organizatio had, prior to 1907, been primarily interested in collecting hi torical materials, preserving historical landmarks, and otherwi: engaging in a number of harmless, and sometimes laudable, civi purposes. After 1907, however, it became actively interested in th anti-Oriental movement.

A glance at the list of prominent leaders of the anti-Orient: agitation in California from 1907 to 1941 will show that mo: of these men were members and in most cases officials of th Native Sons of the Golden West. Hiram Johnson, James I Phelan, U. S. Webb, V. S. McClatchy (the doyen of all anti Oriental leaders in California), J. M. Inman (State Senator an President of the California Oriental Exclusion League), Mayo Eugene E. Schmitz, Abe Ruef, Aaron Altman and James I Gallagher (members of the San Francisco Board of Educatio in 1906), Anthony Caminetti (formerly a State Senator an United States Commissioner-General of Immigration in 1913) - all of these leaders of the anti-Oriental agitation were member and officials of the Native Sons. They were also active and suc cessful political figures in California. As a matter of fact, score of legislators, judges, state officials, Congressmen, and Senator received their initial support and owed their election (or appoint ment) to public office in California in the years 1907–1924 t the Native Sons of the Golden West. The organization, in turn acquired its great political potency by cleverly using anti Oriental feeling to solidify its own ranks and to build a compac political organization.

While glorifying the state of California, its history and tradi tions, the Native Sons has always been a strictly "lily-white" organization. Although making birth in California a conditio of membership, the organization always excepted Chinese, Jap anese, Negroes, and Mexicans (although a few elegant pseudo Mexicans of the "early" and therefore the "best" families wer admitted to membership). According to its philosophy, the State of California should remain what "it has always been and Go

Himself intended it shall always be — the White Man's Paradise." [12]
t has always been committed to the interesting proposition that
he "31st Star shall never become dim or yellow." For years it
maintained that citizenship should be restricted to "native-born
Californians of the white male race." In its official publication, the
Grizzly Bear, it has adhered to the practice of referring to Mexicans as "cholos" and "greasers" and to Chinese as "chinks." In a
brief filed in the Ninth Circuit Court of Appeals it recently reiterated its stand that the Constitution refers to "white people
only" and that the phrase "We, the people of the United States,"
means "we, the white people." [13] It has consistently maintained
that we made a "grave mistake" when we granted citizenship to
the Negroes after the Civil War. [14] While its membership has today fallen to 25,000, it has been, in the past, an extremely powerful political organization.

To appreciate the importance of a "native" organization of
this kind in California, one must realize that the population of
the state has been doubling nearly every decade since 1849. Most
of this net growth in population has been due to migration: the
movement into California of persons born elsewhere. California,
as James Bryce observed, "grew like a gourd in the night." It
has not been peopled by settlers from some near-by state, as
people moved from Illinois to Minnesota, but by people from
all over the world. At the height of the anti-Japanese agitation
in California, there were in the state 90,000 people who had
been born in Illinois; while 80,000 had been born in New York;
68,000 in Missouri; 67,000 in New England; 51,000 in Pennsyl-
vania; 41,000 in Indiana; 35,000 in Wisconsin; 20,000 in Texas;
and 20,000 in Kentucky. There was no county in the state, in
1913, in which fewer than twenty states were represented. The
legislature that passed the first Alien Land Act consisted of
eighty members, equally divided between native-born Californians and those born in some other state. It is significant, as Dr.

[12] Grizzly Bear, March, 1920.
[13] See brief in the case of Reagan vs. King, No. 10,299, Appellant's Brief,
p. 47.
[14] San Francisco Hearings, Tolan Committee, February 21, 1942, pp. 11085,
11074.

Eliot Grinnell Mears has pointed out,[15] that sentiment in California is influenced to a major degree by persons who were not born and brought up in their most impressionable years in the state.

The real significance of this unique population is, however, that in such a heterogeneously constituted state an in-group organization, with a substantial degree of internal cohesiveness, can exercise a political influence out of all relation to its actual membership. For such an organization will represent one of the few *organized* mass groups. Working in conjunction with the State Federation of Labor, the California Grange, and the American Legion, the Native Sons of the Golden West became a real power in California politics. All of these organizations used anti-Oriental feeling as a means of solidifying their membership; of uniting this membership by posing the existence of a common enemy; and of rallying their joint membership around a single issue. Not only was the Native Sons a highly organized in-group in a state made up largely of outsiders, but it had possession of all the symbols of the homeland. It waved the flag of the Bear State Republic; it identified itself with the heroic forty-niners; it paid annual homage to the aging survivors of the Donner Party. Making much of "traditions" in a state that was as new as a fresh nickel from the mint, it easily bluffed the newcomers into thinking that it knew something about a state of which they were admittedly ignorant. Actually, as Ruth Fowler has pointed out, these organizations created more anti-Oriental opinion than they reflected.

Discovering the political potency of anti-Oriental agitation, the Native Sons permitted its attitude on this issue to color its thinking about almost every other issue. It opposed the Child Labor Amendment upon the extraordinary ground that the white American farmer must be free to work his children in the field in order to meet the competition of Japanese labor. It opposed our entrance into the League of Nations out of a deep-seated fear that Japan would bring the issue of racial equality before the League. It has consistently opposed the admission of Hawaii as a state, because of its large population of Oriental ancestry. In preparing the history of its participation in the anti-Oriental move-

[15] *Resident Orientals on the American Pacific Coast*, 1927.

nent, the organization points with pride to the fact that Eugene Schmitz and Abe Ruef were members of Niantic Parlor and Grand Trustees. So great is its pride in this fact that it neglects to mention that these men were convicted of felonies and that they were corrupt public officials.[16]

Given this situation, it is not surprising that the "peak" years of anti-Japanese agitation should have been years in which Presidential elections were held: 1908, 1912, 1916, and 1920. Dozens of California Congressmen were repeatedly re-elected to Congress by their sponsorship of this agitation. Some of them — Mr. E. A. Hayes is a case in point — made this issue the primary basis of their re-election campaigns. The adroit manner in which he manipulated this particular issue is a major explanation of the remarkably successful political career of Hiram Johnson.

It should be noted that not all areas of the state have been equally interested in anti-Japanese agitation. Prior to Pearl Harbor, there had never been much organized anti-Japanese sentiment in Southern California. Even the gradual concentration of the Japanese in Los Angeles County which took place after 1908 failed to produce the same degree of agitational activity that existed elsewhere.[17] At the outset, the "anti feeling" was largely confined to San Francisco. Later the mountain-fruit section in Placer County, the area around Sacramento, and the Stockton delta region, became the hotbeds of organized activity. While other factors would have to be appraised in accounting for this variation of sentiment, it is worthy of mention that the percentage of native-born Californians is greater in the northern than in the southern part of the state. It is also interesting that there should be little correlation between the number of Japanese in a particular area and the virulence of anti-Japanese sentiment.

3. The School-Board Affair

The people around the rim of the Pacific always seem to be momentarily united whenever an earthquake occurs. The Japa-

[16] See *The History of California's Japanese Problem and the Part Played by the Native Sons of the Golden West in Its Solution* by Peter T. Conmy, Grand Historian, July, 1942.

[17] See *Waving the Yellow Flag in California* by John B. Wallace.

nese government contributed over $250,000 to the relief of San Francisco after the earthquake and fire of April 18, 1906. For brief period after the fire, anti-Japanese agitation abated. But i was not long until the wave of crime and violence which de veloped after the fire began to be directed against the residen Japanese. With a construction boom developing in the city, th Japanese community began to expand economically and geo graphically. The number of Japanese restaurants increased fron eight to thirty and a number of Japanese residents bought home: outside the Little Tokyo settlement. Noting this development the Exclusion League called for a boycott of all Japanese estab lishments. At the same time, two distinguished Japanese visitors Dr. F. Omori, of the Imperial University, Tokyo, and Dr. T Nakamura, were assaulted in San Francisco; and, on a subsequen trip to Eureka, Dr. Omori met with similar treatment. The *San Francisco Chronicle* promptly approved of these assaults. The assaults upon these visiting scientists were, according to Ray mond Leslie Buell, "immediately and widely reported in Japan, where they had a profoundly irritating effect." By this time, the program of the Exclusion League had been endorsed by organiza tions composed of nearly four and a half million members; and both political parties had, in 1906, declared themselves in favor of excluding Japanese immigration.

On May 6, 1905, the school board had gone on record in favor of segregating Oriental students in the San Francisco schools, but, for lack of funds, the resolution had been tabled. Now, on October 11, 1906, on the eve of the indictment of Messrs. Schmitz and Ruef for sundry felonies, the school board suddenly decided to carry the resolution into effect: it ordered all Oriental students to attend a segregated school in Chinatown. Not only were the graft investigations pending at the time, but a state election was scheduled for November. The conclusion is ines capable that the school board, which was completely dominated by Ruef and Schmitz, acted at this time to divert public atten tion from the graft scandals. There were only ninety-three Japa nese students out of a total school population of 25,000. A contemporary observer has stated that "no oral or written pro-

26

sts were ever made against the Japanese pupils by the parents
f white pupils"; and, furthermore, educators throughout the
ate joined in voicing an emphatic protest.

"When word of this action reached Japan, there swept over
he country," writes Dr. Bailey, "a wave of resentment against
hat was commonly spoken of as both a treaty violation and an
isult." That the action violated the treaty of 1894 with Japan,
here can be no doubt. Secretary of State Elihu Root admitted
s much when he cabled our ambassador in Tokyo that "the
United States will not for a moment entertain the idea of any
reatment of the Japanese people other than that accorded to
he people of the most friendly European nations." From this
ime forward, America ceased to be *Dai On Jin*, "the Great
Friendly People," in the eyes of the Japanese masses. So intense
vas popular indignation in Japan that one newspaper, the
Mainichi Shimbun, exclaimed editorially: "Why do we not insist
on sending ships?" While it cannot be determined how much
of this resentment was spontaneous and how much was inspired,
t is apparent that the Japan government took advantage of the
ncident to create a diversion at Washington and to create popular sentiment in Japan in favor of increased military and naval
appropriations.[18]

When formal protests were filed in Washington, the Japanese
in San Francisco immediately called a mass meeting and began
to raise funds to fight the issue. In the meantime, Japanese parents
refused to send their children to the segregated school. There is
good reason to believe that this action on the part of the resident
Japanese was in large part instigated by the Japanese consul in
San Francisco. The Japanese vernacular press in San Francisco
proceeded to publish, at this time, some extremely foolish and
highly inflammatory editorials.[19] "When National dignity is
called to question," read one of these editorials, "the sword of
Masamune is unsheathed for action." For the next twenty-five
years these editorials were quoted in California as proof of the

[18] See *Japan and America* by Carl Crow, 1916; and *The Menace of Japan*
by Frederick McCormick, 1917.
[19] See the *Japanese-American* of October 25, 1906, and the *New World*
of October 25.

menacing character of the resident Japanese. One can at lea
draw an inference, however, that these editorials were inspire
by the consul, whose influence was admittedly great with th
editors of both publications. In retrospect, it seems altogeth
unlikely that such provocative statements would have been mad
without the approval of the consul.

Faced with this crisis, President Roosevelt promptly dispatche
Secretary of Commerce and Labor, V. H. Metcalf (a Californian
to the Coast to make a thorough investigation. Without waitin
for a report, however, he sent a message to Congress on Decem
ber 3, 1906, in which he condemned the action of the San Fran
cisco School Board as "a wicked absurdity." In this same messag
he urged Congress to make it possible for the Japanese to becom
citizens and suggested that the President should be authorized t
protect the treaty rights of aliens.

The Metcalf Report (dated December 18, 1906) clearly estab
lished that there was no factual justification for the action of th
school board. It also documented some nineteen cases involvin
serious assaults against Japanese residents of San Francisco. Th
action of the school board was, in fact, merely the first of a lon
series of discriminatory measures adopted in California for th
purpose of forcing Congress to exclude Japanese immigration
None of these acts was aimed at correcting a particular situation
they were all deliberately provocative in character. "The schoo
question," said the *Coast Seamen's Journal*, "is a mere inciden
in our campaign for Japanese exclusion."

Coming soon after the Treaty of Portsmouth, the school-board
affair proved most embarrassing to the national government, and
it remained a source of embarrassment since no effective remedy
was available to the government. On January 17, 1907, the fed
eral government filed two suits in California by which it sought
to enjoin the school board from carrying its order into effect.
Had these suits ever been pressed to trial (they were later dis
missed), it is extremely doubtful whether the federal government
could have prevailed. For by 1907 the Supreme Court stood
firmly committed to the notion that segregation, on the basis
of race, is not unconstitutional, if equal and separate facilities are

28

rovided. This strange constitutional doctrine had been devel-
ped as part of the campaign to emasculate the Fourteenth
.mendment in the years immediately subsequent to the Civil
Var.

Discussion of the San Francisco School Board "incident" on
he floor of Congress showed clearly enough that the Japanese
uestion in California was intimately related to the Negro ques-
ion in the Deep South. "Because of their Negro problem, south-
rners were in sympathy with San Francisco's views; southern
congressmen as a whole were decidedly with California in her
ace struggle." [20] Congressman Burnett of Alabama stated that "we
iave suffered enough already from one race question" and similar
views were echoed by Senator Bacon of Georgia, Senator Tillman
of South Carolina, Senator Underwood of Alabama, Senator Bur-
gess of Texas, and Senator Williams of Mississippi. One Congressman from Mississippi stated: —

> "I stand with the State of California in opposition to mixed
> schools. [Applause] I stand with Californians in favor of the
> proposition that we want a homogeneous and assimilable
> population of white people in the Republic." [Applause] [21]

While these gentlemen were Democrats and doubtless aware of
the fact that the Republican President faced re-election in 1908,
the real basis of their action was obviously the racial situation in
the South. In attempting to cope with California, President
Roosevelt suddenly discovered that he faced the opposition of
the Solid South.

In defying the President of the United States, California stood
on firm legal grounds. The *San Francisco Argonaut*, in a bitter
and mocking editorial of November 10, 1906, put the issue up
to the President in these words: —

> It was on December 18th, 1865, that the 13th Amend-
> ment to the Constitution went into effect, abolishing slavery.
> It was in July, 1868, that the 14th Amendment went into
> effect, making the Negroes citizens, giving them civil rights,

[20] See Tupper and McReynolds, p. 29.
[21] Quoted by Bailey, p. 72.

and enumerating certain of their civil rights. This amendment also cut down the representation in Congress of such states as denied to Negroes the right to vote. But no Southern state as a result of this penalizing ever enfranchised the Negro. It was on Feb. 26, 1869 that the 15th Amendment was proposed to Congress. . . . Does President Roosevelt think Negroes freely exercise the right to vote in Southern states? We do not think so. It is thirty-eight years since the 14th Amendment gave to Negroes civil rights. Does President Roosevelt think Negroes are granted equal rights in theatres, hotels, railway trains, or street cars in all the states, Southern or Northern? We do not think so. It may be said that the Federal Court can coerce the states into giving "equal rights" to the Negroes. We do not think so. But if there may be those who doubt the soundness of our judgment, we may add that the U. S. Supreme Court in the celebrated Slaughterhouse Cases decided that the 14th Amendment does not deprive the states of police powers; that court upheld the right of states to regulate domestic affairs; it decreed that there is a citizenship of the states as well as of the United States; it decided that the states could vest certain privileges and immunities upon their citizens. This decision was opposed by many extremists, as the war feeling still ran high. Congress thereupon passed a measure known as the Civil Rights Bill, which was intended to extort from the white citizens of the Southern states the recognition of the Negroes' "equal rights." This law, when brought up before the Supreme Court, was declared to be unconstitutional.

Obviously this editorial was correct in stating that, if the federal government could force California to abandon its policy of segregation, it could force compliance with the same policy in the South.

At a large mass meeting called in San Francisco, just before Christmas, Mayor Schmitz shouted defiance of the federal government; claimed that he was being unjustly prosecuted in the courts; and contended that he had been indicted, not for his crimes (which were legion), but because of his anti-Japanese views. In the course of this speech, the Mayor stated that, if

30

necessary, he would lay down his life in battle with the Japanese. The *Los Angeles Times* was prompted to remark that "it is a notable fact that his Honor has never laid down anything of value. His promise, however, would almost reconcile anyone to a war with Japan." In the November elections of 1906, California politicians were volunteering by the score to fight Japan. "If we are to have war with Japan," advised Congressman E. A. Hayes, "let's have it right away. We are ready and they are not." P. H. McCarthy believed that the "states west of the Rockies could whip Japan at a moment's notice."

Suggesting that the ordinance be suspended, Mr. Roosevelt invited the school board to Washington. It took Mayor Schmitz a full week to decide whether he would permit the board to accept the invitation. When he finally agreed, he decided to accompany them himself. In February, 1907, the party left for Washington amidst much excitement and fanfare. The Mayor's followers, according to Franklin Hitchborn, "were frankly delighted with the prospect of the indicted Mayor returning from the national capitol covered with glory and acclaimed the savior of the country from a war with Japan."

It would be difficult, indeed, to imagine a more ludicrous spectacle. Heading the delegation was the Mayor, a bassoon player by profession, under indictment for numerous crimes. He was accompanied by the Superintendent of Schools, Roncovieri, a trombone player, close personal friend of the Mayor, and by Aaron Altman, President of the School Board, a brother-in-law of Abe Ruef. Here were Altman, Schmitz, and Roncovieri — all descendants of recent immigrants to the United States, all members in good standing of the Native Sons, one of them under indictment — going to "treat with" the President of the United States as though they were the ministers of a sovereign political power.

The *New York World* (February 14, 1907) found the situation rather amusing: "The Mayor and the Board of Education of a single American city summoned to the White House, asked to approve the forms of a settlement with Japan proposed by the President and his Secretary of State, and allowed to make condi-

31

tions and changes of international policy with the manner of an independent power." Years previously, Lord Bryce had pointed out that "California, more than any other part of the nation, is a country by itself, and San Francisco a Capitol." The state had acquired, he remarked, "a sort of consciousness of separate existence."

In this instance, California was simply practising an old technique. With the aid of the Deep South, it had forced the federal government to adopt the Chinese Exclusion Act in 1882. Since the Supreme Court had held the Civil Rights Statute unconstitutional, the federal government was powerless to prevent discriminatory acts or to safeguard even the treaty rights of aliens. It could no more protect the rights of Chinese and Japanese in California than it could uphold the civil rights of Negroes in the Deep South. The dilemma was directly related to the nation's capitulation to the South on the Negro question in 1876. During their terms of office, Grover Cleveland, William McKinley, Theodore Roosevelt, William Howard Taft, and Woodrow Wilson all had occasion to lament this latent weakness in the federal government.

As Mayor Schmitz and party neared Washington, the newspapers carried sensational headlines about the "inevitable" conflict with Japan. Throughout this period, Captain Richmond P. Hobson was conducting an inflammatory anti-Japanese campaign, on the lecture platform, in Congress (1907–1915), and in the press. "We know," he wrote, "that the Japanese in California are soldiers organized into companies, regiments, and brigades." [22] While the Mayor was en route to Washington, the California legislature convened and the usual spate of anti-Japanese legislation was promptly introduced. By direct appeals to Governor Gillett, President Roosevelt managed to have these bills tabled while he was negotiating a settlement with California's ambassadors. The agreement finally reached in Washington provided that the school board would withdraw the offensive ordinance and that the President would negotiate with Japan for a suspension of further immigration. On March 17, 1907, the ordinance was withdrawn;

[22] *New York Herald*, February 3, 1907.

and shortly afterwards the President, by executive order, stopped further Japanese immigration by way of Hawaii, Canada, or Mexico. The moment this agreement was announced, the anti-Japanese forces in California attacked Mayor Schmitz as a traitor — even the Catholic Archbishop of San Francisco felt that he had been "betrayed."

No sooner had the delegation returned to San Francisco than mobs began to assault the Japanese. Within two weeks after these riots, newspapers in Japan were speaking openly of the possibility of war with the United States, and France informally offered its services as a mediator. This particular outburst in Japan seems to have been inspired by internal political considerations.[23] In June the Board of Police Commissioners in San Francisco refused to issue licenses to Japanese establishments, but this action provoked no outburst in Japan. The behavior of the Japanese press, at this time, was extremely puzzling. One episode in California would produce a flood of denunciation; and other episodes would be greeted with complete silence.

The outburst in May, 1907, was provoked by an incident much less serious than the school-board affair. Coming just as it did, at a time when a settlement of the "Japanese question" had apparently been reached, it provoked angry annoyance in this country. The inference is, I believe, that Japan seized upon the riots of May, 1907, to launch a new anti-American campaign in the press so that the Japanese people would not conclude that a settlement had been reached; in other words, they wanted to keep the issue alive on both sides of the Pacific. All the evidence indicates that, by 1907, the Japanese had become experts in manipulating the situation in California to their advantage. While most of this ranting in the Japanese press in 1907 was probably officially inspired, nevertheless we were actually near war with Japan. At a later date, Mr. Iichiro Tokutomi stated that if Japan had fully recovered from the war with Russia, she would never have accepted the Gentlemen's Agreement.[24]

[23] See Bailey, p. 201; and summary of opinion in the *Literary Digest*, June 22, 1907.
[24] *Japanese-American Relations*, 1922, p. 76.

President Roosevelt thought that we were on the brink of war with Japan. "I am concerned about the Japanese-California situation," he wrote Henry White on July 10, 1907, "and I see no prospect of its growing better." In a letter of about the same date to Henry Cabot Lodge, he said: "I do not believe we shall have war; but it is no fault of the yellow press if we do not have it. The Japanese seem to have about the same proportion of prize jingo fools that we have." The "crisis" itself had the effect of solidifying West Coast opinion. Only three West Coast newspapers — the *Seattle News*, the *Tacoma Daily News*, and the *Los Angeles Times* — supported the President on this issue.[25] It is amazing to note, in retrospect, that so few American newspapers suspected that Japan might be deliberately fomenting the situation on the West Coast and using it for its own advantage. The *San Francisco Call* was one of the few newspapers that suspected as much. "In the solemn game of diplomacy," to quote from an editorial of November 13, 1906, "it is the ancient policy to cultivate and even cherish open sores. Japan wants an offset to our claim that American trade is not being fairly treated in Manchuria. Further, the Japanese do not want extreme measures taken against their sea poachers in the Aleutians."

4. The Episode of the Fleet

If Japan had taken the lead in instigating rumors of war in 1906, the initiative passed to this country in 1907. In May of 1907 the *New York Times* published a translation of a book originally published in Germany, predicting war between the United States and Japan. At the same time, *Collier's* carried a piece by a French publicist predicting war in the near future. Charlemagne Tower, our ambassador in Berlin, reported to the President that "the California troubles were merely a symptom" seized upon by Japan "for the purpose of inflaming public sentiment against America." Charles Denby, American consul in Shanghai, reported that Japan might attack the United States and that her position with respect to the disturbances in Cali-

[25] See *Literary Digest*, January 12, 1907.

fornia was a mere pretext.[26] The German ambassador in Washington, Speck von Sternberg, repeatedly suggested to his good friend, President Roosevelt, that Japan was instigating disturbances in Mexico preparatory to an attack on the United States. In a survey published in the *Literary Digest* (July 27, 1907) the consensus seemed to be that war was inevitable.

Attention was momentarily diverted from the situation in California when, on September 7, 1907, serious anti-Japanese riots broke out in Vancouver; but on October 14 another riot took place in San Francisco. The *New York Times* of September 29, 1907, carried a story about Japanese designs on the Philippines; the *New York Tribune* published a serial story depicting war between the United States and Japan, and the *New York Sun* announced that war was "inevitable." [27] The campaign reached such proportions that President Roosevelt publicly denounced "the wanton levity, brutality and jingoism of certain California mob leaders and certain yellow journals." Although the stock market reacted most unfavorably to these rumors, Dr. Bailey notes that, "strangely enough, the Japanese appear to have made no diplomatic representations whatever." [28] This developing situation showed a curious counterpoint: in the fall of 1906 the Japanese press was furious over the school-board affair; in February, 1907, the American press began to assume a belligerent tone while the Japanese remained silent; in May and June, 1907, the Japanese press was again on the rampage, but as the crisis mounted its tone became extremely moderate.

While the financial crisis in October, 1907, momentarily diverted public attention from the "inevitable" war with Japan, the war stories soon reappeared when, on December 16, the American fleet departed on its famous cruise around the world. At this juncture, Viscount Aoki, the Japanese ambassador, was recalled. On his way home, he announced in San Francisco that the Japanese government had undertaken to regulate immigration. This was the first public intimation of the Gentlemen's Agreement which was confirmed on January 25, 1908. Even the announcement that a "satisfactory agreement" had been con-

[26] Bailey, p. 239.   [27] *Ibid.*, p. 256.   [28] Page 255.

cluded failed to quiet the press, since, by that time, the fleet was already on its way.

The departure of the fleet occasioned a great outburst of jingoism. On the eve of its departure, "Fighting Bob" Evans had said: "Whether it proves feast, a frolic, or a fight, we are prepared." In January, 1908, Ambassador Tower relayed to the President a message from the Kaiser to the effect that the Japanese were drilling "thousands of soldiers in Mexico." Some observers believed that Germany was trying to precipitate a war between the United States and Japan as a means of forcing Great Britain to repudiate the Anglo-Japanese Alliance. Despite these rumors of war, the reception which the fleet received in New Zealand and Australia, and its terrific reception in Yokohama, tended to break the tension. The Root-Takahira notes were exchanged in November, 1908; and by February, 1909, the fleet was back in Hampton Roads.

While the fleet was on its way to the Orient, the anti-Japanese forces in California had been conducting a violent campaign against the Gentlemen's Agreement. A boycott was declared against all Japanese laundries, and billboards in San Francisco carried the notice: —

Foolish woman!
Spending your man's
Earnings on Japs.
Be Fair, patronize
Your Own.
We support you.[29]

Then, as the fleet was nearing home waters in January, the legislature convened in California. At this crucial juncture in relations between the United States and Japan, the legislature proceeded to nullify the good effect created by the fleet's cruise. Bills were introduced to segregate the Japanese in the public schools; to prevent them from owning land; to segregate them in certain residential sections; to prevent them from serving as directors of corporations. On January 16, 1909, the President, whose pa-

[29] Buell, p. 59.

tience was nearly exhausted, wired Governor Gillett that there was "no shadow of excuse" for this continued agitation. Then, on January 30, 1909, a mob in Berkeley assaulted Japanese residents. As a consequence, it took some twelve wires and telegrams from the President to Governor Gillett to force the withdrawal of most of these measures. Throughout this particular crisis, Southern Congressmen and the Southern press publicly "sympathized" with California and consistently endorsed whatever racist measures were sponsored on the West Coast.[30] After this experience, President Roosevelt became convinced that the agitation in California was primarily racial in character and that it had little relation to economic considerations.

During this flurry of excitement, the press of Japan, for the most part, remained silent. "This somewhat unexpected absence of resentment," notes Dr. Bailey, "cannot be definitely explained, but it would seem as if the fleet demonstration and satisfaction with the Root-Takahira agreement were not altogether dissociated from the Japanese reaction." Here, again, is convincing proof that the Japanese were manipulating the situation in California, pressing the question when it suited their purposes and remaining silent when nothing was to be gained. Usually the Japanese became very excited about the "California situation" on the eve of some new adventure in Korea or Manchuria; or on the eve of elections in Japan. For example, there was a considerable outburst of anti-American sentiment in Japan in 1909, at the time of the Manchurian railroad negotiations. "To a certain extent," wrote Mr. A. M. Pooley, "the hostile sentiment aroused in Japan and so vehemently expressed, was spontaneous, but to a greater extent it was generated from official and semi-official sources. It was then, and still is, used by the bureaucratic authorities as the basis of constant and insistent demands for military and naval expansion. The furnace of popular indignation was deliberately fanned by the militarists for the rolling of armour-plate and the drawing of heavy cannon." [31]

As though to serve notice that it did not intend to be forever

[30] See Tupper and McReynolds, p. 47.
[31] *Japan's Foreign Policies*, 1920.

frustrated, the California legislature in 1909 appropriated funds for a general investigation of the Japanese in agriculture. When the report, prepared by the State Labor Commissioner, was submitted in May, 1910, the legislature was horrified to discover that it was quite favorable to the Japanese. "The Japanese land owners," read a portion of the report, "are of the best class. They are steady and industrious, and from their earnings purchase land of low value and poor quality. The care lavished upon this land is remarkable, and frequently its acreage value has increased several hundred per cent in a year's time. Most of the proprietors indicate an intention to make the section in which they have located a permanent home, and adopt American customs and manners." Senator Caminetti (Commissioner General of Immigration in the Wilson administration) immediately proposed the following resolution which was quickly adopted: —

> Whereas, the State Labor Commissioner has in his report concerning Japanese laborers, expressed his opinion of the necessity of such laborers in this state, and thus without authority misrepresented the wishes of the people of this commonwealth, therefore, be it Resolved, that the opinion of such Labor Commissioner is hereby disapproved by this Senate.

Not only was the State Labor Commissioner publicly reprimanded, but his report was never published and the full text of the report is not, to this day, available.[32]

Throughout 1910 and 1911, anti-Japanese agitation continued unabated in California. When the treaty of 1911 between Japan and the United States was under consideration, President Taft had to intervene to prevent the passage of anti-Japanese legislation when its enactment might have had the most serious international implications. It so happened that San Francisco was preparing for the Pan-Pacific Exposition; and the possibility that Japan might not participate in the exposition served to muzzle the anti-Japanese guns momentarily. Japan's annexation of Korea in 1910 and its trial of the Korean nationalists in 1912 served,

[32] See Vol. 54, La Follette Committee Reports, p. 19836.

however, to keep public feeling at the fever pitch in California. The wildest rumors continued to circulate: —

In 1911 it was widely reported in this country with thrilling details, that Japan was taking steps to secure from Mexico a naval base at Magdalena Bay, in Lower California. This had followed a report in 1910 that the Japanese had sunk our drydock Dewey in Manila Bay, after planting mines which imperiled our navy at the station. They had also secretly charted our California harbors. Then there were numerous plottings with Mexico for a position from which this country could be attacked. A combination with Germany to destroy the Monroe Doctrine was the pabulum served up to the American public in 1912. In the same year Japan was forming an alliance with the West Coast Indians to gain a military foothold in this country. In 1915 Japanese spies were seen in the Panama fortifications and in the next year Japan was found conspiring to get a foothold in Panama by getting control of the San Blas Indian lands. Japan's diplomats penned Carranza's protests against our invasion of Mexico, after there had been landed in that country two hundred thousand Japanese troops, who had already fired on American troops at Mazatlan.[33]

Whether these rumors were true or untrue is beside the point. The sensational manner in which each and all of them were featured in the West Coast press served to keep the anti-Japanese issue very much alive. It is certainly not improbable that Japan planted some of these rumors for the express purpose of nurturing this valuable diversionary issue. In connection with subsequent happenings in California, it is interesting to note that, in the 1912 Presidential election, Woodrow Wilson, speaking in the state, declared: "The whole question is one of assimilation of diverse races. We cannot make a homogeneous population of a people who do not blend with the Caucasian race." Over one hundred thousand copies of this statement were distributed throughout California by the Democratic Party.

[33] From the *Independent;* quoted in *Japan and America* by Henry W. Taft, 1932, p. 111.

5. The Yellow Peril

"The conflict of classes, or of races," writes Dr. Robert E. Park, "in becoming forensic and political, ceases to be a mere clash of blind force and assumes a form and character that Herr Hitler has described as 'spiritual,' that is, a kind of psychic warfare in which the weapons are words, slogans, so-called 'vital lies' and other forms of propaganda, not excluding the news and the editors' and columnists' interpretation of it." Anti-Chinese agitation in California represented the initial or "conflict" stage in the development of a fixed racial ideology on the West Coast. The characteristic view of the Chinese was that expressed by a famous West Coast editor, Frank Pixley, in 1876, when he said: "The Chinese are inferior to any race God ever made." The Chinese were never feared in California: they were despised. It was with the appearance of the Japanese, and more particularly with the appearance of "the yellow peril" propaganda, that racial conflict on the West Coast entered the "forensic" stage and began to be discussed in "spiritual" terms.

"The yellow peril" is one of the most influential "vital lies" of our time. Like most lies, the origin of the phrase has been completely forgotten or historically misplaced. Turning to the *Dictionary of American History* (Vol. V, 1940), one finds this reference: "yellow peril . . . grew out of the ethnocentric, hypernationalistic attitude of Americans toward Oriental immigrants . . . had its genesis in the early contacts between Americans of European ancestry and Chinese immigrant laborers on the Pacific Coast." Although the first use of the expression has not been verified, it is quite clear that "the yellow peril" originated as a weapon in *European* power politics. Originally, it had no relation to the immigrant situation on the West Coast.

Shortly after the Sino-Japanese War, the Kaiser sent his cousin the Czar a cartoon entitled: "Peoples of Europe, Guard Your Most Precious Possessions!" The cartoon depicted an ogre arising in the Far East and stretching menacing hands toward the West. The cartoon was the work of the Kaiser himself. By promising

to guard Russia's western front, he had already laid the foundation for the Russo-Japanese War. Throughout the summer of
1900, the Kaiser orated, from time to time, about "the yellow
peril." Emil Ludwig notes that he was quick to realize that he
had invented an extremely effective lie. "So it works!" he wrote
in his diary; "that is very gratifying."

Sensing the likelihood of war with Japan, the Russians began
to make effective use of the same idea. As a matter of fact, Russia
and Germany (and later Japan itself!) planted learned essays,
from time to time, in the European press which elaborated upon
the newly invented peril. "No more popular theme," commented
a writer in the *Living Age* (February 8, 1904), had been con-
cocted in modern times. Seeking to capitalize upon its recently
acquired reputation as a "menace," Japan did nothing to dissipate,
but, on the contrary, had a hand in cultivating, the myth. In its
inception, therefore, the phrase had no relation to the situation
on the Pacific Coast.[34]

At an earlier date, however, the ideological content, to invest
the phrase with meaning, had been formulated. The first formulation of the doctrine itself was made in 1893 by C. H. Pearson in
a book entitled *National Life and Character*. After conjuring up
the horrible spectre of the yellow races sweeping over *Europe*,
Pearson concluded that "it is idle to say that, if all this should
come to pass, our pride of place will not be humiliated." Pearson's
formulation of this idea has been termed the "classic statement"
of the doctrine itself;[35] and he is credited with being the first
person to call attention to the "peril."[36] However, it was a Californian, Homer Lea, who first combined the phrase with the
doctrine and applied the argument specifically to the West Coast.

Lea was a Californian. He knew the "feel" of anti-Oriental
agitation. He was that rare bird among Californians, namely, one
who knew something about the Orient at first hand. He had been

[34] See *The Kaiser's Memoirs*, 1922, pp. 79–81; *Review of Reviews*, August,
1905, p. 218; *Living Age*, July 16, 1904; *Wilhelm Hohenzollern* by Emil
Ludwig, 1926, p. 252.
[35] See *Of Our Blood* by Robert E. Speer, 1924.
[36] See *Japanese Expansion and American Policies* by James Francis Abbot,
1916, p. 155.

in China as a soldier and Sun Yat-sen had visited in his home in Santa Monica. Prior to writing *The Valor of Ignorance*, he had inspected the California coastline and studied its terrain with great care. When the book was published in 1909, it was immediately seized upon by the Hearst Press and utilized effectively as a major prop in the developing anti-Oriental agitation. Lea correlated the domestic "peril" and the overseas "peril": he made them one. Some 18,000 copies of the book were sold in this country, but in Japan it went through twenty-four editions within one month of publication. Going out of print in this country in 1920, it was revived in 1942 with an introduction by Clare Boothe Luce.

Lea was not a Japanese-baiter. He set the tone for much of the ensuing agitation by the respectful attitude which he showed toward the Japanese people. He did not underestimate their capacities: he indulged in no name-calling. On the contrary, he implied that it was precisely because of their better qualities that the Japanese were to be feared. (Their virtues made them dangerous.) It was this argument that V. S. McClatchy, and others, were to use so effectively at a later date. At the same time, the book was essentially racist in character. "A nation," Lea argued, "may be kept intact only so long as its ruling element remains homogeneous." Racial similarity was the cornerstone of national security; a naturalized citizen was an anomaly. Assimilation was out of the question, since "racially there existed no relationship between the people of Japan and of the United States." This argument was extensively used by anti-Oriental leaders in California; [37] it formed the core of the racial views of Madison Grant and Lothrop Stoddard; and, through the work of these men, it again reverberated in California.

While Lea was a racist, he saw the essential vice in our policy toward Japanese immigration. By making the Japanese ineligible to citizenship, we had created that anomalous condition — "caste in a republic." The secondary consequences were of even greater importance. For "the creation of an inferior caste by political

[37] See *The Japanese Conquest of American Opinion* by Montaville Flowers, 1917.

disfranchisement soon permeates every phase of daily existence. Those who are disfranchised are treated by the populace, not alone with social unconcern, but with indignities. Municipalities direct restrictive ordinances against them so that they become the natural prey, not only of the lawless elements, but the police. Their status being already fixed in public opinion, their voice in protestations soon die away in hoarse and broken whispers. . . . When a class or race finds itself in a republic without political franchise, then as a race or class its rights are ground into broken dust. To expect the Japanese," he warned, "to submit to indignities is to be pitifully incomprehensive of their national character. And the American people should realize that it is this cumulative memoranda of wrongs that they must, on some certain sombre day, make answer to. . . ." He saw quite clearly that the military in Japan were using the situation in California to lay the foundation, among the people, for a future war against this country.

No one had a better comprehension than Homer Lea of the fact that little change could be expected in California's attitude toward the Japanese. For Lea realized that the feeling against the immigrants had become part of the traditions, the mores, of the people. "Anti-Japanese sentiment," he noted, "may have been dormant prior to the conclusion of the Russian War, but since then it has openly manifested itself, and is not restricted, as may be supposed, to union-labor or socialistic elements, but *permeates the entire social and political fabric of the West.* [Italics mine.] In the wild gorges of Siskiyou," he wrote, "on moss-grown boulders, and half effaced by the lichens of two decades, can even now be deciphered this legend: 'The Chinese Must Go, Vote for O'Donnell.' We have seen it on the redwood shacks of Mendocino; on the outhouses of cities and towns; on the board fences in the Valley of the Santa Clara, and from there to the Mojave Desert. Even by the borders of Death Valley, in the dreariest of solitudes, the West stencilled the epitome of its racial hatred, a hatred that was taken up and put into public ordinances — into the statute-books of the state, and finally, finding its way to Washington, violated under political pressure such treaty stip-

43

ulations as existed between the United States and China." [38] He called attention to the fact that all political parties in California, in 1908, were united in their opposition to further Japanese immigration. He divided public opinion in California into four groupings: 8 per cent pro-Japanese; 22 per cent indifferent; 30 per cent hostile; and 40 per cent belligerently hostile.

Not only had a firm ideological basis been laid for anti-Japanese feeling by 1909, but malicious stereotypes were being created which tended to solidify anti-Japanese sentiment. From the school-board incident in San Francisco, Wallace Irwin received the inspiration for his popular fiction about the Japanese schoolboy, Hashimura Togo.[39] First published in *Collier's* in 1907, these letters long enjoyed considerable popularity on the West Coast. In them the "Jap" stereotype was clearly outlined: the buck-toothed, bespectacled, tricky, wordy, arrogant, dishonest figure of the comic strips and pulp magazines. It was Mr. Irwin who invented the stereotyped speech of the Japanese-American or "Jap." It was Mr. Irwin who coined all the funny parodies on the use of Japanese honorifics, such as "Honorable Sir," and the "so sorry, please." Thereafter people saw, not the Japanese immigrants, but the stereotype "Jap."

So deep-seated had these group attitudes become by 1927 that Ruth Fowler concluded: "For an interminable length of time they will remain unfavorable to the Japanese as a people of a different race who are physically different and culturally different. . . . The habit of the emotional reaction of fear," she wrote, "will remain for many years." Minnie Inui, a Japanese girl raised in a Caucasian West Coast home, once stated that these attitudes were so pervasive that, by the time she reached maturity, she was definitely anti-Japanese. Writing of her experience as a girl in California during the First World War, Helen Sloan Stetson has said: —

This was the time it was going to happen: while we were busy fighting in Europe. This was when it was going to hap-

[38] *The Valor of Ignorance* by Homer Lea, Harper's, 1909, quoted by permission of the publishers.
[39] See *Letters of a Japanese Schoolboy*, 1909.

44

pen — the Japs were going to take over California. Because we feared greatly, we began to hate greatly. We hated the vegetable and fruit-stand men. We hated the laborers in our groves. We hated because we feared and we feared because we had seen them in the groves, moving and working and living like mechanical men without heart or mind or soul. Because they were machines, and we were only human, and easy going, and wasteful. It didn't happen that first war. But it is happening now: the Japs are coming to take California away just as I knew they would when I was little.[40]

6. The 1913 War Scare

One of the first measures proposed in the January, 1913, session of the California legislature was the so-called Webb-Heney Bill or Alien Land Act. Previously all such proposals had been aimed at aliens in general; but these earlier proposals had encountered the strong opposition of important landowning corporations controlled by British capital. This particular measure, however, was ingeniously drafted: it was aimed not at aliens generally, but at "aliens ineligible to citizenship." Since the existing treaty with Japan did not refer to agricultural lands, it could be argued that the act was not in violation of the treaty. President Wilson sought to prevent passage of the bill. He sent William Jennings Bryan to Sacramento to plead with the legislature and with Governor Hiram Johnson. Unlike the situation on prior occasions, however, the federation administration was now Democratic and the Governor was a Progressive-Republican with Presidential aspirations. The bill promptly passed both houses (35 to 2 in the Senate, 72 to 3 in the Assembly) and was signed by the Governor. The importance of this bill is that it represented the *first official act* of discrimination aimed at the Japanese. The sponsors of the bill freely admitted that it was aimed, not at preventing further Japanese expansion in agriculture, but at driving the Japanese from the state; as a step in the campaign for exclusion.

[40] "Us and the Japs" in *Woman's Day*, August, 1942; see also *"I Can Tell"* by Joan Fontaine, *Liberty*, April 11, 1942.

The land act could not have been passed at a more inopportune time. Shortly prior to its adoption, this country had aroused considerable resentment in Japan by its recognition of the newly established Chinese Republic. Charles W. Eliot reported that, "with a single exception," the American naval officers he had met in the Orient in 1912 "expected war between the United States and Japan within a few months; and most of them thought it was high time." [41] Furthermore the land act was passed, as Mr. A. M. Pooley has pointed out, "shortly after the Tokio mob had succeeded in shattering the third Katsura Ministry." Passage of the bill occasioned violent resentment in Japan. "Revelling in the recent discovery of its power," writes Mr. Pooley, "the mob, inflamed by the opposition, endeavored to use the same methods to force a settlement of the California question on the government" that it had used in ousting the Katsura Ministry. Throughout April and May, 1913, the Japanese press adopted a most threatening and truculent tone. California newspapers on April 18, 1913, carried a dispatch from Tokyo to the effect that "a demand that Japan resort to arms was hysterically cheered at a mass meeting here tonight to protest against the alien land bill now pending before the California legislature. Twenty thousand persons assembled."

"More unfortunate still," observed Mr. Pooley, "the wave of excitement grew under the stimulus of anti-American societies formed by men in responsible positions. The agitation of April and May, 1913, became a national movement and of such volume that the Government had to pay respect to it. The anti-American movement spread, associations sprang up like mushrooms to deal with the matter. Commercial circles agitated for a boycott of the Panama Exposition, and the Department of Agriculture and Commerce unofficially expressed its approval. National demonstrations were held in the principal cities to protest and to threaten. The leaders of the mobocracy boasted of their late victory over the clans, and asserted that the time had come to settle once and for all the question of racial prejudice. Members of Parliament invoked the old *jio* (anti-foreign spirit), advocated a policy of

[41] *Friendship Between the United States and Japan.*

yakiuchi (incendiarism), and invited the people to burn the American embassy. Insulting placards were posted on its walls and a police guard without." Political spokesmen advocated "sledge-hammer" blows against America; and the Marquis Okuma demanded the expulsion of American missionaries. "The missionaries," adds Mr. Pooley, "as usual, blew the Japanese trumpet, conferred together and with the authorities, and enriched the cable companies by innumerable telegrams to the States denouncing their own countrymen and eulogizing the Japanese." The Panama Canal had not been completed and Japan was sorely tempted to declare war. Mr. Pooley states that the Japanese government put out feelers, to see if a foreign loan might be raised to finance a war against America; it was in large part because the funds were not forthcoming (Europe was preparing for war at the time) that Japan did not declare war.

Later in 1913 the Japanese government sent a mission to this country to "allay the bitter feelings of the Japanese in California." [42] Mr. J. Soyeda, a member of this commission, subsequently published a report entitled *Survey of the Japanese Question in California*. In this report he took occasion to urge the Japanese in California to assimilate. He urged them to abandon those customs and habits which set them apart from other residents and to act the part of good citizens, even though they were ineligible to citizenship. The reception accorded this courteous and tactful pamphlet in the California press is indicative of the attitudes which then prevailed. "Honorable Pamphlet," stated the *San Francisco Examiner* on October 2, 1913, "informs us that Honorable Japanese is truly morally superior to unfortunate American inhabitableness, being truth, firmness, uprightness and faithfulness in gentlemen's agreement, therefore is perfectly agreeable to naturalization and intermarriage, which afford happy solution to Honorable Immigration Question not yet impacted upon yellow American press."

The ingenious feature of the Webb-Heney Act of 1913 was that the prohibition ran against "aliens ineligible to citizenship." Although some lower federal courts had ruled that Japanese

[42] See *The Japanese Crisis* by James A. B. Scherer, 1916.

47

were eligible to citizenship, it was generally assumed in 1913 that they were ineligible. The Supreme Court had not, as yet, decided the question. Just how had it come about that Japanese and Chinese were "ineligible to citizenship"? Since 1790 our naturalization laws had defined aliens eligible to citizenship as "free white persons." In a memorable speech in the United States Senate, Charles Sumner had moved to strike out the word "white" which he denounced as a "requirement disgraceful to this country and to this age. I propose to bring our system into harmony with the Declaration of Independence and the Constitution of the United States." Neither the Constitution nor the Declaration of Independence, he noted, uses the word "white." During this famous debate on the naturalization laws in 1870, Congress made aliens of African nativity and persons of African descent eligible to citizenship. But Congress went further and, on Sumner's suggestion, actually struck out the word "white." The word was restored, however, in 1875, largely because of anti-Chinese agitation in California. It has since remained in the statute. Even after 1875 codifiers felt that the word no longer belonged in the statute since it was distinctly out of harmony with, if not actually violative of, the sweeping declarations of the Fourteenth Amendment.

It is extremely significant, as Mr. Max J. Kohler has pointed out in his *Immigration and Aliens in the United States* (1936), that the phrase "free white persons," although on the statute books since 1790, was not construed by the courts until 1878. In a case involving a Chinese, Judge Sawyer, of the federal district court in California, held in that year that the word "white" referred to a person of the Caucasian race. This decision, as all subsequent decisions, completely ignored the circumstances existing when the phrase was adopted. Actually the phrase "free white persons" was designed to exclude "slaves," whether they were red, white, black, or brown, and it was intended to exclude Indians living in tribal organizations. It will be noted that not all *white* persons are eligible; but only *free* white persons. Thus the phrase, as originally used, was utterly devoid of racist implications. It was not *races*, as such, that were excluded; but rather all persons who were not *free*. In an article written in 1894, Professor John H. Wigmore had argued that the word "white" was utterly meaningless if it was construed as importing the idea of "race." He had contended that the Japanese were, in fact, eligible for citizenship. Thus a century after the phrase was first used, it was given, by construction, an intention completely at variance with its original significance. Once established in law, this meaning was extended and broadened by the alien land acts and it led eventually and directly to the passage of the exclusionary Immigration Act of 1924. It should be noted, also, that the prohibition affected many other groups beside the Japanese. It applied equally to Chinese, Filipinos, native Hawaiians, and Hindus. "The implication of inferiority, based upon the alien-ineligible-to-citizenship status," wrote Dr. Mears, "is the greatest grievance which the peoples of Eastern Asia have against this country."

By way of an aside, it might be mentioned that the Webb-Heney Act was actually meaningless. It merely prevented the acquisition of property in the future. It divested no Japanese holdings. It permitted the Japanese to lease agricultural lands, in unlimited amounts, for a period of three years. There was nothing in the act to prevent the indefinite renewal of leases. It had no effect whatever upon the land situation in California. The men who drafted the act conceded that it was intended as "an irritant" — a warning to the Japanese, a step in the campaign for exclusion. However the bill was very effective political material for there did exist in California *a real* land problem.

Visiting California in the eighties, Lord Bryce had been impressed with the extremes of wealth and poverty. He believed that the ostentatious display of wealth by the newly created, and socially irresponsible, millionaires of San Francisco had contributed to the social unrest of the time. Speculation in Spanish land grants was widespread. Great landed estates had come into existence in California and the land was being steadily monopolized. "Latifundia perdunt Californian," was the way he summarized his impressions.

Anti-Japanese agitation in California had the effect of focusing public attention upon what was in reality a minor aspect of the

49

land problem; and, on the other hand, it diverted attention from the problem of large-scale land ownership and operation. When Walter B. Pitkin visited the state in 1920 to report on the Japanese problem, he observed that many of "these royal estates and a hundred others of princely extent and richness" still existed in California. The holders of these vast estates, he noted, continued to behave, despite changed conditions, with a reckless disregard of social responsibility. During the debate on the 1920 Alien Land Act, for example, the *Los Angeles Times* had suggested that the problem might be solved by the importation of 1,000,000 Chinese coolies! [43] The small farmer sensed that the employment of cheap Oriental labor on these large estates constituted, insofar as he was concerned, a type of unfair competition. To some extent, therefore, his anti-Japanese views were an expression of a misplaced social or class consciousness.

Also these California *Junkers* had long displayed such a princely contempt for farm laborers that as late as 1920 "no self-respecting man who could have earned a living at any other form of work would have followed the California ranches." California, Mr. Pitkin observed, was "made up of large ranch holdings and small fruit-ranches. During the harvest season men are employed for only a short period at one place, and then move on to another job. On the large grain-ranches and fruit-farms the hands are usually paid a certain amount a day and board. Until the State Commission of Immigration and Housing took the matter in charge, the men slept almost anywhere. . . . Men slept in barns, on haystacks, or out of doors. All men carried their own blankets. . . . They ate in the cook house surrounded by thousands of flies from scattered manure piles." Conditions were so miserable, in fact, that about the only white men the farmers could attract to the fields were chronic drunks and bindlestiffs who had been following the "dirty-plate route" for years.

Given this state of affairs, it required only a minimum amount of agitation to arouse these men against the Japanese. Their vehemence on the subject, like that of the small farmer, was a

[43] See editorial quoted in *Must We Fight Japan?*, p. 245.

form of unrecognized class hatred diverted from its real object — the *Junkers* of the San Joaquin Valley — toward a scapegoat, the Japanese. Certain of these large concerns such as the California and Delta Farms — with 50,000 acres in the heart of the delta region — and the Rindge Land and Navigation Company — were among the largest employers of Japanese farm labor. There can be little doubt that it was "these great land monopolists and land speculators," as Mr. Jabez T. Sunderland noted, who were "California's real foes — these and not the small farmers, the hard-working market gardeners and the skillful orchardists who, though born in Japan, are loyal to California, and are doing so much to make her waste places to bud and blossom as the rose." [44] Despite this aspect of the matter, however, even such outstanding advocates of land reform as Elwood Mead joined forces with the anti-Japanese movement, thereby investing the movement with something of the aura of a liberal, progressive, and reformist crusade. In fact, most of the progressive political leaders in California were identified with the movement.

7. The Lord of San Simeon

With the entrance of Japan on the side of the Allies in the First World War, anti-Japanese agitation momentarily subsided in California. The war greatly increased the demand for food and not too much emphasis was placed on enforcement of the newly enacted Alien Land Act. It was not long, however, before various interests began to fish in the troubled waters of the time.

The Hearst newspapers had, of course, always been anti-Oriental. The senior Hearst had not hesitated to use anti-Chinese politics as one means of acquiring a seat in the United States Senate. His son had long shown promise as an amateur anti-Japanese agitator; but, with the First World War, he began to show professional talent. At the outset of the war, Hearst was pro-German, and violently anti-Japanese and anti-Mexican. It has been suggested that his ownership of the Cerro de Paseo

[44] *Rising Japan: Is She a Menace?*, 1918.

mining property in Mexico — which could only be profitably operated in the event of war in the Pacific — had something to do with his attitude.

During the early stages of the war, two German agents contributed regular features to the Hearst newspapers. One of these agents, Edward Lyell Fox, wrote a letter to the infamous Nazi intriguer, Franz von Papen, in which he pointed out that the United States had been close to war with Japan in 1913. "The source of that situation," he wrote, "was California. *Cleverly handled, California can be used to create the same situation today.* . . . The public mind must be diverted from Europe to the Orient. Pro-German publicity is futile. The Hearst papers will lead in the attack on the Japs." [45] Incidentally, it is interesting to note that this is precisely the line used today by the Fight Japan First elements. If a first-class war scare could be promoted, Fox advised, it would tend to interrupt the flow of American munitions to Europe. Mr. Hearst soon provided the "scare." [46]

The attack was launched by an elaborate piece which appeared in the *New York American*, and other Hearst newspapers, on September 28, 1915, entitled: "Japan Plans to Invade and Conquer the United States Revealed by Its Own Bernhardi." The article purported to be a translation of a book published in Japan by "the Japanese Military Association." It was illustrated by pictures purporting to show Japanese troops practising landing operations preparatory to an assault on the California coast. Investigation revealed that: (*a*) the purported translators could not be located or identified; (*b*) the pictures were retouched illustrations used during the Sino-Japanese War of 1895; (*c*) the original story published in Japan had been a "dream story" — of the pulp magazine variety — which had sold about 3000 copies instead of the 500,000 copies represented; and (*d*) that the text had been distorted in translation. [47]

[45] Quoted in *Imperial Hearst* by Ferdinand Lundberg, 1936, p. 239; italics mine.

[46] Note that anti-Japanese propaganda during the First World War was financed by German money. See *Annals, American Academy of Political and Social Science*, January, 1921, p. 73 and 116.

[47] See *Hearst, the Lord of San Simeon* by Oliver Carlson and Ernest Sutherland Bates, 1936, p. 179.

Throughout 1915 and 1916, sensational anti-Japanese stories continued to appear in the Hearst press.[48] The *New York American* of July 23, 1916, carried a "Hymn of Hate," one stanza of which read: —

> They've battleships, they say,
> On Magdalena Bay!
> Uncle Sam, won't you listen when we warn you?
> They meet us with a smile
> But they're working all the while,
> And they're waiting just to steal our California!
> So just keep your eyes on Togo,
> With his pockets full of maps,
> For we've found out we can't trust the Japs!

As part of this campaign, interests which Mr. Hearst controlled in the motion-picture industry made a serial film entitled "Patria," starring Mrs. Vernon Castle. After he had seen a section of it in Washington, President Wilson wrote the producers. He complained that the picture was "extremely unfair"; that it was "calculated to stir up a great deal of hostility." He asked that it be withdrawn.

At a later date, Walter B. Pitkin stated that he had examined hundreds of items which appeared in the Hearst press during this period and had found the allegations "so ridiculous that only children and morons could take them seriously." Precisely the same statement, of course, might have been made about sections of the Japanese press for the same period. In any case, it was this contemptible race-mongering of the Hearst press in 1915 and 1916 that set the stage for the next outbreak of anti-Japanese feeling in California.

8. The Protagonists

At this time, V. S. McClatchy was editor and publisher of the powerful *Sacramento Bee*. The McClatchys were a pioneer Irish-Catholic family related by marriage to the tightly knit "first

[48] See *Los Angeles Examiner* for the month of October, 1915.

families" who, for so many years, have dominated Sacramento. The McClatchy newspapers — the *Sacramento Bee*, the *Fresno Bee*, and the *Modesto Bee* — have always exerted exceptional political influence in the San Joaquin Valley. There is no doubt that, on the whole, this influence has been exercised in the interest of the people. The McClatchy newspapers have fought for public ownership; for good government; for many liberal and progressive measures. Just because of this fact, however, they were extremely influential when they began to support anti-Japanese agitation.

Eight miles from Sacramento was the town of Florin, one of the few communities in the state completely dominated by the Japanese. Near by were important Japanese settlements at Walnut Grove and Mayhew. As a boy, V. S. McClatchy had driven through these districts in horse and buggy, delivering copies of the *Sacramento Bee* to a typically American farm community. While he always insisted that economic interest had little to do with anti-Japanese feeling, it is interesting to note that, in one of his numerous pamphlets, Mr. McClatchy complained that "no American newspaper" was being distributed in the Florin section in 1919. It is altogether possible that he was not even aware of the fact that his hatred of the Japanese might be related to the decline of the *Sacramento Bee's* circulation in Florin. In any case, Mr. McClatchy was an honest, sincere, courageous man.

In 1919 this provincial-minded gentleman made his first trip to the Orient. He happened to be in Seoul when the independence demonstration occurred; in fact, he returned with one of the first copies of the Korean Independence Manifesto. As an experienced newspaperman, Mr. McClatchy was deeply impressed with the tight censorship that the Japanese exercised over virtually all news reaching the West Coast papers. He arrived back in California determined to lead a holy crusade against the resident Japanese. In September, 1919, he formed the California Joint Immigration Committee (sponsored by the Native Sons of the Golden West, the Grange, the State Federation of Labor, and the newly formed American Legion); withdrew from his business, and devoted the balance of his life to anti-Japanese propaganda. In effect, he *was* the California Joint Immigration Committee. He financed its operations; he directed its activities. As a publicist, he was shrewd, resourceful, and thoroughly plausible. His hatred of the Japanese was of the sublimated variety: he never engaged in name-calling and he consistently paid tribute to the "better qualities" of the people themselves.[49] In later years, he often exchanged friendly letters with some of the Nisei leaders in California,[50] and on occasion invited them to his San Francisco apartment.

His principal opponent in a decade-long debate on the Japanese question in California was the Reverend Sidney Gulick. Born in Japan of missionary parents, Gulick had resided in the Orient for over thirty years. Prior to his return to America in 1913, he had lived all of his life in the Far East and most of the time in Japan, where he had lectured at Doshisha University and the Imperial University at Kyoto. Not only was he hopelessly out of touch with the current of events in America, but he was decidedly pro-Japanese in his views. His arguments were frequently unscientific and his thinking was generally illogical and fuzzy. He defended Japanese policy in Korea and publicly supported Japan at the time the famous Twenty-one Demands were served on China.[51] Much the same position, incidentally, was taken by the Reverend Frank Heron Smith, another "missionary spokesman" for the Japanese in California.[52]

Around 1914 the Federal Council of Churches, working in collaboration with the Japan Society (which had been formed in 1907), set up a special committee to deal with the Japanese question in California. It was said at the time that approximately one fifth of the council's revenues was set aside for the work of this Committee on Relations with Japan. In setting up the committee and financing its activities, the Federal Council was pri-

[49] See, for example, his pamphlet, *The Germany of Asia*, based on a series of articles which appeared in the *Bee*, March, 1919, after his return from the Orient.
[50] See letters to Saburo Kido dated July 5, 1935, and May 23, 1933.
[51] See Tupper and McReynolds, pp. 97, 115.
[52] See *The Other Side of the Korean Question*, published in Seoul, May, 1920.

marily acting in response to pleas from missionary groups in Japan, who complained that anti-Japanese agitation in California was prejudicing their work.

The Reverend Sidney Gulick was selected, in 1914, to direct the work of this committee. Not only were ample funds available, but the committee had open sesame to the pages of the *Outlook* and *Independent* (controlled by Mr. Hamilton Holt, one of the organizers of the Japan Society). As a consequence, the Japanese question in California became inseparably linked with a strong pro-Japanese policy in the Orient; in other words, *Japan* was defended as well as the Japanese immigrants in California. Such a policy played directly into the hands of the anti-Japanese forces in California. The side of the Japanese immigrants in California needed fair presentation to the public; but this type of presentation was worse than none. Dr. Gulick consistently tried to prove too much and thereby incurred additional antagonism.

Throughout the long controversy that ensued after 1914, he worked in the closest possible collaboration with K. K. Kawakami, whose subsequent career leaves no doubt that he was an official apologist for the Japanese government.[53] Books, pamphlets, and articles flowed from the pens of Messrs. Gulick and Kawakami. They were assisted by another Japanese agent, Dr. T. Iyenaga, who was on the payroll of the Japan Society.[54] Such an alignment confirmed the worst suspicions that Mr. McClatchy ever entertained about the resident Japanese. He saw through the flimsy arguments advanced by the missionaries; and he knew perfectly well that Kawakami was running more than "a bureau of literary service" in San Francisco.

It should be noted, for the record, that it was these pro-Japanese forces who laid the foundation for the passage of the Immigration Act of 1924. Dr. Gulick thought it would be good strategy to secure the passage of a quota immigration measure before the anti-Japanese forces in California could secure the passage of an exclusion bill. The anti-Japanese forces promptly denounced the strategy as an attempt to nullify the Gentlemen's

---

[53] See *The Menace of Japan* by T. O'Conroy, 1934, pp. 99–100.
[54] See Pooley, p. 54; Flowers; and Crow, p. 197.

Agreement and began to clamor for exclusion. Ignoring the un-
mistakably aggressive direction of Japanese policy in the Far
East and talking about peace in abstract terms, Dr. Gulick, and
the groups he represented, gave the race bigots a polemical advantage which they were quick to utilize. Commenting upon the
proposal for a quota immigration system, Max J. Kohler writes: —

> It is not without interest that this national quota scheme
> was first suggested by the Rev. S. L. Gulick, a missionary
> who had resided in Japan for a long time, and who evoked
> this scheme in order to avoid friction with the Orient. I
> had occasion to warn him about fifteen years ago, that it
> would not solve the Japanese question, but it would cause
> untold mischief for other race groups as well, and would
> also do serious injury to our country at large.[55]

9. The Postwar Campaign

During the 1915 and 1917 sessions of the California legislature
attempts had been made to pass additional anti-Japanese measures; but these proposals were held in abeyance and later tabled
when we found ourselves in the war as an ally of Japan. But
on April 1, 1919, while the Peace Conference was in session in
Paris, two California Senators sought to introduce a number of
anti-Japanese bills. A cablegram was sent to the Secretary of
State in Paris, asking his views on the advisability of pressing such
legislation at the time. Mr. Lansing immediately replied that it
would be particularly unfortunate to have the bills introduced
and requested that they be withdrawn. But the moment the
Treaty of Versailles was signed on June 28, 1919, a wave of anti-
Japanese agitation swept California.[56]

This renewed agitation differed, in important respects, from
earlier movements. To an extent that had not previously been
true, this agitation was anti-Japan rather than anti-Japanese.
Elements that had never been previously interested now became
violent partisans of the "anti" movement. This shift in opinion

[55] *Op. cit.*, p. 161.
[56] See *Japanese Immigration* by Raymond Leslie Buell, 1924.

was largely due to Japanese action in Korea, Siberia, China, and Shantung. The publication of a number of books about the Korean situation contributed to the shift.[57] Also various government reports dealing with Hawaii served to arouse general apprehension.

Organized labor, which had taken a leading part in all previous agitations, now began to dissociate itself from the anti-Japanese movement. After 1910 the Japanese had been driven from the cities toward the land. Now it looked as though they were going to be driven from the land back to the cities, and labor did not relish this possibility. The Federated Trades Council of Sacramento, on September 10, 1920, passed a resolution condemning anti-Japanese "propaganda now being spread by designing parties to the detriment of labor." In 1916 the American Federation of Labor failed, for the first time in years, to pass an anti-Oriental resolution. Speaking in California, Hugo Ernst, a leader of the San Francisco labor movement, had said: "This sort of resolution gets us nowhere. Why can't we face the question more squarely and organize the Japanese workers in our midst, which is the only solution to the question?" Walter MacArthur, another influential labor leader, condemned the idea of "racial inferiority." "You can't charge the Japs with unassimilability," said Richard Caverly of the Boilermakers Union; "the same charge used to be directed against the lousy Irish." Despite labor's growing disaffection, however, the postwar anti-Japanese agitation was founded upon a broader popular base than at any previous period.

"The origin of the agitation which developed in 1919," write Tupper and McReynolds, "was a purely political move with an eye on the 1920 election."[58] United States Senator James D. Phelan, a Democrat seeking re-election when every sign pointed to a Republican landslide, premised his entire campaign upon the issue of White Supremacy. Writing in the *Grizzly Bear* for February, 1920, he said: "Imagine a Japanese seeking the hand

[57] See *The Case of Korea* by Henry Chung, 1920; *The Rebirth of Korea* by H. H. Cynn, 1920; and *Korea's Fight for Freedom* by F. A. McKenzie, 1920.
[58] *Op. cit.*

of an American woman in marriage! . . . If you knew," he said in the same article, "how these people raise their garden truck, you would never let a bite of it pass your lips." To aid the sorely pressed Senator, his colleagues arranged for the Committee on Immigration and Naturalization to hold hearings in California during the summer of 1920. The hearings were opened in San Francisco on July 12, 1920, by Senator Phelan himself. He testified that the "Japanese are an immoral people"; proceeded to confuse Buddhism and Shintoism; charged that California was headed toward "mongrelization and degeneracy"; claimed that mysterious threats had been made upon his life; and urged that the Japanese be ousted to save the state from the threat of Bolshevism! A man of great wealth, Senator Phelan financed the Anti-Asiatic League and the Oriental Exclusion League, both of which organizations were integral parts of his political machine.

After the Treaty of Versailles had been signed, the California legislators began to clamor for a special session so that they might pass the bills which had been tabled at the request of Mr. Lansing. Governor William D. Stephens refused to call a special session. The Native Sons immediately demanded his removal from office; denounced the opposition as "Jap-lovers," and rallied their forces to save "California — the White Man's Paradise." In an effort to sidetrack this agitation, Governor Stephens caused a special report to be prepared on the Japanese question. When this report (*California and the Oriental*) appeared in June, 1920, it was found to be a characteristically rabid document. It also appeared that the Governor himself had finally decided to mount the anti-Japanese bandwagon. Seeking to punish him, however, for his failure to call a special session of the legislature, the "anti" forces immediately placed two initiative measures on the November ballot: an alien poll-tax bill and a new Alien Land Act. Both measures were approved by decisive majorities: the Alien Land Act by a vote of 668,483 to 222,086.

The agitation accompanying the 1920 election and the campaign over these measures occasioned widespread resentment in Japan. In the autumn of 1920, the Marquis Okuma called a meeting in Tokyo to organize a publicity campaign against "the unlawful attitude of the California-Americans." Viscount Takahira Kato had said of the 1920 Alien Land Act: "We can never overlook this act." Students in Tokyo began to debate the question "Shall We Declare War against the United States?" and in this country Walter B. Pitkin raised the question: "Must We Fight Japan?" This 1920 agitation rapidly assumed national proportions. "The spread of the agitation throughout the country," observe Tupper and McReynolds, "encouraged the anti-Japanese agitators to renew their movement against the Japanese immigrant, and the old issues were once again brought to the front pages of the press." [59] The California Oriental Exclusion League began to send speakers throughout the East and Middle West, and to cover the nation with its pamphlets and leaflets. Coming as it did, when the ink was scarcely dry on the Treaty of Versailles, this agitation did incalculable harm. It brought us, as a matter of fact, to the brink of war with Japan. [60]

In point of virulence, the 1920 agitation far exceeded any similar demonstration in California. In support of the initiative measures, the American Legion exhibited a motion picture throughout the state entitled "Shadows of the West." All the charges ever made against the Japanese were enacted in this film. The film showed a mysterious room fitted with wireless apparatus by which "a head Japanese ticked out prices which controlled a state-wide vegetable market"; spies darted in and out of the scenes; Japanese were shown dumping vegetables into the harbor to maintain high prices; two white girls were abducted by a group of Japanese men only to be rescued, at the last moment, by a squad of American Legionnaires. When meetings were called to protest the exhibition of this scurrilous film, the meetings were broken up. [61]

Two influential novels appeared which were planned as part of the campaign: *Seed of the Sun* (1921) by Wallace Irwin and *The Pride of Palomar* (1921) by Peter B. Kyne. [62] The Irwin novel, I am informed, was prepared at the instigation of V. S.

[59] *Op. cit.*, p. 177.
[60] See *Japan in Recent Times* by A. Morgan Young, 1929, p. 221.
[61] See Buell, p. 71.
[62] See also *The Interlopers* by Griffing Bancroft, 1917.

McClatchy. Both novels had appeared as serials in national publications of large circulation in 1920: the Irwin novel in the *Saturday Evening Post* and the Kyne novel in the *Cosmopolitan*. Both novels, according to Ruth Fowler, were long in active demand in the California public libraries. Mr. Cornelius Vanderbilt, Jr., sent copies of the Kyne novel to a list of important Americans and requested their comments. These were published in a pamphlet entitled *The Verdict of Public Opinion on the Japanese-American Question*. The Kyne novel was largely based upon Mr. Montaville Flowers' *The Japanese Conquest of American Opinion* (1917), and was dedicated to Mr. Flowers.

Here are some of the charges made against the Japanese in Mr. Kyne's novel: their manners are abominable; they are greedy, selfish, calculating, quarrelsome, suspicious, crafty, irritable, and unreliable; they have no sense of sportsmanship, no affection for their wives, and they have never shown the slightest nobility or generosity of spirit.[63] These remarks were directed, of course, at immigrants living in America. "When a member of the great Nordic race," observes the hero of the novel, "fuses with a member of a pigmented race, both parties to the union violate a natural law." This hero, a Native Son, angrily argues with another character that "we ought to have Jim Crow cars for these cock-sure sons of Nippon." The book is one long paean of praise for the Anglo-Saxon copied almost verbatim from Homer Lea and Montaville Flowers. Amusingly enough, however, it is an Anglo-Saxon character who, in conspiracy with a Japanese, attempts to defraud the hero (who is part Mexican, but a "high-class" Mexican). "How about John Chinaman?" one character asks the hero. To this query he gives the stock California answer: "Oh, a Chinaman is different. He's a regular fellow — he appreciates the sanity of our position." When the Declaration of Independence is mentioned, the hero counters with the charge that that document was written by "sublimated jackasses."

Josiah Royce once observed, apropos of anti-Oriental agitation in his native state of California, that "trained hatreds are par-

[63] Pp. 124-125.

ticularly pathetic and peculiarly deceitful." By 1920 the people
of California had been thoroughly trained to hate the Japanese
and other Oriental people. Charges advanced against the Chinese
in 1876 — when the first Congressional committee inquired into
the Oriental problem on the Coast — had been repeated, with
scarcely a single modification, in every subsequent hearing or investigation. The people of California had listened to these charges;
had heard them repeated by responsible public officials; had seen
them in the newspapers and on the billboards; and had become
familiar with them in every political campaign. For seventy-five
years, writes Dr. Charles N. Reynolds, the people of California
had "lived in an atmosphere of racial consciousness." [64] Surveying
the files of one small-town newspaper, Dr. Reynolds found 2877
news item about the Japanese, totaling 20,453 inches of space.
The general attitude reflected in these items was that of "irritation verging on hostility." He also found that there were "peaks"
and "depressions" in the amount of space devoted to the Japanese
(which he was able to correlate with election years and periods
of economic depression). "The almost complete disappearance
of unfavorable news in the breaks between high levels," he wrote,
"is eloquent proof of the fictitious character of the anti-Japanese
movement."

The 1920 agitation in California was so violent that it over-
flowed, so to speak, and began to affect other groups. In the
summer of 1920, roadside signs appeared in Fresno stating: "No
Armenians Wanted"; and at the same time petitions were circulated, around Lodi, against the Armenians, Turks, Greeks, and
Hindus, as well as against the Japanese.[65] On the night of July
18, 1921, a band of several hundred white men, with the "apparent connivance of the police," [66] rounded up fifty-eight Japanese
laborers in Turlock, "placed them on board a train, and warned
them never to return." The repercussions in Tokyo were instantaneous. "No recent development," wrote Louis Seibold, "has
ever caused more excitement among the Japanese than the recent

[64] "Oriental-White Relations in Santa Clara County," unpublished dissertation, Stanford University, 1927.
[65] *San Francisco Examiner:* June 20, 1920.
[66] Buell, *Japanese Immigration.*

driving out of 700 Japs from the fruit section around Turlock, California. The leading newspapers of Tokio, Osaka, Kobe and Nagasaki seized upon the incident to demand from the United States an indemnity for the damage done to the feelings of the former subjects of the Mikado by the citizens of California." [67] The Turlock "incident," notes Mr. Buell, was "a direct result of the campaigns of incitement against the Japanese which have featured in many California elections. The incident shows that the means employed by the Pacific Coast to 'solve' its Japanese problem merely increase the ill-feeling between the Oriental and the whites, and still further alienate the Japanese from American life." Later Japanese were driven out of the Merced area [68] and still later from Hopland and other parts of the state.[69]

These "incidents" in California in 1920 and 1921 had international significance. The Washington Naval Conference convened on November 12, 1921, and was in session through February, 1922. Prior agitation in California threatened to interfere with the plans for the conference. The people of Japan were certainly not in a position, in these years, to follow the devious diplomatic moves of their rulers; but as Mr. Buell has pointed out, the agitation in California "was perfectly comprehensible to the people of Tokyo." [70] Surveying the work of the conference itself, Mr. Buell said: "As long as we continue this pin-pricking policy toward Japanese legally resident in this country, the Japanese in Japan will naturally be led to believe that the anti-Japanese agitation in the United States is wholly illegitimate and caused by racial prejudice alone. More important still, they will be led to believe by the military party in Japan, that America's protests against Japanese imperialism in Asia are a mere mask behind which are hidden the 'real' designs of the United States in the Far East." [71] The main reason for popular Japanese suspicion of American policy consisted in "our domestic policy toward the Japanese." [72]

[67] *Op. cit.*
[68] *San Francisco Examiner*, July 15, 1921.
[69] *Ibid.*, July 29, 1924.
[70] *The Washington Conference*, 1922, p. 365.
[71] Page 364.   [72] Page 362.

10. Another Pyrrhic Victory

The Alien Land Act, passed as an initiative measure in 1920, was represented as the "final solution" to the Japanese problem; as designed to eliminate every "loophole" in the 1913 statute. Following its adoption in California, much the same statute was adopted in Washington, Oregon, Arizona, Colorado, Delaware, Nebraska, Texas, Idaho, and New Mexico. As soon as the act went into effect in California, an appeal was immediately taken to the United States Supreme Court. Pending an outcome of the appeal, its enforcement was stayed. It was not until December, 1923, that the Supreme Court handed down its decision upholding the constitutionality of the act. The decision created great consternation in California, for most of the large land-holding companies had been advised that the act was unconstitutional. Newspapers carried sensational headlines about 30,000 Japanese preparing to abandon 500,000 acres of valuable farm lands.[73] At long last, the Japanese were going to be "ousted" from the fields.

Actually the Japanese continued to dominate the production of small-fruit and vegetable crops. A comparison of the percentage of the crops controlled by Japanese in 1920 with the same figures for 1940 shows that, in the twenty-year period, the Japanese had lost control of certain crops (lettuce) and gained in others. In general, the Japanese occupied much the same position in California agriculture in 1940 that they had in 1920. The average acreage of Japanese farms in California was reduced from 80.1 acres in 1920 to 44 in 1940; from a total of 361,276 acres in 1920 to 226,094 in 1940. The total value of their production, however, had increased from 1920 to 1940. The number of Japanese employed in agriculture declined somewhat after 1920 and a drift back toward the cities developed. But it was soon discovered that non-Japanese farmers could not, on a competitive basis, farm these lands successfully; and gradually the Japanese

[73] See *Literary Digest*, January 12, 1924, and "California Uproots the Japanese" by Robert Welles Ritchie, *Country Gentlemen*, December, 1923.

moved back into substantially the same position which they had occupied in 1920.

Enforcement of the Alien Land Act of 1920 was vested in local law-enforcement officials. When a "white person" in one of these counties wanted to lease land to a Japanese, he usually had no difficulty in doing so. Local district attorneys enforced the act when they wanted to enforce it; and they obligingly ignored evasions of the act when it suited their interests to do so. The act was easily evaded: title to farm land was placed in the names of Hawaiian or American-born Japanese; verbal agreements were entered into — "gentlemen's agreements" — that ran counter to the terms of written documents; Japanese were employed as "managers" instead of as "tenants." By these and other devices, and with the connivance of law-enforcement officials, the act was blithely ignored. The amount of land escheated to the state under this statute is wholly negligible. With the large-scale importation of Filipino workers after 1924, production was steadily increased — the Filipinos becoming farm laborers and the Japanese being promoted to managerial positions.

It would be extremely difficult to determine precisely what groups profited by the passage of this act, the agitation for which had jarred two continents and nearly precipitated a war. Land-owners certainly did not profit, for they were forced (at least momentarily) to accept lower rentals. Agricultural workers did not profit, for their wages declined to an all-time low by 1933. In the long run, the non-Japanese produce growers did not profit, since, after 1920, production became increasingly organized on a nation-wide basis. California growers were, therefore, competing with Italian vegetable growers in New Jersey and Mexican workers in Texas. The competitive position of the California farmer was not improved. The general public did not benefit; on the contrary, it paid the bill. Prior to the passage of this act, Japanese growers had forced the cost of vegetables to the consumers in West Coast cities to decline from 10 to 50 per cent (in some crops) at a time when food prices generally were rising. "With the exception of a few groups," writes Dr. John Rademaker, "the struggle was academic to all factions supporting the acts. The

65

benefits these groups derived from the acts were not dependent upon the actual presence or absence of the Japanese farmers, *but rather upon the process of opposing them.*" [74] (Italics mine.) That is, the business of opposing the Japanese had political value to the organizations involved.

11. Exclusion

Although it was generally assumed that Japanese were "ineligible to citizenship," a test case did not arise until after the passage of the Alien Land Act of 1920. The Japanese consuls seemed reluctant to obtain a decision on the question, apparently preferring to keep the issue alive for propaganda purposes. After the passage of the Alien Land Act, they concluded that a test could no longer be avoided. The test case itself, the Ozawa case, was decided by the Supreme Court on November 13, 1922. In this case, the Court held that Takao Ozawa, graduate of Berkeley High School, three years a student at the University of California, was not a "free white person" and was therefore ineligible to citizenship. The case was one of great importance, since it had a bearing on the decision in the Alien Land Act case and opened the door, so to speak, for the passage of the Immigration Act of 1924.

The decision provoked wild resentment in Japan. In commenting upon the decision, the *Osaka Mainichi* said that "Americans are as spiteful as snakes and vipers — we do not hesitate to call that government a studied deceiver." The *Tokyo Jiji* published a cartoon with the caption: "The Broken Promise" — referring to the promise of citizenship made those aliens who served in the First World War.[75] The adverse effect of this decision was somewhat mitigated by the quick and generous fashion in which California contributed to the relief of the Japanese at the time the great earthquake and fire of September 1, 1923, devasted Tokyo. But a still greater explosion was about to burst.

[74] "The Ecological Position of the Japanese Farmers in the State of Washington," unpublished dissertation, University of Washington, 1939.
[75] See, generally, *Oriental Exclusion* by R. D. McKenzie, 1927.

When the so-called "quota immigration act of 1924" was introduced in Congress, Senator Samuel Shortridge, from California, moved an amendment to exclude "all aliens ineligible to citizenship." The amendment was based upon the decision in the Ozawa case. While the bill as a whole was pending before Congress, Ambassador Hanihara wrote a letter to Secretary of State Hughes in which he mentioned that "grave consequences" might follow if the bill, with the Shortridge amendment, was enacted. The letter touched off a blast of rhetorical fireworks led by Senator Henry Cabot Lodge and, on March 15, 1924, the bill was adopted by a decisive vote. Mr. Hughes had stated that passage of the bill would be likely to nullify the work of the Washington Conference and President Coolidge signed the measure with, as he expressed it, "stated reluctance." While California was responsible for the inclusion of the "ineligible-to-citizenship" provision in the act, the vote on the bill represented an affirmative national, not sectional, vote. The race riots of 1919–1921 had, in the opinion of Dr. Ray Lyman Wilbur, "a considerable effect" in securing passage of the bill; for they had made the entire nation extremely race-conscious. It is also a matter of record that the racist views of Madison Grant, Lothrop Stoddard, and Henry Fairfield Osborn were influential in securing passage of the act.[76]

"By a curious coincidence," wrote Yusuke Tsurumi in *Contemporary Japan* (1927), "the Immigration Act broke in upon the meditations of the Japanese people at a moment when the nation was bleeding from the wounds inflicted by the greatest calamity ever visited upon mankind by earthquake and fire. . . . A tremendous amount of the national capitol lay in utter ruins, more than two hundred thousand people had been killed by falling buildings or burnt to death in a raging whirlwind of fire, industries were prostrate, vast regions devastated, and national economy subjected to awful strains at every point. In the midst of our afflictions, the nation that had literally shaken open our gates — waived aside a long standing agreement with us and

[76] See *Japan and America* by Henry W. Taft, 1932; and *Congressional Record*, March 20, 1924, p. 4573.

slammed its own gates shut in our face." To the Japanese, passage of the act was as "unexpected as it was incomprehensible."

The consequences, in Japan, were momentous. "The news of the enactment aroused the nation for several weeks to a dangerous pitch of excitement," writes Professor Toynbee. "On the 31st of May and the 4th of June two persons committed suicide as a protest against the passage of the Act, and on the 10th of June the funeral of one of them was the occasion of a great popular demonstration. On the 5th June, Mr. Woods (our Ambassador) sailed for the United States. In Tokyo, on the 7th June, a dance at the Imperial Hotel, at which Japanese as well as westerners were present, was interrupted by a party of men, several of them dressed in Samurai costume, who protested to their fellow countrymen against dancing and dressing like Americans and keeping western company. On the 1st July, an unknown Japanese entered the precincts of the American Embassy, lowered the American flag, cut it in two, and escaped without being arrested." [77] "The signing of the Immigration Bill," writes Harry Emerson Wildes in *Japan in Crisis* (1934), "coincided with the 1924 elections to the Diet. Revengeful anti-foreign candidates, pledged to enact retaliatory laws, were swept overwhelmingly into office." It is important to remember that the Immigration Act represented the first *federal action* of discriminatory character aimed at the Japanese. "Whatever may have been the attitude of individual Californians," observes Robert Aura Smith, "the government of the United States repeatedly committed itself to the position that it was the desire of the United States to secure and preserve a strong, independent, and friendly Japan." [78] It is impossible to escape the conclusion noted by Mr. Smith, "that the American attitude toward Japanese immigration has had a major influence on everything that has taken place in the relationship of the two countries since that time." Whatever liberal potential existed in Japan expired with the passage of this act. [79]

[77] Quoted by Taft, *op. cit.*
[78] *Our Future in Asia*, 1940, p. 201.
[79] See *Fire in the Pacific* by Simon Harcourt-Smith, 1942, p. 77; *Behind the Face of Japan* by Upton Close, 1942, pp. 318 and 299; *The Menace of Japan* by T. O'Conroy, 1934, pp. 43–44; *Eyes on Japan* by Victor Yakhontoff,

68

Toward the end of September, 1924, Japan reopened the immigration question at Geneva for much the same reasons that she had sought to raise the issue of racial equality at the Versailles Conference — namely, as a bargaining point in her diplomacy.[80] Passage of the Immigration Act set off a series of minor explosions on the West Coast. In 1925, a mob of American citizens forcefully deported a small group of Japanese workers from their homes in Toledo, Oregon. Suits were promptly filed against those responsible and damages were ultimately collected. Here, again, our position was equivocal. "The nation," wrote one observer, "continues to make treaties which the states or their citizens are to violate and the best the Secretary of State can do is to explain our Constitution and ask Congress to vote compensation to the injured aliens and their families." (It should be observed, by way of final comment, that passage of the Immigration Act provoked widespread opposition in this country. Some of the editorial comment is contained in the volume by Henry W. Taft previously cited.)

Shortly after the passage of the act, the Pacific Coast Chambers of Commerce began to look with favor upon some modification of its exclusionary features. But early in 1929 both houses of the California legislature passed a joint resolution "against any character of action designed to modify the present immigration laws relating to the exclusion of Asiatic laborers." Despite this rebuff, the California Council on Oriental Relations was formed in 1931 in an effort to bring about some change of attitude in California. With the Mukden incident of September 18, 1931, and the attack on Shanghai on January 27, 1932, it became apparent that nothing could be accomplished and, late in 1934, the council was disbanded. Passage of the act, which had been the real goal of the anti-Japanese forces for a quarter of a century, did bring about a stabilization of relations in California. During the depression years after 1929, virtually no agitation developed.

1936; *Japan and America* by Henry W. Taft, 1932, p. 192; *Japanese Immigration* by Raymond Leslie Buell, 1924, pp. 314-315; *Literary Digest*, July 12, 1924.

[80] See Young, p. 160.

Anti-Japanese feeling became dormant, but, as subsequent events demonstrated, any change in the existing relationships promptly revived the tense attitudes of the earlier period.

With the appearance of the Japanese as real competitors on the world markets and with the crisis in Far Eastern affairs which developed after 1931, the *status quo* in California was immediately threatened. In 1935, 1937, and 1939, various anti-Japanese measures were introduced in the California legislature; in 1934 mobs assaulted the Japanese in Arizona; and in the spring of 1935 the Hearst press began to inveigh against "inequitable Oriental competition sapping the economic life of America and retarding recovery." [81] At the same time, a mysterious Committee of One Thousand was formed in Southern California. It began to repeat in its publication, the *American Defender*, the familiar calumnies: Japanese truck-gardeners were spraying their vegetables with arsenic; using human excrement as fertilizer, thereby creating epidemics of "bacillary dysentery"; they were training an army in Peru, and so forth. Typical of its utterances was this passage from the issue of April 27, 1935: —

> Wherever the Japanese have settled, their nests pollute the communities like the running sores of leprosy. They exist like the yellowed, smoldering discarded butts in an over-full ashtray, vilifying the air with their loathsome smells, filling all who have misfortune to look upon them with a wholesome disgust and a desire to wash.

On April 9, 1935, West Coast newspapers blazed with headlines when a mess boy on the army transport *Chaumont* was found to be an alien Japanese. On April 29, a Santa Barbara company announced that it had applied for permission to manufacture gas masks: "We believe that the time is now here when we should be as prepared as the Japanese." Incidents of this kind continued to be reported in the press throughout the period 1935 to 1939, but they did not disturb relationships within the state between Japanese residents and non-Japanese residents.

In reviewing the California-Japanese war, it is important to

[81] See my article in the *Nation*, June 26, 1935.

remember that, as the tension mounted over the years, anti-Japanese agitation developed an opposition. Issues were joined, after a fashion, and the controversy was hotly debated for years. This ideological warfare was conducted in the local, state, and national press; on the lecture platforms; from the pulpits; it echoed in legislative forums; it was discussed at international conferences; it found reflection in a series of books, pro-Japanese being countered by anti-Japanese, favorable with unfavorable views. At the same time, various ostrich-like groups, both in this country and in Japan, were maintaining a ridiculous fiction that the two nations were devoted to each other and that no point of real controversy existed to mar their traditional friendship. Japan sent a continuous parade of good-will missions, visiting "interpreters," and miscellaneous cultivators of amicable relations; we, in turn, sent several important missions of this character to Japan. America published a volume of tributes to Japan in the form of a "Message" from America to Japan; the Japanese immediately countered with an elaborate "Message" from Japan to America. Viewing this rashly optimistic spate of books and "tributes," one is inclined to agree with Hashimura Togo, the Japanese schoolboy in Wallace Irwin's book, when he observes: —

"Some frequent Professors are asking the question now: Will White Man and Yellow Man ever Mix? Yes because I have knowledge of the affair. They mix once in San Francisco; they mix once in Vancouver. But such mixing is not good-healthy for the human race because it make broken-glass, pistol-shot, outcry, militia and many other disagreeable noises. Japanese gentlemen mixes race with Jiu Jitsu, Irish gentlemen with gas-pipe."

At the very moment that Japanese good-will missions arrived in this country uttering protestations of enduring friendship, the Japanese press would be denouncing Americans as bullies, hypocrites, thieves, cowards, double-faced, arrogant, designing, and unscrupulous. American missions no sooner docked in Yokohama than the California press would unleash another venomous assault upon the resident Japanese. When Americans returned from the Orient with realistic accounts of what was happening in Japan, they were promptly attacked as war-mongers or as disgruntled correspondents with axes to grind. Nearly every book by an informed correspondent was immediately countered with a volume by the Reverend Sidney Gulick or Mr. K. K. Kawakami. The Japanese propaganda machine in this country, with Chugo Chira operating the "East and West News Bureau" in New York and K. K. Kawakami conducting a "bureau of literary service" in San Francisco, was quick to intervene in all these journalistic controversies. Later the Japanese government added a few California journalists to its payrolls.[82] For years the fires of controversy were kept burning. Thus, as Ruth Fowler observed, "California residents gradually found opposition to the Japanese an ever-present issue, being applied to almost all their political, social, and economic problems. . . . It colored every direct and indirect contact that they had with the Japanese." Caught in the continuous crossfire of this California-Japanese war were the resident Japanese. Always the victims of this weird transpacific struggle, they were the first casualties on the mainland after December 7, 1941, when the real war began.

[82] See *With Japan's Leaders,* by Frederic Moore, 1942, p. 64.

CHAPTER III

The West Coast Japanese

WHILE years of agitation served to lay the foundation for a fixed racial ideology on the West Coast, the character of the Japanese immigrants and the circumstances of their settlement gave a color of justification to the agitation. The typical point of view of the Californians toward the Japanese was summarized by Dr. Edward Alsworth Ross at the first anti-Japanese mass meeting in the state. Dr. Ross was neither a professional agitator nor a politician: he was a professor of sociology who then, and later, enjoyed a national reputation. If such a man, a social scientist, could place his approval upon the age-old charges leveled against Oriental labor, then it may well be argued that there must have been some substance to these charges.

There was some substance to the charges; but the substance was of a quite different character from what it was represented to be. Basic cultural differences were mistakenly and habitually labeled as racial differences. Noting the somewhat slower rate of assimilation of Japanese immigrants by comparison with some (but by no means all) other immigrant groups, the conclusion was hastily drawn that the Japanese were "incapable of assimilation." Actually, assimilation is a second-generation process. It is seldom that a first-generation foreign-born group has become thoroughly assimilated, particularly where sharp cultural, linguistic, and racial differences are involved. The West Coast made the mistake of not recognizing that the first generation was, after all, an *immigrant* generation. Because of their racial difference, the Japanese were never regarded as immigrants, but always as interlopers. Not only were the Issei immigrants; they were late immigrants. In California they were branded as "unassimilable" before they had resided in this country for a decade. Furthermore, the West Coast failed to recognize, in its polemics, that there was a second generation. This oversight is not surprising, because the second generation made its appearance at a comparatively late date (long after the charges summarized by Dr. Ross had become part of the orthodox racial creed of the area).

The second generation was just reaching maturity in 1941. Had war been delayed for another decade, it is altogether probable that evacuation might have been avoided. For by that time most of the Issei generation would have passed away and only the second and third generation would have remained. The tragic aspect of the evacuation program is that the attack on Pearl Harbor occurred just when new elements were beginning to emerge from the old; when America had begun to speak through its new sons, the Nisei. To appreciate this situation, it is necessary to find out something about the Japanese immigrants. Who were they? What were they like? What brought them to America?

1. The Immigrants

From 1900 to 1910, about nine tenths of the immigrants were males. Most of them were under thirty years of age. They came to this country for purely economic reasons and not as refugees in quest of religious or political freedom. Japan had undergone a period of economic and psychological expansion after the Sino-Japanese War of 1895. New vistas had suddenly opened up before the eyes of the people. In semi-feudal Japan, however, these newly stirred ambitions could not be realized except by a small section of the population. The immigrants who came to Hawaii and the West Coast were "birds of passage": not one in a thousand intended to remain. They planned on returning to Japan as soon as they had accumulated a nest egg. This was the explanation for their driving intensity, their passionate addiction to hard manual labor. The motive back of emigration was "to make money — and nothing more."[1]

[1] *Immigration: Cultural Conflicts and Social Adjustment* by Lawrence Guy Brown, 1933, Chapter XV.

While various trades were represented among the immigrants, nearly two thirds were farmers or farm laborers (who had considered themselves lucky to make sixteen cents a day in Japan). They were by no means illiterate. Most of them had the equivalent of an eighth-grade education. They came from the lower economic and social groupings in Japan, not a few belonging to the so-called "outlaw" or Eta class. Those who came by way of the Hawaiian Islands had, in many cases, been dulled and broken by years of unspeakable drudgery. As a group, they were exceptionally hard workers, habituated by experience to the most strenuous physical labor.

As in all migration movements, a selective factor was involved. The youngest and the most energetic were the first to leave. Word-of-mouth rumor, reports from relatives, and the general reputation of America as the land of plenty, were the chief stimulants to migration. Immigrants from the same prefectures in Japan tended to settle in the same areas in America. Twenty-eight per cent of the Japanese around Palo Alto, for example, were from Hiroshima. While certain prefectures in Japan were heavily represented, they were not, in most cases, those in which the pressure of population upon resources was greatest.

Since few women were involved in the initial immigration, most Japanese men married late in life and an estimated 20 per cent never married. Feeling that their stay in America was temporary, they gave little thought at the outset to establishing homes. Even after they acquired families, they drove their wives and children with the same intensity that they drove themselves. More than a third of the marriages were of the picture-bride variety. Most of the picture brides, in fact most of the women immigrants, arrived in the period from 1910 to 1921 (in 1921 Japan voluntarily stopped the issuance of further passports to women — the so-called Ladies' Agreement). Arriving in San Francisco by the boatload, dressed in native costumes, their faces powdered to a deathly pallor, their hair done up in huge pompadours, the picture brides provided the newspapers with material for endless feature stories. Most of the women came from substantially the same social classes and from the same prefectures as the men. Arriving in this country nearly a decade later than her husband, the wife was retarded in her assimilation from the outset. Through closer contact with the children, however, she was later able to make perhaps a better adjustment than her husband.[2]

Three distinct phases of settlement were involved: "the pioneer" phase; the "settling down" phase; and the "second generation" phase. While 20 per cent of the male immigrants went directly into agriculture, most of them worked as general migratory laborers for a period of from five to eight years. As they arrived, they were routed by their countrymen from the steamship to the Japanese boarding house to the labor contractor or "gang-boss." Fitting the needs of the West Coast economy, the gang-labor system solved the language problem and provided immediate employment.

Working first in sugar beets and grapes, Japanese immigrants soon found general employment in agriculture: by 1909 they constituted 41.9 per cent of the agricultural labor supply in California. The large farms in California not only showed a lively interest in Japanese workers: they "welcomed them."[3] As late as 1907, these interests were quite favorable to the Japanese. For the purpose of urging Congress to permit further immigration, they founded the International Equality League and conducted an active lobby in Washington. Aside from agriculture, Japanese immigrants were to be found, from Vancouver to San Diego, in three basic industries: fishing and canning; mining; railroad construction and maintenance.

As immigration increased, opportunities were created for service centers in the ports of entry such as Seattle and San Francisco. With savings accumulated from gang-labor employment, the earlier immigrants began to open small shops, boarding houses, and hotels, and a few began to enter the trades. These service centers (which later became the Little Tokyos) were usually located near an already existing Chinatown, which, in turn, was

[2] On the women immigrants generally, see *My Lantern* by Michi Kawai, Tokyo, 1936, Chapter XII.
[3] See Dr. Varden Fuller's paper, Vol. 54 LaFollette Committee Reports.

located in the "skid-row" section of the particular city. In the early years of the century, there existed on the West Coast a definite demand for cheap boarding houses, hotels, barbershops, and restaurants that could cater to the needs of a large floating population of single men as well as to the immigrants themselves.

After 1908 these nascent service centers were hard hit by the restriction on immigration and the various boycott movements organized by the unions. Many immigrants became discouraged and returned to Japan; others would have done so had they possessed the means. Meeting with considerable success in agriculture, many immigrants decided to get married and to make their home in America. As a consequence, a marked movement from urban to rural areas occurred after 1908. With this shift to agriculture, "the settling down" phase really began.

During the boom which developed on the West Coast after 1914, both urban and rural groups made rapid headway. Some of the earlier pressures and prejudices began to abate. This short-lived phase ended with the rising hostility of the postwar years, the passage of the Alien Land Acts, and the enactment of the Immigration Act of 1924 — developments which prompted many immigrants to give up the idea of settlement and to return to Japan. Gradually abandoning all thought of returning to Japan, those who remained after 1924 became increasingly preoccupied with the future of their children. The "second-generation" phase dates from around this period.[4]

2. Cultural Luggage

The Japanese immigrants who came to America had only a few dollars sewed in their clothing and a handful of personal belongings in a dilapidated suitcase. But they did bring some highly important, if invisible, luggage — the culture of their homeland. Just what were some of the more important items making up this invisible luggage?

[4] See *Social Solidarity Among the Japanese in Seattle* by Frank Miyamoto, December, 1939.

Like most insular peoples, the Japanese, as John Embree has pointed out,[5] regard themselves as a race apart, unique in origin and achievement. There was a definite "pride of race" in these immigrants which proved intolerably offensive to the white residents of the West Coast. There was, also, as Frank Miyamoto has said, "a proud heritage of homogeneous culture" with a strong emphasis upon traditional social values. As a group they were held together, not only by their pride of race, but by the fact that their culture was "integrated like a mosaic."

Group relationships had great meaning to them. They thought of the family and of the group as realities more concrete than the individual. Their enlarged family system, supported by strong traditional ties, was quite unlike the family system they encountered in California. Numerous social forms, such as the *ken* organizations, and such customs as the *tanomoshi* (a kind of self help mutual financing arrangement), served also to hold them together as a group. All of these and other factors tended to make for a remarkable internal solidarity which as much, perhaps, as external pressures set them apart from other groups. What the Californian inconsistently denounced as "clannishness" (inconsistent because he refused to accept the Japanese as an individual) was really the product of these cultural factors.

Japanese immigrants to America came from a society only recently — and partially — released from the rigid class demarcations of a feudal society. As Dr. John Rademaker has observed, this factor naturally placed a premium upon success in the struggle for position and status. Observers have noted the same trait in Japan. "It is as though," writes Helen Mears, "while living in Japan, repressed in their small islands, crowded for space, fed on a limited diet, breathing a thick steamy vapor, they have become closed in on themselves like a bulb, the life-germ dormant, so that when they are freed from the special and peculiar conditions of their own land, taken out into full sun and crisp air, given proper nourishment, they develop with astonishing swiftness." So quickly were these latent potentialities released in America that, within a few years after their arrival, most of

[5] *The Japanese*, Smithsonian Institute, January 23, 1943.

he immigrants began to make remarkable progress under the most severe handicaps of prejudice and hostility.

Numerous factors assisted in furthering their rapid economic expansion. Their arrival on the West Coast coincided with a period of spectacular economic development. The emphasis that existed in Japan on small-scale individual enterprise served them well in a region which was, at the time, replete with opportunities. The antagonistic attitudes of the dominant group, however, intensified in relation to the success that they achieved. The remarkable progress which they had made was denounced as "aggressiveness," which, when coupled with the aggressiveness that Japan was showing in the Orient, began to assume a menacing aspect. In Japan it was customary for husband and wife, the family as a unit, to work together in field and shop. When immigrants pursued this custom in California, they were accused of operating "sweatshops," engaging in unfair competition, and mistreating their women. Even the Japanese "pride of race" was resented. Since Japanese showed virtually no tendency toward intermarriage with other groups, they were accused of regarding themselves as "superior," although intermarriage had been prohibited by law as early as 1905. Since these traits and customs were uniformly regarded as racial and not cultural in origin, it was assumed that they were inherent and unchangeable. Whatever was odd or different about the Japanese immigrant was attributed to his slant eyes, black hair, and brown skin.

The immigrants also brought with them a knowledge of intensive cultivation that was new to the West. They possessed a remarkable knowledge of soils and of how to treat soils for the production of certain crops; an expert knowledge of the use of fertilizers and of fertilizing methods; a great skill in land reclamation, irrigation, and drainage; and a willingness to put in the enormous amount of labor required in intensive farming operations. They pioneered in the production of many crops. They reclaimed vast areas of the West, including the cut-over timber lands of the Northwest and the valuable delta lands in California. Even the *San Francisco Chronicle* readily conceded that "the most striking feature of Japanese farming in California has been

79

the development of successful orchards, vineyards, or gardens on land that was either completely out of use or employed for far less profitable enterprises."

It was George Shima, an immigrant, who taught the Californians how to develop a good potato seed. It was Japanese farmers who developed berry production in the West by increasing the yield four and five times over what it had been (planting strawberries and grapevines at the same time so that when the strawberries were replanted three years later a profitable vineyard would be in production). It was the Japanese who took over the semi-abandoned community of Livingston and made it a profitable farming area, and who succeeded in the mountain-fruit section in Placer County after other groups had failed. "In the Imperial Valley and the Delta country," observed Robert Welles Ritchie, "the Japanese never displaced white men, for white men would not work there; and in the mountain fruit district, the Chinese and after them the Japanese came in, after nearly every white man had quit, and made a go of a crippled industry." [6] In later years the Californians contended that the Japanese were monopolizing the best lands; but candor should have compelled the admission that most of these lands were originally marginal in character.

Entering the fishing industry around 1897 — an industry that has always been an immigrant industry on the West Coast — they revolutionized methods of production. Many of them were born fishermen. They ventured into deeper waters far off shore; they used gasoline-driven vessels; developed new types of nets, sails, baits, and hooks, and enormously increased the average haul.[7] Their most important contribution to the economy of the West, however, was the manner in which they organized produce production on a year-round basis so as to provide a steady flow of produce to the markets.

[6] *Country Gentleman*, December, 1923.
[7] See *Facts About the Japanese in America* by Janzo Sasamori, 1921.

3. The Californians

No sharper contrast could be imagined than that between the traditional culture of these Japanese immigrants and the culture they discovered in California. The two cultures were "sensationally contrarious." The homogeneous, highly integrated culture of the Japanese (the end product of centuries of isolation and a scarcity of resources) was confronted in California with a highly heterogeneous and oddly assorted culture based on ample resources, unlimited space, and an ever-expanding economy. California was as large as the total land area of the Japanese islands. Immigrants on arriving in America were actually frightened by the *size* of the country. They were terrified by "the large buildings, big trees, tall people, vast plains, and material plenty of North America." [8] Nearly everything they saw seemed weirdly out of scale.

In 1900 California was an expanding frontier region. It had been settled, as Lord Bryce observed, by "a mixed multitude" which had brought with it "a variety of manners, customs, and ideas," resulting in a society "more mobile and unstable, less governed by fixed beliefs and principles" than any area in America. The tightly knit social organization of the Japanese stood out in bold relief against the loosely constituted, and highly unorganized, character of social forms in California. The deeply traditional aspect of Japanese culture was sharply at variance with the practices of a community too new to have acquired many traditions, much less a respect for tradition. The Japanese respect for authority was incongruous in a state where, as Lord Bryce noted, "a great population had gathered before there was any regular government to keep it in order, much less any education or social culture to refine it. The wildness of that time passed into the soul of the people, and has left them the more tolerant of violent deeds, more prone to interferences with, or supercessions of, regular law, than are the people of most parts of the Union."

[8] *My Narrow Isle* by Sumie Seo Mishima, 1941, p. 153.

Where the Japanese were thrifty, the Californians were care-
less; where the Japanese specialized in intensive, the Californian
specialized in extensive, farming. California had grown rapidly
in semi-isolation. For years it had been remote from what Lord
Bryce called "the steadying influence of eastern states." More
than any other state it possessed, in his judgment, "the character
of a great country, capable of standing alone in the world. What
America is to Europe, what Western America is to Eastern
that California is to the other Western States. California is the
last place to the west before you come to Japan."

In part, the character that the Japanese settlements assumed
in California must be explained in terms of the unintegrated, unstable, mobile, and loosely organized character of the state itself.
There was really no force in the state capable of molding, transforming, or integrating these immigrants. There was nothing to
integrate them to, since California itself had not achieved integration. Migration, as Dr. Robert E. Park has observed, has "had
a marked effect upon the social structure of California society.
For one thing, it has dotted the Pacific Coast with Chinatowns
and Little Tokyos, not to mention the large Mexican colony in
Los Angeles and the transient fruit camps all up and down the
valley. Here a large part of California's population, which comes
from such diverse and distant places, lives in more or less close
communities, in intimate economic dependence, but in more o
less complete cultural independence of the world about them.
Elsewhere in this illuminating article, Dr. Park speaks of California as "a congeries of culturally insulated communities." [9] No
better characterization of the state has ever been made.

For this characterization can be applied not merely to the
foreign settlements, but to other communities as well. Chinatown
and Little Tokyo were culturally insulated communities; but
so, in a sense, are Pasadena and Santa Barbara. In such a heterogeneous and unrelated society, crises precipitate violent "anti"
movements. For there is lacking a general sense of community
purpose and responsibility. During the depression years, "Old
Stock" — that is, white, Protestant, Anglo-Saxon Americans from

[9] *American Journal of Sociology*, May, 1934.

Oklahoma, Arkansas, and Texas — were roundly denounced in California as "interlopers." The same charges were made against them that were made against the Japanese: they were "dirty"; they had "enormous families"; they engaged in unfair competition; they threatened to "invade" the state and to "undermine" its institutions. During these turgid years (1930–1938) California attempted *to exclude*, by various extralegal devices, these yeoman farmers just as it had excluded the Chinese and the Japanese. "Okies" were "inferior" and "immoral." There was much family discord when Okie girl met California boy, and vice versa. In attempting to get a foothold in California, Okies and Arkies acted much as the Chinese and the Japanese had done: they established "Little Oklahomas" and "Little Arkansases" on the periphery of established rural communities. At the outset, they, too, were compelled to take marginal positions and to underbid established wage rates. The prejudice against the Okies was obviously not "race" prejudice; yet it functioned in much the same manner.

4. Areas of Settlement

One remarkable aspect of Japanese immigration (which had a decided influence upon the accumulation of prejudice) was the tendency toward geographical concentration. In 1940 there were 126,947 Japanese in this country of whom 112,533 resided in the three West Coast states (nearly 80 per cent in California and most of these in Los Angeles County). Unlike other immigrant groups, the Japanese showed no tendency toward dispersal; on the contrary, they were more densely concentrated on December 7, 1941, than they had been twenty years previously. In 1910, 57.3 per cent of all the Japanese in this country resided in California; in 1920, 64.8 per cent; in 1930, 70.2 per cent; in 1940, 73.8 per cent. They tended to concentrate not merely in California, but in a limited number of areas within the state.

When pressures began to develop against them, the Japanese did show some tendency to disperse. The number of Japanese in the inter-mountain states increased to 20 per cent of the total in the United States and then declined to 8.22 per cent in 1930.

It is extremely important to note, here, that the Japanese consuls deliberately discouraged the idea of dispersal, giving as their reason a desire to localize areas of competition and of friction.[10] The consuls persisted in this policy even after further immigration had been suspended. It is perfectly obvious, however, that the concentration of the Japanese in California had a tendency to magnify, rather than to minimize, whatever potential friction existed. I find it exceedingly difficult to believe that the consuls were merely mistaken about the effects of dispersal. To be sure, the tide of migration has always been westward in America so that, even if the Japanese had been more inclined to disperse, they would have been moving upstream. Nevertheless the fact that they were, for a period, attempting to resettle over a wider area, and that they were discouraged from doing so by the consuls, leads me to the conclusion that the consuls wanted to keep the "Japanese question" alive in California.

This tendency toward concentration also prevailed in Canada, where the consuls pursued a similar policy. Most of the Japanese in Canada — three fourths of them in fact — resided within a radius of from fifty to seventy-five miles of Vancouver. This concentration of immigrants created an illusion of greater numbers than the facts warranted. It also created an impression that settlement was being "ordered and controlled as though from some central source."[11] Naturally this impression did not make for improved relations. Both in the cities and in rural areas, the Japanese were conspicuously located. Much of their garden farming was around the peripheries of cities, along main highways, near packing plants and railroad sidings. They were more conspicuous than the Chinese huddled together in their Chinatown settlements. In residential areas, they were hedged in by racial restrictions. Since only certain soils were suitable for intensive farming and since it was necessary to locate as near the large urban markets as possible, the Japanese were also concentrated in rural areas. Thus, as Dr. John Rademaker has observed, their

---

[10] *The Japanese Invasion* by Dr. Jesse Steiner, 1917, pp. 85–86.
[11] *The Japanese-Canadians* by Charles Y. Young and Helen R. Y. Reid, 1938.

84

ecological position influenced their social position. Concentration and visibility increased the prejudice against them and this prejudice, in turn, increased the degree of concentration.

Furthermore, the Japanese population in California tended to increase relatively faster than other so-called "colored groups." The Chinese and Indian groups decreased in relation to total population between 1900 and 1920. The Negro group showed only a slight increase (from .07 per cent of the total to 1.1 per cent). But the Japanese increased from .07 per cent of the total in 1900 to 2.1 per cent in 1920. While there was a 54 per cent increase in the number of all Japanese in the United States between 1910 and 1920, there was a 300 per cent increase in the number of women during the same period (for picture brides were not excluded under the Gentlemen's Agreement). In their first years of settlement, Japanese immigrants showed a high birth rate (such as other immigrant groups have shown and for the same reasons). The increasing concentration of Japanese in particular areas in a single state, coupled with what appeared to be the alarming possibilities of future increase, greatly disturbed white residents in California. The increase in the number of Japanese, however, was at all times insignificant when compared with the general increase in population. In any case, it was always this possibility of *future* competition, of *future* conflict, rather than the existing situation, which made for mounting race tension in California.

Geographical concentration tended to accentuate those aspects of Japanese culture which made for group solidarity. It tended to preserve the Japanese family system. It made possible the continuance of a highly organized group life (there were 350 Japanese organizations in Los Angeles; 230 in Vancouver). Segregation was, in part, responsible for the "intense gregariousness" which characterized the West Coast Japanese. The fact that, unlike some immigrant groups, the Japanese had a homogeneous and self-satisfying culture tended to make them more content with the restricted world in which they lived. Their highly centralized organizations not only aided them in creating a socially satisfactory world, but also permitted them to compete effectively as a group. Group competition was, however, immediately denounced as sinister and conspiratorial. Since their group life was so highly organized, they could appeal to the consuls for assistance; and every intervention by the consuls further aggravated the prejudice against them. The patterns thus established tended to persist since they created at least a tolerable world within which the immigrants could exist. While Little Tokyo was a ghetto, still it was the best ghetto in California. Its residents were obviously the most prosperous colored minority in the state. The minorities in California have always tended to arrange themselves in a hierarchical order: Indians, Mexicans, Filipinos, Negroes, Chinese, and Japanese (in ascending scale). By 1920 the Japanese had become the bourgeoisie of the minority groups.

Special concentration was matched by occupational concentration. Some 43 per cent of the gainfully employed Japanese on the West Coast in 1940 were to be found in agriculture, more particularly in the production of vegetables, small fruits, and greenhouse products. This concentration resulted from a trial and-error experimentation with other types of agriculture. Over the years, the number of Japanese-operated farms devoted to the production of berries and vegetables sharply increased. By 1930 they had abandoned almost every other type of agriculture. Experience had shown that they could not compete successfully in other types of farming. It is this admitted fact, moreover, which disposes of the contention that Japanese competition was unfair or that it was based on a lower standard of living. If it had been true that their standard of living was so much lower as to constitute a real factor in competition, then they should have been able to succeed in other types of farming. It is obvious, I think, that the advantage which they enjoyed in the types of farming in which they did succeed was primarily a cultural advantage, and one which redounded to the benefit of virtually every other group in the community.

The concentration upon agriculture was even greater than have indicated. In addition to the 22,027 employed in agriculture in 1940, there were some 11,472 (26 per cent of those gainfully employed) engaged in wholesale and retail trade which, for the most part, was largely confined to the distribution of Japanese-grown produce. About 17 per cent of the gainfully employed were to be found in the service industries and trades — domestic service, cleaning and dyeing, barbershops, restaurants, rooming houses, and hotels. Here, again, many of these people were dependent upon agriculture since they catered primarily to the Japanese community. Few Japanese were to be found in manufacturing or in the construction industries. Those in the professions were also dependent upon the patronage of the Japanese community.

Within this narrow orbit, the Japanese had been highly successful. In 1940 there were 5135 Japanese-operated farms in California, embracing about 226,094 acres, which, including buildings, were valued at $65,781,000. While most of these farms were small, Japanese production, because of its intensive character, represented a substantial proportion of total production. In 1941 the Japanese controlled 42 per cent of the commercial truck crops in California, their production being valued at $35,000,000. Although they operated only 3.9 per cent of the land in farms and harvested only 2.7 per cent of all crop land harvested, they produced from 50 to 90 per cent of such crops as celery, peppers, strawberries, cucumbers, artichokes, cauliflower, spinach, and tomatoes. By and large, the Japanese had acquired a near-monopoly on the production of fresh vegetables on a small-acreage basis for the large urban markets on the West Coast. They figured only to a minor extent in the production of staple crops on a large-acreage basis by mechanized methods; and, except in Oregon and Washington, they figured only slightly in the large-scale production of produce crops for out-of-state shipment.

This monopoly on the fresh-vegetable market was strengthened by the fact that the Japanese had organized wholesale and retail outlets for Japanese-grown produce. Thus in 1941 there were some 1000 Japanese-operated fruit and vegetable stores in Los Angeles employing around 5000 people (mostly all Japanese), and doing a business of $25,000,000 a year. The industry had been thoroughly organized and integrated from the fields to the wholesale markets to the retail outlets. The timing and planning of year-round production to meet the needs of these markets had been carefully worked out. The Little Tokyos were primarily service centers for people who were engaged in, directly or indirectly, or were dependent upon, this single industry.

By 1941 the Japanese population had outgrown this narrow economic base. There were too many Japanese service trades and retail stores, and too many Japanese in the professions, to be supported by the income available in the Japanese community. Many of the retail stores had been able to survive because they catered to the peculiar tastes and buying habits of the older or Issei generation. As this generation began to die off (their median age was 50.1 years), stores were faced with the necessity of changing the character of their merchandise in order to hold the patronage of the second generation. When, therefore, these stores began to cater to the Americanized tastes of the second generation, they came into direct competition with large chain-store organizations. For years prior to 1941, observers had noted the high incidence of business failures and bankruptcies in Little Tokyo. "The Japanese business shops have a good front," one merchant told Frank Miyamoto, "but when you get inside, you find out how bad the whole thing is." Many of these businesses were behind the times, offered inferior merchandise, and were badly managed. Of 138,-834 Japanese in the United States in 1930, 50.2 per cent were foreign-born; but of 126,947 Japanese in 1940 only 37.3 per cent were foreign-born. Thus without its being generally realized, a death sentence had been imposed on Little Tokyo prior to December 7, 1941.

As the Nisei reached maturity, there was a significant trend away from Little Tokyo. In 1928 one observer reported that, in Los Angeles, there were 203 Japanese-operated fruit stands, 292 grocery stores, 74 florist shops, 69 nurseries, 108 restaurants, and 68 dry-cleaning establishments which had most of their dealings with non-Japanese customers. Over a period of years there was unquestionably a slow but steady expansion out of Little Tokyo, a gradual reorientation of the Japanese-operated business toward the Caucasian public.

This trend was apparent throughout the Pacific Coast. In Vancouver, according to Young and Reid, the economic activity of the Japanese had become by 1938 "dispersed and scattered throughout the city. The Japanese are found in commercial enterprises in significant numbers not only in their own areas of settlement, where, incidentally, they cater to Whites as well as to Japanese, but also to a remarkable extent all over the city where their only customers are Whites." Seven out of twelve drygoods stores in Vancouver were Japanese-operated. A study of Japanese vegetable markets throughout the West Coast cities in 1941 would clearly have shown that most of these markets were catering exclusively to a "white" clientele. The owners and employees of these markets continued to live in Little Tokyo, but they were working outside the area.

It was also apparent that the Nisei did not necessarily follow in the footsteps of their parents. They showed little interest in becoming nurserymen, hotelkeepers, and gardeners. Anxious to obtain white-collar jobs that conferred status, they sought employment as salesmen, clerks, and managers in Japanese-operated markets. Since they spoke excellent English, were well-educated, and had many friends in the Caucasian world, they were gradually displacing the Issei in all positions that involved direct dealings with the public. They had also begun to take over many Japanese-operated businesses. In the wholesale produce markets in Los Angeles, there were 50 per cent more Nisei in 1934 than in 1928; in the retail vegetable markets there were three times as many Nisei in 1934 as in 1928.

As a matter of fact, they had begun to push the Issei out of nearly every characteristically Japanese enterprise with the exception of the wholesale florist shops, the importing and exporting concerns, and the art shops. Knowledge of the Japanese language continued to give the Issei an advantage in these lines. This general development away from self-sufficiency and toward a broader economic base, and from Issei to Nisei direction, became pronounced after the group began to shift from rural to urban areas. As late as 1927, the Japanese had been described as the least urbanized immigrant group in America; but by 1941

50 per cent of the West Coast Japanese lived in urban areas. The trend was not only toward the cities, but toward Los Angeles in particular. After 1930 some 3000 Japanese moved from Seattle to Los Angeles.

It was this trend which, if it had continued, would sooner or later have eliminated the group competition of the Japanese and thereby, perhaps, reduced the prejudice against them. For as Young and Reid point out, "the more rapid the economic expansion of an immigrant group, the more quickly it is likely to be assimilated. The speed of assimilation in the case of the Japanese, however, is offset to a certain extent by the fact that the discrimination which results from their economic expansion tends to drive them in upon themselves for protection and postpones their ultimate attachment to the community. Paradoxical as it may seem, the more rapidly the Japanese are assimilated, the sooner will they be unable to outstrip the native population in economic competition." For as they became better assimilated, they tended more and more to adopt the living standards and customs of the dominant group.

Actually what had happened over a period of forty years' residence on the West Coast can be summarized, in the words of Dr. John Rademaker, as follows: at the outset of settlement "the extraordinarily great differences between the languages of the Japanese and of the white population, the distinguishing racial characteristics, the divergences between the ceremonial customs and etiquette of the two peoples, the diversity in family relationships, especially in regard to the number of relatives included within the intimate group and the division of labor within the family, contrasts in food habits and differences in cultural values, all contributed to the crystallization of a feeling of difference which both peoples have felt toward each other." [12]

Over a period of years, however, these very cultural differences tended to create a complementary division of labor characterized by a measure of good will and understanding, integrating "Japanese and whites in a single, well-articulated economic organization." The competition which at first existed, between Japanese

[12] *American Journal of Sociology*, November, 1934.

farmers and non-Japanese farmers, between Japanese laborers and non-Japanese laborers, had made the distinguishing racial characteristics useful to both groups in identifying competitors. The competitive feeling was noticeably increased during periods of economic depression, such as 1907 and 1920, and was kept alive by recurrent political agitation. This initial competition had resulted in a "turning in upon itself of the Japanese group, and the erection of a barrier by the white population against the threats, imagined or real, of the Japanese against white economic and social status."

The complementary division of labor based on cultural differences had resulted in the Japanese residents' becoming an "integral part of the economic organization," but "in practically all other aspects of social organization, with the exception of public school education," remaining a discrete element. While the Japanese unit in the society was "well integrated internally," it existed mainly as "a separate system unincorporated in the organization of the dominant white population for political, religious, recreative, kinship, and fraternal functions."

Subsequent to 1924, however, these barriers were being quietly and gradually lowered, despite a tendency for the habits and institutions, which had been developed during the earlier period of isolation, to persist. The rapid growth and maturity of the Nisei, or second generation, was bridging this gap. Paradoxically the cultural differences which had originally separated the two groups had made for social acceptance since they tended to minimize direct competition. Full integration was, therefore, at least foreseeable in 1941.

"At the present time," observed Dr. Chitoshi Yanaga (1939), "social contacts are limited largely to the schools, but social distance is growing less and less. In five or six years, there will be rather free social intercourse." The conflict between the two groups was, in the last analysis, primarily cultural. As Dr. Rademaker has said, "there is no evidence that racial characteristics in themselves are responsible for prejudicial attitudes. When these racial characteristics occur in combination with other factors, such as economic and social competition, they serve as distinguishing marks which identify Japanese and whites and permit each to develop distinctive responses to the other."

5. What the Trade-Unions Forgot

During the nineties, when times were hard, "white" labor had indulged in open violence against the employment of Orientals in agriculture. In 1893 and 1894, mobs assaulted the Chinese in many rural areas; and a so-called "Industrial Army," as part of these disturbances, had driven Japanese farm laborers from the Vaca Valley.[13] But, at a very early date, the Japanese themselves began to strike for higher wages. Strikes were reported at Hayward,[14] and in Sutter County they struck for an increase from $1.25 to $1.40 a day.[15]

On one occasion, more than a thousand Mexicans and Japanese struck in the sugar-beet fields in Ventura County. In connection with this strike, the Los Angeles Labor Council passed a resolution favoring the organization of Oriental labor of all types. The secretary of the council stated at the time that "this is one of the most important resolutions ever brought to the attention of the council. It virtually breaks the ice on the question of forming the Orientals into unions, and so keeping them from scabbing on the white people." [16] By the end of the 1903 season, employers were grumbling about "the saucy, debonair Jap, who would like to do all his work in a white starched shirt with cuffs and collar accompaniments." In 1906, H. Shera of Upland, California, wrote to the Chicago Federation of Labor suggesting that it boycott shipments of lemons and oranges harvested by nonunion labor.[17] At the same time, the Japanese struck in the walnut industry.[18] "The Japanese," complained the *Pacific Rural Press* on June 11, 1910, "have no scruples in striking for higher wages." Their

[13] See *Sacramento Record-Union*, May 18 and 24, 1894.
[14] See *Oakland Tribune*, August 4, 1902.
[15] *Pacific Rural Press*, August 15, 1903.
[16] *Oakland Tribune*, April 1, 1903.
[17] *California Fruit Grower*, March 3, 1906.
[18] *Pacific Rural Press*, October 13, 1906.

own countryman, the famous George Shima, observed that "it's discouraging — all the time they strike." [19]

In an early report of the Industrial Commission [20] it is stated that "the Japanese although unorganized in the sense in which the word is used today, act in complete agreement among themselves." A subsequent report [21] stated: "They have reduced the workday from 12 to 11 hours and by means of strikes have *raised the wages of all races.* At a later date, Japanese farm laborers in San Jose were clamoring for the trade-unions to organize them.[22] From 1930 to 1935, a handful of Japanese were active in forming the Cannery and Agricultural Workers Industrial Union. One T. Hariuchi, a charter member of this union, was deported because of his organizational activities in Imperial Valley.[23] This long record of incipient trade-union activity certainly shows that the Japanese were not "coolie laborers"; and that they sought to improve working conditions rather than to destroy existing labor standards. As a matter of fact, they might easily have been integrated into the trade-union movement but for two considerations: the movement was concentrated in San Francisco; and its leaders were deeply involved in the politics of anti-Oriental agitation.

6. The Issei

No immigrant group ever made a more determined effort to succeed in America than did the Japanese. The reports of the Immigration Commission consistently paid tribute to their eagerness to adjust themselves to their new environment. The progress of the Japanese, reads one report, "is due to their greater eagerness to learn, which has overcome more obstacles than have been encountered by most other races, obstacles of prejudice, of segregation, and wide differences in language." At the outset, they showed a remarkable willingness to adopt American folk-

[19] *Ibid.*, September 16, 1911.
[20] Vol. 25, Pt. IV.
[21] Vol. 25, Pt. II, p. 25.
[22] *San Jose Mercury-Herald,* May 13, 1917.
[23] *Daily Worker,* February 4, 1930.

ways; to adopt American clothes, habits, furnishings, and even religious practices. They conducted themselves with admirable fortitude in the face of a bigoted opposition. There was no crime problem among them (a remarkable fact for an immigrant group); they paid their debts; they supported their own indigents. They conducted good-citizenship campaigns; they organized special campaigns against prostitution and gambling. When objections were made to the type of homes in which they lived, they organized Better Homes and Gardens campaigns. When objections were raised to the language schools, they took the initiative in suggesting that these schools be regulated or that the Japanese language be taught in the public schools. When objection was raised on the issue of dual citizenship, they asked the Japanese government to liberalize its expatriation laws.

They were, as one witness testified, "the great approachers — they are more ardent students of our economy than any other class; they are better students of our history than any other immigrants." They sought to co-operate, in an organized way, to achieve better race relations. "Japanese who have lived abroad," writes Helen Mears, "seem to become curiously indistinguishable from the natives of their adopted country." "Precisely because of their historical traits of allegiance and organization," writes Dr. Robert E. Park, "the Japanese are capable of transforming their lives and practices more rapidly than any other group . . . they are inclined to make more far-going concessions than any other group in order to overcome American prejudice and to secure status here . . . whether we like them or not, no other foreign-language group is so completely and intelligently organized to control its members, and no other group has at all equalled them in the work of accommodating themselves to alien conditions."

But it is also true that they showed a deep-seated reluctance to divest themselves of the entirety of their cultural heritage. It was not so much a question of their desire to divest themselves of one heritage and to assume another as it was of their ability to do so. The old ties were too strong and too meaningful. But even so, *there was a time*, as Frank Miyamoto has suggested, when they might have broken completely away from these ties. That moment occurred during the First World War when it seemed as though some of the pressures against them might abate. Encouraged by this momentary lull in hostilities, they sent for wives and began to establish homes. But by 1924 the Issei had become convinced that they would never win final acceptance. Writing in 1933, Saikichi Chijiwa concluded that the immigrant "never will be accepted since his race and physical features will always set him apart."

It was the decision of the Supreme Court in 1923 holding that Japanese were "ineligible to citizenship" that forced the Issei to abandon all hope of acceptance. Not only was this an insurmountable barrier, but it meant that agitation against them would continue. For, as David Starr Jordan once observed, "a permanently alien non-voting population makes for social and political disorders." [24] "So long as these people are foreign citizens," he wrote in another connection, [25] "they must be controlled from home by consular agents. Any act concerning them, if affecting their accepted rights, is international in character. The international interests of the United States cannot be safely left at the mercy of haphazard local referendum. That all races resident in our country should have means of becoming citizens is vital to the integrity of the nation. We should condemn no race of men to permanent outlawry, a line of policy disastrous wherever it has been tried."

All first-generation immigrant groups in America are inclined to be nationalistic. Until 1924, the Issei were probably no more inclined in this direction than any other immigrant group; but afterwards they did develop, in some cases, what has been termed a "suppressed nationality psychosis." Nationalistic tendencies increased. They fought to retain the language schools despite the fact that the schools themselves were an admitted failure. They thought that the schools would be one means of instilling in their children a sense of pride in their background. They thought they might assist in bridging the chasm that had begun to separate the

[24] *Out West*, March, 1907.
[25] *New Republic*, May 14, 1924.

two generations. Their children, they said, were in danger of developing an inferiority complex and of sinking "to the level of Indians." They heard themselves and their children described by a California legislator as "bandy-legged bugaboos, miserable craven, simian, degenerated, rotten little devils." The sting of discrimination must have cut these proud people very deeply. Yoshio Markino, the artist, told in his book, *When I Was a Child*, of being stoned in Golden Gate Park in San Francisco in 1893 by a mob that shouted "Jap!" and "Sukebei!" Such experiences are not easily forgotten.

The hardest and heaviest blow for the Issei, however, was the realization that their children were turning away from them. They had pinned all their hopes on these children; it was for the Nisei that they "sweated and slaved without thought of personal betterment, of good clothes, homes, cars; they lived in the hopes of their children." [26] The rebuffs they had experienced in California, even the final blow of evacuation, were minor tragedies when compared with the growing realization that they lived in one world and their children in another.

7. Issei *vs.* Nisei

The professional California patriots who are forever talking about the "unassimilable character" of the Japanese usually refer to the Issei or immigrant generation, although they are never at pains to make this point clear. In fairness to this widely prevalent notion, it should be conceded that there were, among the Issei, many immigrants who showed few marks of assimilation. Their English was poor; they lived restricted, narrow lives; they were in touch with no vital currents of thought either in this country or in Japan. Some of them were sentimentally attached to Japan, but to a Japan that, in most cases, they had not seen for many years. It was with reference to such individuals and to the Issei generation as such that the legend of the "unassimilable character of the Japanese" arose.

[26] "These Are Our Parents" by George Morimitsu, *Asia and the Americas*, October, 1934.

The Reverend Paul B. Waterhouse was the first Californian to examine the facts upon which this legend was predicated. In the early twenties he was commissioned by Mr. Morris, our ambassador in Tokyo, to make a study of some 1500 Nisei in California under fifteen years of age to determine if they were being assimilated. Waterhouse discovered that over two thirds of these youngsters were enrolled in Protestant Sunday schools. He found that they were associating with other children in the schools "with practically no consciousness of race distinctions." Despite the fact that it was traditional for the Japanese child to follow in the trade of his father, Dr. Waterhouse discovered that the majority of these children "did not wish to follow their father's occupation, no matter what it was." Nisei girls, he found, would *not* work in the fields. "The evidence," he wrote, "is overwhelmingly conclusive that the second generation of Japanese not only can but actually are assimilating American ideals and customs and standards of living. All the facts go to show that these children, no matter how backward their parents may be, are most rapidly assimilating American life and are being assimilated by us." [27]

The proof of assimilation existed in the enormous gap that separated the two generations. The abnormal age gap that separated the Issei from the Nisei (due to late marriages) merely served to emphasize the cultural cleavage. Culturally the Nisei were much closer to the dominant groups than they were to their own parents. This cleavage was not only apparent: it was notorious. For years the vernacular newspapers had featured the split between the two generations; [28] for years Little Tokyo had echoed with family discord and bickering. The Nisei were customarily denounced by the Issei as upstarts, smart alecks, mannerless, disrespectful, and worthless.[29] To one excited elder, the Nisei appeared as nitwits, immoral ("committing sexual liberties with sublime faith in the science of drug store preventives"), dance-mad, extravagant, hopelessly addicted to American clothes,

[27] *The Future of Japan-American Relations in California*, 1922.
[28] *New World Sun*, January 1, 1933.
[29] *The Great Northern Daily News*, January 1, 1940.

beauty parlors, and movies. It is amusing to note that while Californians reiterated the slogan "Once a Jap, Always a Jap," and persisted in the belief that the Japanese were the most clannish people on earth, the Japanese communities were echoing with internal dissension. All manner of differences in belief and opinion existed and Japanese families were, in many cases, hopelessly divided by these differences.

The rift was widened by the fact that the parents had been so intensely preoccupied with their stores and shops that they had neglected the children. In the eyes of these children, the Japanese home was not an overly attractive institution. They tended to shift for themselves; to live outside the world in which they slept. Lack of understanding was a constant irritant. "You wouldn't understand, skip it," was a familiar Nisei rejoinder. Almost everything their parents did or said irritated the Nisei and served to turn them, not only against their parents, but against all things Japanese. It was in an effort to preserve some semblance of control over the Nisei that the parents clung so tenaciously to their culture. Small wonder, then, that one Issei should have observed: "There is little harmony in many families because of the gap between the two generations. There is no understanding, no sympathy, each of them walking his own way." [30] "The community elders voice no optimism," he wrote, "in the future of the Nisei in the United States. They hold to the belief that a dark, forbidding end awaits them."

In some cases, the Japanese father had sent the wife and children back to Japan; or, in other cases, the child had been sent to Japan to live with relatives at an early age. When these children subsequently returned to America, their parents were complete strangers; there was not even the bond of affection. Nisei raised and educated in Japan as Japanese found the culture of America "unreal and terrifying"; they were particularly thin-skinned and sensitive to discrimination. In still other cases, the wife and children were permanently separated from the father by the passage of the Immigration Act of 1924. The children (usually American-born) continued to reside with the alien

[30] *Nisei Tragedy* by Kanichi Niisato, Tokyo, 1936.

mother in Japan; less frequently, with the father in America.

The usual Japanese-American home was itself a hybrid institution. "The culture of my parents' homeland," writes George Morimitsu, "ended with the songs we heard and the foods we ate and the holidays my parents observed. We never engaged in long talks as other families do, because we never understood each other well." One Nisei, Aiji Tashio, has given a vivid impression of the mixed character of such households. "I sat down," he wrote, "to American breakfasts and Japanese lunches. My palate developed a fondness for rice along with corned beef and cabbage. I became equally adept with knife and fork and with chopsticks. I said grace at meal times in Japanese, and recited the Lord's prayer at night in English. I hung my stocking over the fireplace at Christmas and toasted 'mochi' at Japanese New Year. The stories of the 'Tongue-cut Sparrow' and 'Momo-taro' were as well known to me as those of Red Riding Hood and Cinderella. As I look back upon it now, I see that my parents indulged in this oriental side of the family life with a certain amusement and tolerance. I rather think that they were good showmen and had no serious idea of making Japanese citizens of their children. On some nights I was told bedtime stories of how Admiral Togo sent a great Russian fleet down to destruction. Other nights I heard of King Arthur or from *Gulliver's Travels* and *Tom Sawyer*. I was spoken to by both parents in Japanese and English. I answered in whichever was convenient or in a curious mixture of both." [31]

The Japanese-American communities on the West Coast were as curiously mixed as the homes. "The Japanese immigrant," write Young and Reid, "is a citizen of two worlds; the one which he shares with his fellow immigrants, and the one which he and they have in common with the remaining groups in the Canadian community. The first of these worlds is more intimately associated with the affairs of the immigrants because it is so definitely linked with their past in Japan. While its origins derive from Japan, its present setting is Canadian and its essential characteristics are consequently modified. It is really, indeed, neither

[31] *New Outlook*, September, 1934, p. 37.

Japanese nor Canadian. It is a marginal world or society between the two civilizations, with customs and institutions peculiar to itself and an atmosphere all its own. The most appropriate name for this society is Japanese-Canadian, for while its roots are in the soil of Japan, its structure and content are increasingly altered by unceasing adaptation to the environment of the New World." [32]

Even such institutions as the Buddhist Church were profoundly modified in the process of transplantation. The Reverend J. Mizuno has described Buddhism in America as "a mixed religion," increasingly assuming the forms and adopting the practices of a Christian church. The Buddhist churches had Sunday schools, regular Sunday services, and societies paralleling those to be found in the Christian churches. In these Buddhist churches, people sang Christian hymns with a few words changed, such as, "Buddha loves me, this I know." Many of the immigrants and most of the Nisei were Christians. Owing to the initial language problem, however, the Japanese-Christian, or segregated church, had developed. By 1940 there was considerable agitation in favor of dissolving these churches, the racial character of which had come to be regarded as an influence retarding assimilation.

Biological adaptation paralleled social adaptation. It has been repeatedly demonstrated (by Dr. H. L. Shapiro, Dr. Inui, Dr. Ichihashi, and others) that the children of Japanese immigrants differ from their parents physically as well as culturally. They are taller, larger, and heavier than children born and reared in Japan. As a result of better dental care, the shape of their mouths is different. Once the absence of important vitamins from the native diet is rectified, they respond with astonishing rapidity. Dr. P. M. Suski and Dr. Paul Frampton of Los Angeles measured, weighed, and examined hundreds of American-born Japanese and found many physical points of difference from children born in Japan.

The second generation on the West Coast grew to maturity under fairly favorable circumstances, as anti-Japanese agitation

[32] Op. cit.

100

began to wane somewhat after 1924. There were only a few segregated schools on the Coast and these were the result of the geographical concentration of Japanese in certain rural areas, as around Florin and Walnut Grove. In most of the schools, Japanese youngsters passed through the secondary grades with little friction and, in many cases, with practically no consciousness of racial differences. They were everywhere highly regarded by their teachers and extolled for their excellent application and not infrequent brilliance. Through high school and into college and university, they mingled freely with other groups (they were never ostracized as were the Negroes); formed enduring friendships (usually, however, of boy for boy, girl for girl); took an active part in athletics and other school activities; and were frequently elected to class offices. As one high school graduate said: "In all my school days when I have mixed and intermixed with my American schoolmates and teachers, I have found no differences. Our similarities of interest were so innumerable that they overshadowed and even hid my inheritance."

A consciousness of difference usually developed only after graduation from high school or in the first years at college or university. In the high schools, the Nisei belonged to all the athletic and social and scholastic organizations; but in college a measure of social segregation existed. Since they usually applied for employment with Japanese-operated firms, they were not made to feel conscious of discrimination after graduation. The fact that they experienced so little discrimination, in fact, was a circumstance that tended to widen the breach between them and their parents.

There were, of course, some instances of prejudice. John Aiso, a brilliant Nisei, was elected president of the student body of a Los Angeles Junior High in 1922 by a vote of three to one. Egged on by indignant parents, some Caucasian students instituted a recall election which was sponsored by several local newspapers. The incident did not appear to bother Aiso for he went on to Brown University, where he graduated with high honors. Such cases were, however, extremely rare. The principal of one rural high school in California, where the student body was nearly one-third Japanese, told me that in the twelve years that he was there he never had occasion to reprimand a student for racial prejudice or intolerance.

Nisei college and university graduates found it increasingly difficult after 1930 to find positions for which they were trained. And as they sought employment outside the Japanese community, they did encounter discrimination. By 1941 they had begun to talk about a "return to the land" as a solution of their problem; and both the Nisei and their Caucasian advisers had come to recognize that dispersal over a wider area was essential.[33] "For the majority of the Nisei the range of opportunity is definitely limited," said the *New Canadian;* "the local Japanese community cannot continue to absorb all the Nisei entering the labor market as the saturation point has been reached. It is becoming increasingly apparent that the Nisei will have to expand outside the community for their livelihood."

By no means all the difficulties faced by the Nisei could be traced to external pressures and discriminations. One of the principal influences retarding acceptance was the character of the Little Tokyo community itself. The Japanese-American communities on the West Coast were, perhaps, the most gossip-ridden communities in America. Mr. William Himmel was quite correct when he wrote, in an unpublished manuscript, that "the greatest aid to assimilation that the Nisei could adopt would be to liquidate gossips and gossiping and to break loose from the strangleholds of home and community."[34]

The Japanese immigrant had discovered that assimilation was not essential to economic existence. He was inclined, therefore, to adopt a "modified position" toward America and to induce his children to do likewise. The Issei were able to bring considerable influence to bear upon the Nisei because they held the economic purse-strings. As a consequence, there was sometimes an appearance of incongruity and compromise in the attitude of the Nisei for which they were not directly responsible. In high school orations, they spoke in glowing terms of American citizenship (but frequently as something external to themselves). Then

[33] *Japanese-American Times*, May 6, 1941; *New Canadian*, May 9, 1941.
[34] See *New World Sun*, January 1, 1933, where the same point is discussed.

their proud parents would proceed to have the orations published in book form and to request the local Japanese consul to write the introduction! Without always being aware of the fact, the Issei in many cases sought to bring their children up as compromise Americans, capable of living in either of two worlds. To the extent that they succeeded — which in my opinion was negligible — they did limit the opportunities for assimilation which existed.

Like other immigrants, the Issei had sought patrons in the Caucasian world. They had attempted to identify themselves with the particular social groupings that seemed to have the greatest prestige and influence. They curried favor with the Daughters of the American Revolution, the Chambers of Commerce, and the American Legion and fondly imagined that these groups, which invariably participated in all their ceremonial celebrations, would rally to their defense in a crisis. It was only natural that the Nisei should seek advice and guidance from these same groups. Also the political beliefs of the Issei tended to influence the Nisei. In Los Angeles, the Japanese business world was intimately linked with the most reactionary sections of the American business world. Its leaders were strongly anti-labor, joined the Merchants and Manufacturers Association in promoting "red" scares, and were consistently conservative on all social and political issues. A poll taken in Imperial Valley in 1936 showed that 90 per cent of the Japanese-Americans favored Alf Landon for President.

It is interesting to note that local officials in California worked hand-in-glove with the Japanese consuls in an effort to ferret out the anti-fascists among the Nisei. Captain William F. Hynes of the "Red Squad" of the Los Angeles Police Department received funds, at one time, from the Japanese consul for this purpose.[35] Under these circumstances, only a few Nisei dared to speak out against Japanese aggression in China or to sponsor liberal movements. It is to their great credit that many of them did participate in campaigns to boycott the shipment of scrap metals to Japan. A conspicuous feature of all formal Japanese meetings and banquets in California was the presence, in the

[35] *Los Angeles Daily News,* June 14, 1939.

places of honor, of the most reactionary citizens and officials of the community. These individuals joined with the leaders of the Japanese community in opposing boycotts and sanctions against Japan and looked upon Japanese aggression in China with far less concern than did the Nisei. One could make a fat volume of the effusive tributes paid to the leaders of the Japanese communities by public officials of the State of California in the years from 1930 to 1941. These same individuals were the first to advocate the evacuation of the Japanese.

Not only were the Japanese communities closely knit worlds in which everyone tried to know everyone else's business, and usually did, but they were essentially *petit bourgeois* communities. There was only a small capitalist class and a negligible upper-middle class; and a relatively small working class. The fact that there was really only a single class interest represented in the community made, as Mr. Miyamoto has suggested, for internal solidarity. But it also tended to keep broad currents of ideas and interests out. Little Tokyo was not only a small world: it was essentially a petty world.

It was a world that made for frustration. " 'I've walked up and down this damn street,' " observes a character in a short story by G. T. Watanabe,[36] " 'for twenty years and I'm sick and tired of it!' And, as he stood there cussing the street you could sense his distaste for his surroundings. He stood there cussing, but he could not break away. He was a part and yet not a part, of this street where sensibilities were slowly being killed, where maladjusted and disillusioned Nisei sought to forget their unhappiness in the din of raucous laughter and blatant noise, where restless and gaudily-dressed Pinoys sat sipping their coffee . . . he stood there cussing the street, this shoddy street of dirty gutters filled with lottery tickets; of shops, some old and faded and dusty, and others new and modern and shining; of grocery stores with their peculiar Oriental smell; of pool halls with the sound of balls clicking and with their dimly-lit interiors and faces turned away from the sun; of the cafes with their brightly-glowing neon lights, filling the night air with a hazy blue and red

[36] *New Canadian*, June 5, 1941.

and green, and canned music from the jute boxes; and the speaks with their hot Dixieland bands, their wailing jungle rhythms."

The favorite character in the Nisei short story, in pre-evacuation days, was a Byronic figure, full of frustration and despair; a sensitive, rebellious introvert. There was scarcely an issue of the vernacular press that did not carry a symposium on "The Nisei Problem." The Nisei themselves conducted endless surveys to discover what was the source of their trouble. Their self-criticism ranged over a wide field: they were lacking in assurance; they were too clannish; they were defeatist; they were consumed with a sense of futility, and so forth, and so forth. In many respects, the Nisei were a perplexed and unhappy lot, despite the reputation they had, among the Issei, of being pleasure-mad extroverts engaged in a constant round of social activities. Without quite realizing why, the Nisei were seeking a larger world; they were suffocating in Little Tokyo.

By 1940 the Nisei had begun to emerge from this fog of uncertainty and doubt. A new note had begun to echo in their publications. "So long as the Nisei insists," wrote Kenny Murase, "as he has so doggedly done, upon clinging to the myopic viewpoint, of working only among his own group and ignoring the Italians, Poles, Jews, Chinese, Negroes, and other minorities, his will be a lonely and futile cry in the vast wilderness of apathy and scorn. As long as he does not discard his shell of imposed self-sufficiency and identify himself as a positive and aggressive racial element, he cannot expect acceptance by other elements which have already proved their mettle as dynamic forces in the shaping of American destiny." [37] By 1941 the Nisei were just beginning to make their presence felt on the West Coast. As the war clouds deepened, a glaring spotlight was focused on these bewildered youngsters. All of America suddenly seemed to be staring at them; a great voice seemed to be shouting in their ears: "Will you be loyal? Are you a spy? What will you do if war should come?" They were really not prepared to meet this frightful experience. It came almost a decade too soon. And then on December 7, 1941, their whole world fell apart.

[37] *Japanese-American News*, January 1, 1941.

CHAPTER IV

Exodus from the West Coast

THERE existed on the West Coast on December 7, 1941, a deep fault in the social structure of the area. This fault or fissure separated the small Japanese minority from the rest of the population. Like the earthquake faults that run along the coastal area, this particular fault was deeper in some places than in others; it had been dormant for years, but, in the language of the seismologists, it was still potentially active. While the fracture had begun to heal, the fitting-together process was incomplete. Past history had shown that almost any jar would disturb this fault. The attack on Pearl Harbor was more than a jar: it was a thunderous blow, an earthquake, that sent tremors throughout the entire Pacific area. The resident Japanese were the victims of this social earthquake. This is the root fact, the basic social fact, which precipitated the mass evacuation of the West Coast Japanese — "the largest single forced migration in American history," in the words of Dr. Paul S. Taylor.

Since this fault lay beneath the surface and had not been active for some years, it had been generally ignored. The military, for example, had never contemplated mass evacuation in the event of war. Only one group in the population was fully aware of the existence of this social fault — namely, the anti-Oriental diehards. Knowing of the existence of the fault, they not only anticipated an earthquake, but had laid the foundation, in fear and in fantasy, to capitalize upon the shock when it came. They had kept the old lies circulating; they had revived, from time to time, the old hatreds and the old fears. In March of 1935 a California Congressman had told his colleagues that there were 25,000 armed Japanese on the West Coast ready to take to the field in case of war. The *San Francisco Chronicle*, at the same time, quoted a state official to the effect that the "Japanese in California are training for war." In May, 1936, Bernarr Macfadden published an open letter in *Liberty* addressed to the President in which he increased the number of Japanese "soldiers" in California to 250,000. Throughout these years, the "scare" stories continued to appear.[1]

On February 21, 1940, William Randolph Hearst had written an editorial in the *Los Angeles Examiner* in which he had said: —

> Colonel Knox should come out to California and see the myriads of little Japs peacefully raising fruits and flowers and vegetables on California sunshine, and saying hopefully and wistfully: "Some day I come with Japanese army and take all this. Yes, sir, thank you." Then the Colonel should see the fleets of peaceful little Japanese fishing boats, plying up and down the California coast, catching fish and taking photographs.

The interests who inspired these and other stories knew what they would do the moment the earthquake struck: as early as 1939, Mr. Lail Kane, chairman of the National Defense Committee of American Legion Post No. 278, had stated, "In case of war, the first thing I would do would be to intern every one of them."[2]

Evacuation is over; it is past. No purpose would be served in discussing the matter at this time were it not for the fact that this social fault still exists on the West Coast. Formerly a local, it now threatens to become a nation-wide phenomenon. Evacuation, moreover, is now being cited on the Coast as *proof* of the disloyal and untrustworthy character of this entire minority. It is a cloud that follows the evacuees wherever they go. For these reasons, it requires reconsideration, not for the purpose of reopening the issue itself, but of lifting, if possible, this cloud of suspicion. Just why was evacuation ordered and by whom? But,

[1] See *Focus* for July, 1938; *Friday*, May 9, 1941; *Life* for October 14, 1940 — "Californians cast an anxious eye upon the Japanese-Americans in their midst"; and *Click*, February, 1941, "Japan Attacks the U. S. in 1941."

[2] *Saturday Evening Post*, September 30, 1939.

first, a brief statement of *how* it was effected in order to clarify certain points in the explanation itself.

1. Evacuation

On December 11, 1941, the Western Defense Command was established, the West Coast was declared a theater of war, and General J. L. De Witt was designated as commander of the area. On December 7 and 8, the Department of Justice arrested, on Presidential warrants, all known "dangerous enemy aliens." Subsequently, by a series of orders the first of which was issued on January 29, 1941, the Department ordered the removal of all "enemy aliens" from certain designated zones or so-called "spot" strategic installations, such as harbors, airports, and power lines.

Following the appearance of the Roberts Report on Pearl Harbor, January 25, "the public temper on the west coast changed noticeably" [3] and "by the end of January, a considerable press demand appeared for the evacuation of all aliens, and especially of the Japanese from the west coast." The moment this *press campaign* was launched, a highly significant meeting of the entire West Coast Congressional delegation took place in Washington under the chairmanship of Senator Hiram Johnson (a leader of the old anti-Oriental forces in California). On February 13, 1942, this delegation submitted a letter to the President recommending "the immediate evacuation of *all persons of Japanese lineage*," and suggesting that this might be accomplished without a declaration of martial law (martial law had been proclaimed in Hawaii on December 7). On February 14, 1942, General De Witt submitted a memorandum to the War Department, in which he recommended mass evacuation of the Japanese.[4] On February 19, 1942, President Roosevelt signed Executive Order No. 9066, authorizing the War Department to prescribe military areas and to exclude any or all persons from these areas. The next day Mr. Stimson delegated this responsibility to General

[3] Preliminary report, Tolan Committee, March 19, 1942.
[4] *Final Report: Japanese Evacuation from the West Coast*, 1943, p. 33.

De Witt, who, on March 2, 1942, issued Proclamation No. 1, setting up certain military areas.

Subsequently the General on March 27 prohibited all persons of Japanese ancestry from leaving these military areas, and by 108 separate orders, the first of which was issued on March 24, ordered all such persons to move from Military Areas No. 1 and 2 (embracing the states of Washington, Oregon, California, and a portion of Arizona). Congress, in effect, ratified this action on March 21, 1942, by the passage of Public Law No. 503, making it a criminal offense for a person or persons excluded from military areas to refuse to move. By June 5, 1942, all persons of Japanese ancestry had been removed from Military Area No. 1; by August 7, Military Area No. 2 had been cleared. This is a brief log of events in the evacuation procedure — the *how* of evacuation.

It can be seen from this brief chronology that it was General De Witt who made the decision in favor of mass evacuation, and who, along with the West Coast Congressional delegation, had recommended it. The President and the Secretary of War were naturally preoccupied with more important matters at the time, and relied upon the General's appraisal of the situation. In the last analysis, it was his responsibility; he had to make the decision. Now why did he order *mass* evacuation?

The explanation given at the time was "military necessity." The military necessity itself was not defined. But with the issuance of the General's final report on evacuation, dated July 19, 1943, but not released until January, 1944, it now becomes possible to review the reasons prompting mass evacuation. The report clearly establishes the existence after December 7, 1941, of a grave and serious risk of an invasion of the West Coast. Guam was captured on December 13; Hong Kong fell on December 24; Manila on January 2; Singapore in February. Our fleet had been badly crippled at Pearl Harbor; for a time the disposition of the enemy's fleet was not known. On February 23, 1942, a Japanese submarine had shelled the California coast near Santa Barbara. The risk of imminent invasion was obvious and real, but it was as grave in Hawaii as on the mainland.

General De Witt's responsibility was of the most serious character. He was a military commander and military commanders have to make quick decisions; they have to act on the basis of possibilities as well as probabilities; they cannot weigh considerations with the nicety of a scientist working in a laboratory. The General must, also, have been haunted by the specters of Admiral Kimmel and General Short, who had been charged with dereliction of duty in Hawaii. Clearly, a serious military hazard existed on the West Coast; but what made the General relate the presence of the West Coast Japanese to this hazard?

In his report, two considerations, not strictly military in character perhaps, but certainly related to military security, are stressed: the danger of sabotage and the risk of espionage. The General knew, however, by February 14, that *no acts of sabotage* had occurred in Hawaii. If the Japanese population contained actual saboteurs, it is inconceivable that they would not have made their appearance during the attack on Pearl Harbor, which the Japanese government obviously intended to be a smashing, crippling blow. What is more disconcerting, however, is the fact that General De Witt cites the absence of sabotage as "a disturbing and confirming indication that such action will be taken." [5] In other words, the absence of proof (and no Japanese on the West Coast or in Hawaii have been convicted of sabotage) is taken as evidence of a fact. It is also disturbing to note that the General's suspicions were riveted on one minority and that he minimized the likelihood of sabotage on the part of German and Italian nationals who were possibly in a better position to commit such acts by reason of the fact that their race did not identify them as enemy nationals.

There was strong evidence that espionage was being practised on the West Coast. But the General notes that raids on Japanese communities failed to stop, for example, off-coast signaling. Who was engaged in this espionage? No answer is to be found in the report; but evidence of another character exists which throws some light on the problem. Prior to Pearl Harbor, two native-born white Americans had been convicted of being espionage

[5] Page 34.

agents for the Japanese government: John Farnsworth, a former naval officer, and Harry Thomas Thompson, a former seaman. Later, after the outbreak of war, an indictment was filed against Frederick Vincent Williams and David Warren Ryder charging them with having been unregistered agents of the Japanese government. They were both convicted. David Warren Ryder had, for many years, been a well-known Pacific Coast journalist. Arthur Clifford Reed, another native-born white American, was indicted as an unregistered agent of Japan (he had been a corporal in the Army).[6] Heizer Wright, indicted for being an unregistered agent of Japan for ten years prior to Pearl Harbor, was a member of the editorial staff of the *New York Daily News*.[7] On June 14, 1943, the OWI revealed that the persons who did the actual signaling at Pearl Harbor, on the eve of the Japanese attack, were Nazi agents (not local resident Japanese). Joseph Hilton Smyth, purchaser of the *Living Age*, was certainly not a Japanese-American, any more than were his associates in this camouflaged Japanese propaganda scheme. Ralph Townsend, sentenced to jail for being an unregistered agent of Japan, was a leader in the America First movement. For some years prior to Pearl Harbor, a Los Angeles police captain had received money, from time to time, from the local Japanese consul, for the ostensible purpose of spying on resident citizens of Japanese descent.[8] It has been pointed out that, after the attack on Pearl Harbor, Tokyo relied almost entirely on non-Japanese agents and for obvious reasons.[9] This evidence is, of course, by no means conclusive, but it does indicate that the real betrayal was not "from the east," as suggested by Mr. Alan Hynd, but from sources much closer home. No resident Japanese-American, either in Hawaii or on the mainland, has been convicted of being an unregistered agent or of having engaged in espionage activities. To focus attention on local residents of Japanese descent, actually diverted attention from those who were busily engaged in espionage activity.

[6] See *Los Angeles Times*, January 7, 1944.
[7] *PM*, July 9, 1943.
[8] *Los Angeles Daily News*, June 14, 1939.
[9] See *Sabotage!* by Sayers and Kahn, p. 193.

General De Witt also states that the resident Japanese were in danger of mob violence and that he acted, in part, to protect them. He notes, however, that most of the reports of attacks against them were, upon investigation, "either unverified or were found to be cumulative." [10] What are the facts? With the war clouds becoming increasingly darker throughout 1941, public opinion on the West Coast remained surprisingly sympathetic toward the resident Japanese.[11] Even the shock of the attack on Pearl Harbor failed to produce popular hysteria; and public opinion remained quite unbiased.[12] "Every Japanese," wrote Chester Rowell, "good or bad, is visibly a Japanese; and if there comes a wave of hysteria, caused by the conduct of some Japanese, there are precedents in every country for the psychology that would visit anger on them all. *I am glad to report that, so far, there has been no evidence of any such feeling.*" [13] "Despite the nature of Japan's attack on Pearl Harbor," wrote Dr. Eric Bellquist of the University of California, "there was no immediate widespread reaction of suspicion of aliens and second-generation Japanese." [14] Dr. Bellquist notes that it was not until *after* the "commentators, and columnists, 'professional patriots,' witch-hunters, alien-baiters, and varied groups and persons *with aims of their own*," began inflaming public opinion in January, 1942, that hysteria began to develop. It was then, in his phrase, that "patterned patriotism on the loose" became apparent and the "clamor for un-American restrictive measures became rife." There were no disturbances in the Northwest, reports Selden Menefee,[15] "no disorders of any sort," but, on the contrary, "expressions of sympathy" toward the resident Japanese. (As to the remarkable calmness which prevailed throughout the Pacific Coast on December 7, 1941, see the hour-by-hour report prepared by the correspondents of *Time, Life,* and *Fortune,* entitled

[10] *Report,* page 9.
[11] *Pacific Citizen,* September, 1941; *Seattle Post-Intelligencer,* August 23, 1941; and series of articles in the *Los Angeles Daily News,* August 21, 22, and 23, 1941.
[12] *Portland Oregonian,* for example, editorial of December 16, 1941.
[13] *Survey,* January, 1942.
[14] *California Alumni Monthly,* April, 1942.
[15] *Assignment: U. S. A.,* 1943, p. 67.

The First Thirty Hours.) I know of only two reported instances of violence in California: on December 27, 1941, a fight occurred between Filipinos and local Japanese in Stockton; [16] and on January 1, 1942, unknown persons fired at the home of a resident Japanese in Gilroy, California.[17] And if there was a danger — which the facts do not show — then it becomes pertinent to inquire, Why did the authorities fail to take proper measures to allay *possible* hysteria (as they did, for example, in Hawaii); and why were no authoritative statements issued to negate the widespread and continuous rumors of sabotage in Hawaii?

It develops, also, that a number of nonmilitary considerations entered into General De Witt's meditations. He began to engage in psychological speculation: Were these people loyal? How would they act? "While it was *believed* that *some* were loyal, it was known that many were not." [18] He was not of the opinion, except hypothetically, that *any* were loyal. While much circumstantial proof is cited in support of this hypothesis, the report contains *not one word* of reference to the manner in which these people had tried to demonstrate their loyalty long before Pearl Harbor. Since it is an official report, this omission serves to fix a cloud of suspicion upon the entire group.

In the files of the *Congressional Record*, throughout 1940 and 1941, may be found numerous memorials and petitions from the West Coast Japanese attesting their undivided allegiance to the United States. On October 21, 1940, the entire Japanese population of Imperial Valley, Nisei and Issei alike, assembled on the courthouse steps in El Centro and reaffirmed their loyalty to this country. On March 9, 1941, the Japanese-American Citizens League met with the Los Angeles City Council, pledged their fullest support, and asked to be given a chance to demonstrate, in any manner suggested, their loyalty. A similar meeting was held on March 21, 1941, with officials of the Army and Navy Intelligence Services, at which plans were adopted to put all of the facilities of the J.A.C.L. at the disposal of the authorities and

[16] *Sacramento Bee*, December 27, 1941.
[17] *Los Angeles Times*, April 24, 1943.
[18] *Report*, p. 9; italics mine.

at which the Nisei were complimented upon their patriotic action. These were merely sample demonstrations.

A local resident Japanese, Shuji Fujii, a Kibei, editor of the militant anti-fascist publication *Doho*, consistently denounced the fascist elements among the West Coast Japanese, and frequently by name.[19] The editor of the English section of *Rafu Shimpo* (a Japanese-American daily published in Los Angeles) protested against the drive for contributions for the relief of soldiers wounded in the Sino-Japanese War. Lieutenant Commander Ringle, of Naval Intelligence, has written[20] that many Nisei co-operated with him in his work as an intelligence officer and that, in his opinion, 85 per cent of the entire resident Japanese population was unquestionably loyal. None of this evidence is mentioned in General De Witt's report. Today these prewar acts of loyalty are actually referred to, by such persons as Mayor Fletcher Bowron of Los Angeles, as *suspicious* circumstances.

Undeniably there were dangerous individuals among the West Coast Japanese; undeniably there was a strong current of nationalistic feeling among certain Issei leaders. But the point is that these elements were well known to the authorities. They were promptly arrested on December 7 and 8, both on the mainland and in Hawaii. Writing in *Collier's*, in October, 1941, Jim Marshall observed that "for five years or more there has been a constant check on both Issei and Nisei — the consensus among intelligent people is that an overwhelming majority is loyal. The few who are suspect are carefully watched. In event of war, they would be behind bars at once. In case of war, there would be some demand in California for concentration camps into which Japanese and Japanese-Americans would be herded for the duration. Army, Navy or FBI never have suggested officially that such a step would be necessary. . . . Their opinion, based on intensive and continuous investigation, is that the situation is not dangerous and that, whatever happens, there is not likely to be any trouble — with this opinion west coast newspapermen, in touch with the problem for years, agree most unanimously." Lieutenant Commander Ringle, who was as closely in touch with

[19] See *Doho*, April 1, 1940.   [20] *Harper's*, October, 1942.

the entire problem as any official, did not think mass evacuation was necessary. That the authorities *had never contemplated* evacuation indicates that they had never regarded such a measure as being a matter of "military necessity."

It also develops that "military necessity" involved a judgment, by an army official, on purely sociological problems. "The continued presence of a large, unassimilated, tightly knit racial group, bound to an enemy nation by strong ties of race, culture, custom, and religion," states General De Witt, "constituted a menace which had to be dealt with." [21] Obviously there was a problem involved on this score; but it is interesting to note that West Coast sociologists who had studied the problem for years did not draw the same conclusion as the General and, needless to say, they were not consulted by him. No consideration whatever was given to the possibility of launching a special morale program or a campaign of so-called "preventive politics" in order to cope with the problem. No comparison was drawn between the manner in which these communities were organized and the manner in which German and Italian consuls had, in the most notorious fashion, conducted subversive activities on the West Coast. The problem of weighing these so-called "ethnic affiliations" was hardly one that, as a matter of proper function, should have been assigned to a military commander. Granted a special problem was involved, it by no means follows that mass evacuation was the only method of coping with it.

And it further develops that racial considerations were also regarded as part of the "military necessity." "The Japanese race," states the General, "is an enemy race and while many second and third generation Japanese born on United States soil, possessed of United States citizenship, have become 'Americanized,' the racial strains are undiluted. . . . It therefore follows that along the vital Pacific Coast over 112,000 potential enemies, of Japanese extraction, are at large today." [22] (This was part of the General's initial report.) I can draw but one inference from such a statement, namely, that the General regarded the entire group as potential enemies because they were racially related to the en-

[21] *Report*, page vii.   [22] Page 34.

emy. I do not understand, furthermore, why General De Witt felt compelled, in this instance, to put the word Americanized in quotation marks. Unfortunately, the General has since convicted himself of being deeply prejudiced on the score of race. Testifying on April 13, 1943, in San Francisco before the House Naval Affairs Subcommittee, he volunteered this statement: —

A Jap's a Jap. They are a dangerous element, whether loyal or not. There is no way to determine their loyalty. . . . It makes no difference whether he is an American; theoretically he is still a Japanese and you can't change him. . . . You can't change him by giving him a piece of paper.

This cynical appraisal of citizenship as "a piece of paper" and its brusque disregard of the factor of citizenship in general is rather disconcerting. It certainly demonstrates that it was the *racial* factor which, rather than the so-called "ethnic affiliations," really bothered the General.

Lastly, it now develops that political pressure was exerted on General De Witt. This pressure was (*a*) exerted directly on him; and (*b*) indirectly brought to bear upon him through the technique of an organized campaign. Testifying before the Dies Committee in Los Angeles, Mayor Fletcher Bowron made this interesting comment: —

"I may say that I was quite active in getting the Japanese out of Los Angeles and its environs. I held various conferences with Tom Clark, now Assistant United States Attorney General, who was designated in charge of enemy alien activities on the Pacific Coast, and together with him and the then Attorney General, now Governor Warren, we held a long conference with General De Witt relative to the situation, *and I hope we were somewhat helpful in General De Witt making his decision.*" [23]

After the Pacific Coast Congressional delegation had recommended mass evacuation on February 13, and *before* the President had issued Executive Order No. 9066, the delegation dispatched the Tolan Committee to the West Coast "*so that local communi-*

[23] Vol. 54, p. 9207. Italics mine.

ties could voice their attitude toward the developing program."
The committee came to the West Coast immediately (before the
order was signed) and held hearings (February 21 to March 2,
1942). If this were a matter of "military necessity" it is a little
difficult to understand why it was necessary to take "the pulse of
opinion" on the West Coast. It also develops that, at the time,
the Attorney General of the United States was opposed to mass
evacuation, particularly in the absence of a declaration of martial
law, and that members of the West Coast delegation threatened
to lead an attack against the appropriation for the Department of
Justice unless some satisfactory solution could be reached.

Unlike their confreres in Hawaii, the dominant business interests on the West Coast did not want to see martial law proclaimed.[24] These interests felt that, if some means could be devised to get the Japanese excluded from the West Coast without
a declaration of martial law, then such a declaration might be
altogether avoided. The action of the West Coast delegation in
dispatching the Tolan Committee to the Coast before the President had acted on their demand indicates an intention to exert
public pressure on the administration. This was precisely what
the Tolan hearings did. For, as so often happens, the "pro"
groups, those favoring evacuation, were prepared for the occasion and dominated the hearings. Virtually no Issei testified; and
the Nisei were appearing under a severe handicap for they were
forced, in effect, to agree in advance to whatever was proposed
as a solution, since they were asked to do so "as proof of their
loyalty." Although it was claimed that possible Filipino-Japanese
strife might be a factor in the developing situation, no Filipinos
were called to testify. In general, no minority groups were called.
The German and Italian groups, including the Jewish refugee
groups, were at great pains to distinguish their case from that of
the resident Japanese, including the Nisei.

Through these hearings, definite pressure for evacuation was
carefully organized (not because the committee itself was unfair — it was eminently fair — but because the "pro" groups took

[24] See testimony of Mr. Paul Shoup, President Los Angeles Merchants
and Manufacturers Assn., before the Tolan Committee, p. 11866.

possession of the hearings). Pressure for mass evacuation came from several different sources: from politicians and political units (all seeking to pass the buck to the government); from groups that had an obvious and readily acknowledged economic interest in evacuation; and from the traditionally anti-Oriental organizations, such as the American Legion, the California Joint Immigration Committee, and similar organizations. The mayors of Los Angeles, San Francisco, Portland, and Seattle all favored mass evacuation; various grand juries and city councils and boards of supervisors presented similar demands; and law-enforcement officials, in general, spoke in favor of the proposal. Few rank-and-file citizen groups appeared. The parade of witnesses in favor of evacuation certainly had the appearance of organization. Although the press had been conducting a steady campaign for evacuation since the latter part of January, there was little public interest, as such, in the problem. The hearings in Los Angeles were attended by a handful of witnesses and perhaps a dozen spectators.

In reviewing the testimony of these "pro" witnesses, two considerations become of paramount importance. In the first place, there was an almost unanimous assumption that Japanese should be placed in a separate category from German and Italian nationals; and, second, everyone assumed that sabotage had been practised by resident Japanese in Hawaii. The Attorney General of California (now Governor Warren) was, perhaps, the most forceful advocate of mass evacuation. "We believe," he testified, "that when we are dealing with *the Caucasian race* we have methods that will test the loyalty of them." [25] He professed to believe, as though to emphasize the racial factor, that the Nisei constituted *a more likely danger* than the Issei. Not only did most of the witnesses assume that acts of sabotage had been committed in Hawaii, but the chairman of the committee consistently questioned witnesses on the assumption that such acts had been established. It is also worthy of note that virtually all of these witnesses testified that evacuation was required for the safety and protection of the Japanese themselves; that it was *primarily* for

[25] P. 11015; italics mine.

118

their protection. These same individuals are now strenuously contending that no Japanese should be permitted to return to the West Coast even in the postwar period. Since witnesses were encouraged to believe that sabotage had occurred in Hawaii, considerable credence was given to Mr. Warren's theory that the West Coast faced "an invisible deadline of sabotage." Thus old dormant fears were revived; old suspicions were renewed; and the same clichés that had been echoing on the Coast for fifty years or more were repeated — although awkwardly and in a manner that indicated lack of recent practice.

The point — of which so much was made at the hearing by the introduction of fancy maps — that it was "more than mere coincidence" that so many Japanese were located near "vital installations" requires a special word of comment. There could be no question, for example, that the Japanese fishing colony on Terminal Island, in the center of Los Angeles Harbor, did constitute a potential hazard. But how did the colony happen to be there? It had been established thirty years prior to the attack on Pearl Harbor and by American canning interests, not by the Japanese. Since fishing boats arrive at all hours of the day and night, it is essential, and has always been essential, that cannery workers live near the canneries. They traditionally report for work when the whistle blows at the cannery, announcing the arrival of the boats. The canneries *compelled* these workers to live in close proximity to the plants. Early in 1941, the colony had been attacked as a likely center of espionage activities and the community itself had requested a full investigation. Such an investigation was actually conducted by the FBI, and Naval Intelligence, but no arrests were made. It is certainly a safe assumption that Naval Intelligence officers knew all about the background and activities of every resident of the island, since the island residents had been under surveillance for years.

All of the Japanese fishermen were members of the Seine and Line Fisherman's Union and, long prior to December 7, they had repeatedly made declarations of their loyalty and support in case of war. The devotion of these fishermen to their homes, their children, and to the schoolteachers who taught at the all-Japanese school, had been a favorite topic of local newspaper columnists for years.[26] Yet overnight this colony of fishermen, tied to their island community by the dictates of the canning industry, became sinister proof of the disloyal attitude of the resident Japanese.[27]

Mr. Warren, ruler in hand, also pointed to small Japanese truck gardens shown, by the map, to be located near factories, power lines, and refineries. The Japanese, as previously shown, specialized in the production of fresh vegetables for the urban West Coast markets. By reason of freight and transportation costs, these gardening units had to be placed near the markets themselves. Located around the periphery of the city, they were naturally intermeshed with sites used for industrial purposes. Only the Japanese could farm these small plots successfully since they alone, by their intensive cultivation methods, could pay the high rental demanded for land which was essentially industrial, and not agricultural, in character. Most of this land lay between Los Angeles and the San Pedro–Long Beach harbor area. Inevitably the Japanese farmed, therefore, near oil refineries; near factories; near important strategic installations.

But some of these units were located beneath high-tension power lines, and certainly this was a suspicious circumstance. The answer was revealed by inadvertence at a subsequent hearing. When the power lines were built, the companies had to purchase a thousand-foot right-of-way or easement through the center of which ran the line. The property within the path of the power line could not be rented for residential purposes; nor was it desirable for industrial or commercial use. Concerns such as the Southern California Edison Company found that they could rent this easement land to Japanese at fifteen or twenty dollars an acre. That is how the Japanese happened to be beneath the power lines.

But some of them farmed on the heights at Palos Verdes from which they could overlook Los Angeles Harbor and "flash signals" to boats at sea; they could even see, in the famous Los An-

[26] See *Los Angeles: City of Dreams* by Harry Carr, 1935, pp. 329–330.
[27] On the colony, generally, see "Friends or Spies on Terminal Island?" by Margaret Fowle Rogers, *International Baptist Magazine*, May, 1941.

geles phrase, "Catalina Island on a clear day." Certainly this location was most suspicious. Later it developed that the reason the Japanese farmed on the Palos Verdes hills was because the land was high and free from frost; and because they needed one area near Los Angeles for dry-land farming so that early tomatoes and beans and peas might be placed on the tables of Los Angeles consumers. The Los Angeles County Farm Advisor later testified that there was no other area available which met these requirements. And that is why the Japanese happened to be where they "might see Catalina on a clear day." Italian "enemy alien" truck farmers and Italian "enemy alien" fishermen could have been indicted as suspicious characters by a similar unscrupulous use of circumstantial evidence by prejudiced observers. But no such indictment was made; and its omission is the best proof of the racial bias of the ruler pointers who appeared before the Tolan Committee and had its members gasping and panting over the menace of an "invisible deadline for sabotage."

2. Ethnic Ties

While insisting that mass evacuation was primarily essential to protect the resident Japanese against mob violence — an argument that sounds strange indeed when advanced by high-ranking law-enforcement officials — witnesses before the Tolan Committee advanced the usual stock arguments against the Japanese which had been repeated during all the previous agitations. Particular emphasis was placed on the language schools, the charge of dual citizenship, and the influence of Buddhism and Shintoism upon the resident Japanese.

A sense of ordinary common fairness should long ago have dictated a recognition of the peculiar language problem faced by Japanese residents on the West Coast. Immigrant parents felt the necessity of having their children instructed in the Japanese language in order to preserve family ties and to maintain some basis of communication with children who were speaking English in the schools, on the playgrounds, and in their everyday life. But from the outset there was a difficulty involved in securing competent instructors. The language school, supported by private funds, was devised to meet this clearly recognized need. Knowledge of their language was not only important from their parents' point of view, it was also important to those Nisei who, in later life, might seek employment in Japanese firms or in the export-import business.

It is indeed difficult to read anything subversive into the frankly expressed wish of Japanese parents that their children should know something about the history and culture of Japan. It is probably true, however, that some of these schools used text material that was objectionable. In Hawaii, the Japanese themselves sponsored legislation to bring the vernacular schools under state regulation. And many people have forgotten that in December, 1920, the Japanese Association of America suggested that California should enact similar legislation. In fact, such a bill was enacted in California only to be ruled unconstitutional in 1927. One of the reasons it was held unconstitutional was that the Catholic Church felt that such legislation might be extended to their parochial schools. And what has also been forgotten is that, in Oregon, the Japanese were finally successful in getting one public school to form a Japanese language class. Over a period of years, the vernacular schools were discussed at length in the Japanese-American press on the West Coast and many proposals were made, in the States and in Canada, to integrate these language schools with the public school system. That this step was never taken is to be attributed not to the Japanese, but to our own failure to recognize the existence of a definite educational problem. As to the schools themselves, Mr. Vierling Kersey, Superintendent of Schools in Los Angeles, once said: "We have absolutely no objection to these schools." [28]

The fact of the matter is that these schools were never successful. As one observer has so well said, the Japanese youngster spent a "precious hour and one-half tossing spit balls at his classmates and calling his teacher names in American slang which she pretended not to understand. Physically he was in school; mentally he was making a run around left end for another touchdown.

[28] *Los Angeles Daily News*, August 21, 1941.

He was restless. He counted the minutes. At the gong, he dashed to freedom." Based on three years' experience as an instructor in one of these schools, Saikichi Chijiwa predicted in 1927 that they would soon pass out of existence. That they failed even in their primary purpose of language instruction is shown by the fact that the Army, scouring the relocation centers for Nisei who knew the language, found that only 15 per cent of the Nisei could speak Japanese and that only about 5 per cent could read or write Japanese. Furthermore, parochial schools have taught foreign languages to immigrant children in America for generations; and no serious complaint has ever been filed against them. Prior to December 7, 1941, the Italian consulates had distributed fascist-inspired textbooks and other materials to Italian language schools in California. But, at the Tolan Committee hearings, *only* the Japanese language schools were deemed subversive or otherwise suspect. Later a California legislative committee found that Italians had sponsored similar language schools in which official fascist propaganda was taught and texts were used that were supplied by the Italian consuls.[29]

The "dual citizenship" charge was similarly unrealistic and unfair. The Japanese Nationality Code has always been predicated upon the doctrine of *jus sanguinis* — namely, that a child is Japanese if its father is a Japanese national at the time of its birth. Under the Fourteenth Amendment, we have always followed the doctrine of *jus soli* — except in the case of our own nationals abroad — that persons born in this country are citizens of the United States. That there are two such conflicting doctrines of nationality may be readily explained: countries having a heavy out-migration — the population exporting countries — almost uniformly follow the doctrine of *jus sanguinis;* while countries of heavy in-migration — the population receiving countries — follow the doctrine of *jus soli*. There is nothing peculiar, therefore, about the rule followed by Japan (it has been the rule of many European nations).

What we have forgotten is that the Japanese on the West Coast themselves petitioned Japan in 1914 to modify its law. The law

[29] *UnAmerican Activities in California*, 1943, pp. 316–319.

was, in fact, modified in March, 1916, and again in December, 1925, so as to make it possible for Japanese born in this country to renounce any claim of dual citizenship. It is a little difficult to see how such a claim could arise in actual practice, since we have never recognized the principle of dual citizenship. In any case, after 1925 many Nisei did renounce Japanese citizenship (the Japanese-American Citizens League carried on a ceaseless agitation to this end), and those born after December 1, 1925, were automatically released from such a claim. It is, however, true that many Nisei, largely through ignorance, or indifference, neglected to renounce the claim. While stressing this matter of dual citizenship, the anti-Japanese forces have always failed to note the sharp and obvious cleavage between the first and second generation — a fact of far greater significance.

Not being a theologian, I hesitate to discuss Buddhism or Shintoism as possible factors making for strong currents of nationalism among the resident Japanese population. But it is difficult to believe that Buddhism, as practised in America, is quite the same faith as Buddhism practised in Japan. The testimony of all observers is to the contrary. They point out that, as an imported cultural institution, Buddhism has undergone definite modifications and that the Buddhist churches have tended to parallel the Christian churches, adopting the same institutional paraphernalia, such as kindergarten schools, Sunday schools, some of the same hymns, and most of the same societies. Adherents of Buddhism have pointed out that an appreciation of its rites is largely dependent upon some knowledge of Japanese; and that with the decline of a knowledge of the language there developed a loss of interest in the faith. They also complained that children became involved in Christian practices merely as an incidence of their daily life. Generally speaking, Buddhism seemed to have stronger roots in rural than in urban communities. It had little interest for the Nisei. To them it was "odd" and "difficult" and the very appearance of a ramshackle Buddhist temple was as incongruous to them as it was to most other Americans.

I have examined any number of the proceedings of the Young Buddhist Leagues — the so-called Bussei groups. They read almost exactly like the proceedings of a typical conference of young go-getting Methodists. There is certainly nothing esoteric about the proceedings: government officials appeared and discussed soil problems; social workers orated about the problems of the second generation; and civic leaders exhorted the faithful to take a more responsible part in the affairs of their communities. If there was a tendency, on the part of these churches, to undermine faith in American democracy, it is certainly not reflected in the proceedings themselves. It is, however, probably true that after 1937 some effort was made by Japan to use the vernacular schools and the Buddhist churches for propaganda purposes, both here and in Hawaii. For example, the *Literary Digest* of February 13, 1937, reported that some "forty young missionaries from the Buddhist University in Kyoto, Japan," had recently arrived in the United States. But to make religious faith a test of loyalty or to consider it as evidence affecting the question of loyalty was as unfair as to imply that race could be made a test of loyalty.

More serious than this age-old native-son gossip about language schools, dual citizenship, and Buddhism, was the fact that the Japanese did have a tightly knit pattern of social organization and that most group activity was co-ordinated by the local Japanese Association which, in turn, had close ties with the various consulates. The same type of co-ordination existed in the control which certain Japanese firms exercised over both Issei and Nisei and the relationship which existed between these firms and the consulates. What made this pattern particularly troublesome was the fact that in 1941 the leadership was still 'vested in the Issei. It is important to note, however, that the war had broken this pattern of relationships. The vernacular schools were closed; the consulates were closed; all aliens had been registered in 1940; the assets of the Japanese firms had been frozen in midsummer, 1941; and, immediately after December 7, the leaders of the various associations were in jail. Precisely the same relationship patterns existed in Hawaii. If anything the various Japanese organizations were more closely knit in Hawaii than on the mainland.

There is still another factor involved which has never been discussed in relation to the evacuation problem. The Japanese and the Japanese-Americans had a big economic stake in the security of the West Coast. Their holdings have been estimated as being in excess of $200,000,000. From a strictly economic point of view, what could they possibly hope to gain from a Japanese victory? Even the few deluded individuals who might have believed in the possibility of a Japanese victory must have realized, as did the Japanese war lords, that the most Japan could hope to achieve was a stalemate in the Pacific with Japan retaining a portion of its Far Eastern loot. How could even such a hypothetical victory improve the lot of the West Coast Japanese? Bad as their position was after the attack on Pearl Harbor, it would have become intolerable had Japan, let us say, achieved a stalemate in the Pacific. In such an eventuality, remote as it must have seemed, they could only have expected economic and physical annihilation on the West Coast. Most of the Issei had lived in this country from thirty to fifty years; they had, in a majority of cases, American-born children. Several thousand of these Nisei were serving in the United States Army on December 7, 1941. Assuming that there were strong currents of nationalism among some of the Issei leaders, it should not be forgotten that 72 per cent of the Nisei have never been in Japan. The most powerful economic, family, and personal considerations dictated the necessity of continued allegiance to the United States.

3. Economic Pressures

While the position taken by the various groups before the Tolan Committee cannot be said to follow a clear line of economic interest, it is certainly true that special-interest groups were active in exerting pressure for mass evacuation. The shipper-grower interests in Washington were opposed to mass evacuation, while the Washington Commonwealth Federation, an ultraliberal group, favored it. But the California shipper-grower interests were definitely in favor of mass evacuation and for admittedly selfish reasons. Shortly after December 7, the Shipper-Grower Association of Salinas sent Mr. Austin E. Anson to Washington to lobby for mass evacuation. "We're charged with wanting to get rid of the Japs for selfish reasons," said Mr. Anson. "We might as well be honest. We do. It's a question of whether the white man lives on the Pacific Coast or the brown men. They came into this valley to work, and they stayed to take over." [30] Similarly, so-called "white interests" in the nursery and florist businesses were actively seeking mass evacuation as a means of eliminating unwanted competition.

To appreciate the position that these special-interest economic groups took, however, it is necessary to explain the situation as they saw it. By December 7, 1941, the Japanese had achieved a *tolerated* position in the industries in which they were concentrated, such as the produce industry, the floral industry, the nursery industry. They were tolerated because of an unofficial truce that had been declared: this far they might go but no farther. But with prices rising after December 7, produce interests saw an opportunity to take over the Japanese holdings. For they foresaw that prices would continue to rise (particularly if the Japanese were ousted), thereby creating an opportunity for them to take over and operate successfully types of business which, in "normal" times or in a period of declining prices, they could not possibly hope to operate at a profit. They also realized that, once the Nisei came into possession and ownership of these businesses, they might expand out of the tolerated zone. For the Nisei were American citizens; they were exceptionally well-educated; and they could not, therefore, be expected to stay within the confines into which their parents had been driven. To get all Japanese out of the state would eliminate, so they thought, this potential *future* competition.

These same special-interest groups have, moreover, continued to be most active in urging the permanent exclusion of the Japanese from the West Coast. High stakes are involved: the Japanese produce production in California had an estimated annual value of $35,000,000; their share of the florist business in Los Angeles alone was valued at around $4,000,000 annually. In Washington,

[30] *Saturday Evening Post*, May 9, 1942.

as I have indicated, the situation was somewhat different, because there the Japanese figured more prominently in the production of produce for interstate shipment, whereas in California they were largely confined to the production of fresh vegetables for the local markets. While there was this split in the ranks of the economic pressure groups — not all of whom favored mass evacuation — it is nevertheless incontestably true that certain groups stood to profit (momentarily at least) by the elimination of the Japanese; and that they played a very important behind-the-scenes role in securing mass evacuation.

4. The Earthquake Strikes

By the time the Tolan Committee arrived in California, in February, 1942, the social fault that I have mentioned had begun to jar the Japanese communities loose from their moorings. On July 26, 1941, the assets of Japanese nationals had been "frozen." The restrictions imposed on enemy aliens on December 7 and 8 had begun to hamper the Issei in their business activities and a serious economic crisis had developed. The uncertainty of the situation had created a type of economic paralysis: business transactions were suspended, crops were not being planted, many activities were being held in *status quo*. Landlords had begun to evict Japanese tenants; insurance policies were being canceled; social-security payments could not be released to Japanese nationals. Japanese firms were slowly losing patronage. No new employment fields were opening. The families of those individuals arrested on Presidential warrants were in dire distress. Nisei were being discharged from their positions (they were summarily ousted from city, county, and state civil-service positions without hearings and with no charges being preferred against them). On January 17, 1942, it was reported that most of the Japanese firms in San Francisco would have "to close within a few months." This distress was apparent as early as August, 1941; by January, 1942, it had become acute.

The committee arrived in Los Angeles just in time to observe the disastrous effects of the summary ouster of the Japanese fishing colony — five hundred families — from Terminal Island. On February 15, these families were told that they were expected to move within thirty days; later, they were given twenty-four hours in which to vacate. The utmost confusion prevailed, as families sought to find places into which they might move, and tried frantically to dispose of their effects. Most of these families were without resources. These two developments, the paralysis creeping over the Japanese communities and the ouster of families from spot strategic areas, merely indicated that an earthquake had struck along the fault.

There is one further aspect of the matter, however, that warrants consideration: between February 19 and March 27, 1942, the Japanese were at liberty to depart voluntarily from Military Area No. 1. The failure of voluntary evacuation to effect the desired removal of all Japanese from the area was largely responsible for the subsequent orders for evacuation. During the period mentioned, it is estimated that some 10,231 Japanese voluntarily departed from Military Area No. 1, but, of this number, some 4825 merely moved into Military Area No. 2. In some cases, this involved simply moving a few miles. It also had the effect of concentrating evacuees in certain rural areas in central California where, by their presence, they aroused suspicion and tended to aggravate an already tense situation.

In the nature of things, voluntary evacuation could hardly have been successful, since few resident Japanese had friends or relatives in the Middle West or East and did not know where to go. Many of them lacked the necessary funds to finance a long-distance trip; and, besides, they were uncertain about the kind of reception they might meet. It was a question of fleeing from a known to an unknown evil. Of those who did voluntarily depart, some 5396 went to areas outside both Military Areas Nos. 1 and 2, principally to Colorado and Utah. Of those who did move, during the period of voluntary evacuation, it is estimated that 1200 shortly returned to Military Area No. 1, thereby further complicating an already complicated situation.

In attempting to remove themselves beyond Military Areas Nos. 1 and 2, evacuees either had to cross through the inter-mountain states or to locate in this region. In February, Congressman Tolan had wired the governors of these (and other) states, inquiring about the possibilities of relocating the Japanese. With the exception of Governor Carr of Colorado (who was subsequently defeated in a political campaign), all replied unfavorably. Typical of the replies received was the comment of Governor Homer M. Adkins of Arkansas: "Our people are not familiar with the customs or peculiarities of the Japanese. We are always anxious to co-operate in any way we can, but our people, being more than 95 per cent native born, are in no manner familiar with their customs and ways and have never had any of them within our borders, and I doubt the wisdom of placing any in Arkansas." I know of one family that had been located in New Mexico for almost thirty years prior to Pearl Harbor. Yet it is interesting to note that the pressures became so great in New Mexico (so many of whose soldiers were involved at Bataan) that this family voluntarily moved into a relocation center to secure protection. That this could happen in New Mexico is some indication of what might have happened in California if evacuation had not been ordered, once the flood of agitation had started.

Sentiment in these intermountain states not only was opposed to relocation, but was of such a character as to indicate the kind of reception that evacuees might face if they moved farther eastward. For example, Governor Payne Ratner of Kansas stated that "Japs are not wanted and not welcome in Kansas" and directed the state highway patrol to turn back any Japanese trying to enter the state.[31] One Japanese group, consisting of seven adults and a baby, was stopped at nearly every Colorado town in attempting to cross the state. On March 7, 1942, the press reported that Japanese, attempting to cross through Arizona, were stopped by state highway patrolmen. Similar incidents were reported throughout the area. Typical of the general reaction was the statement of the Nevada Bar Association: "We feel that if Japs are dangerous in Berkeley, California, they are likewise dangerous to the State of Nevada." The *State-Tribune* of Wyoming

[31] Reported in the *Las Vegas Daily Optic*, April 1, 1942.

stated in an editorial of March 8, 1942: "It is utterly unequitable and unfair to subject Wyoming to the bureaucratic dictum that it shall support and find employment for Japanese brought here from Pacific Coast defense zones." In its issues of March 2 and 9, 1942, the *Denver Post* carried similar editorial statements. The mere fact that the governors of these states had been queried on the possibility of relocation brought down upon them an avalanche of mail from irate constituents.

As they retreated eastward evacuees met with unpleasant incidents at many points and were constantly subjected to humiliating experiences. Signs posted in shops read: "This restaurant poisons both rats and Japs"; barbershops carried signs reading "Japs Shaved: Not Responsible for Accidents"; cards were placed in automobile windshields reading "Open Season for Japs"; stores, filling stations, restaurants, refused to serve evacuees.[32] The vigorous expression of such attitudes and the recurrence of such incidents clearly indicated, early in March, 1942, that voluntary evacuation would not be successful. The same evidence indicated that evacuation would have to be federally supervised, that minimum measures of protection would have to be taken, and that further voluntary evacuation would have to be curtailed. As a consequence the first "freezing" order was issued on March 27, 1942.[33]

5. "E Day" Arrives

Just as the federal authorities were pushed into the program of evacuation, so they were compelled to improvise extraordinary devices and expedients to cope with the problem which they had inherited overnight. Not only were there no precedents to follow — no guideposts along the way — but the time element precluded the possibility of a studied consideration of various possibilities and alternatives. Having permitted themselves to be convinced that these people were a menace, it necessarily followed that

[32] See the *Christian Advocate*, October 15, 1942.
[33] See also "The Problem People" by Jim Marshall, *Collier's*, August 15, 1942.

prompt action was required. There is no evidence that the military had ever contemplated, in the event of war, such a measure; certainly they had no concealed Plan X to pull from their files. The whole program was evolved in response to external pressures and developments. It evolved dialectically: by internal and external compulsions.

It is important to remember, as Mr. Dillon Myer has pointed out, that "internment camps were never *intended* in relation to this program." All that was originally contemplated was an order excluding persons of Japanese descent from the area. When it became apparent that these persons were slow to move, that they needed assistance; and when it gradually dawned on the authorities that they did not even know where to move, then and only then were plans prepared which contemplated assistance, supervision, and control of the movement. Voluntary evacuation was then "frozen" and the Wartime Civil Control Administration was created as a branch of the Western Defense Command to supervise the removal of the evacuees. It was essentially WCCA's function to direct the removal — not the relocation — of these people. To this end it was deemed necessary to prevent further voluntary removals; to assemble all evacuees for removal; and to establish temporary reception or assembly centers.

Evacuation proceeded on a regular army timetable. Since removal was ordered on an area-by-area basis, as reception facilities were established, it did not occur simultaneously throughout the West Coast. Civil control stations were established in each area having a minimum of 1000 persons to be evacuated. Evacuees were registered at these stations and to these stations they reported on "E Day," the Army's designation of the date fixed for their removal. E Day will not soon be forgotten by the resident Japanese. The final decision in favor of total mass evacuation occurred only after weeks of uncertainty, debate, agitation, rumor, and conflicting reports. The decision itself came to most Japanese as almost as great a shock as Pearl Harbor. Until the very last moment there was always the hope of a respite or reprieve, or the possibility that some alternative plan might be adopted, or that only certain groups, such as the aliens, would be evacuated. To be forewarned of a disaster is not to be prepared for the disaster itself. As a group, the Japanese were stunned by the final decision; and to most of them it was a major disaster. It was as though they had been engulfed in a natural calamity, such as flood, or fire, or earthquake.

One Nisei underwent plastic surgery in an effort to have his features changed: "I was so ashamed," he said, "of my racial identity." Dreading to meet his Caucasian friends, Koji Kurokawa hid in the basement of his employer's home for twenty-three days. On a Fourth of July prior to evacuation, Hideo Murata, a veteran of the First World War, had been presented by the board of supervisors of Monterey County with a "Certificate of Honorary Citizenship" which read: —

Monterey County presents this testimony of heartfelt gratitude, of honor and respect for your loyal and splendid service to the country in the Great World War. Our flag was assaulted, and you gallantly took up its defense.

When E Day was announced in Monterey County, Murata went to see his friend the sheriff, and asked if it wasn't all a mistake, or perhaps just a practical joke. Finding that the order meant what it said, he went to a local hotel, paid for his room, and committed suicide. The sheriff found the certificate of honorary citizenship clutched in his hand. Not every Japanese, needless to say, felt this keenly about the matter. Most of them tried to accept the bitter intelligence itself in good spirit. Some volunteered to assist in the process; others attempted a show of high spirits about the entire procedure; all of them co-operated in the movement itself.

A curious aspect of E Day in California, as elsewhere on the West Coast, was the kindly complacence shown by the Caucasian residents of the area. While there had been weeks of agitation for the removal of the Japanese, this agitation had been conducted at a relatively high level. Uniformly the stress had been placed on considerations of national security, military necessity, and the well-being of these admirable people, the West Coast Japanese. The friendliest spirit prevailed in virtually every area. In more than one area this spirit verged on tenderness and remorse. Editorials appeared in which the evacuees were wished *bon voyage;* complimented on their excellent behavior; assured of a warm welcome upon their return; sentimental "sayonaras" echoed throughout the area. There were no harsh or strident or bitter denunciations. In areas which have since become hotbeds of anti-Japanese agitation, the departure of the Japanese was the occasion for the expression of heartfelt sentiments. There was virtually no realization, among the generality of citizens, that they were witnessing a unique departure from American tradition.

For those long proclamations ordering removal which appeared in the newspapers, were announced over the radio, and were tacked to telegraph poles and posted on bulletin boards, referred to "all persons of Japanese ancestry." No exceptions were specified; no provision was made for cases involving mixed marriages; and one drop of Japanese blood brought a person within the category defined. Here a group was being singled out for discriminatory treatment *solely* upon the basis of race or ancestry. In Germany, as Dr. Morris Opler has pointed out, the Nazis merely pretended to discriminate against persons on the score of race or ancestry. They were well aware of the fact, as were the German people, that the Jews are not a race. But we premised the discrimination explicitly and solely upon the fact of race or ancestry; more particularly of "ancestry" since the Koreans and the Chinese belong to the same "race" as the Japanese. No phase of our tradition, particularly of our Western tradition, has been more firmly accepted than the proposition that a man is not responsible for his ancestors. Even to inquire about a person's ancestry, in the early days of the West, was to violate an unwritten prohibition firmly implanted in the mores of the people. The acquiescence of the Japanese in this singular procedure was wholly admirable; but the indifference to, the calm acceptance of, the same procedure by their fellow citizens presents a somewhat different problem. It is, perhaps, only to be accounted for in terms of the fact that the Japanese, as such, had never been really accepted as a part of the community.

Their removal was, therefore, accomplished with much the same smoothness that an easily detachable part is removed from a machine.

From the control stations, the evacuees were escorted to a series of hastily improvised assembly centers. In selecting sites for assembly centers, WCCA showed great ingenuity. Use was made of fairgrounds, parks, race tracks, and pavilions. In California, assembly centers were established at Marysville, Sacramento, Tanforan, Stockton, Merced, Turlock, Salinas, Fresno, Pinedale, Tulare, Santa Anita, Pomona, and Manzanar (the only assembly center that was constructed as a relocation project). In the Northwest, assembly centers were established in Portland and at Puyallup; and in Arizona at Cavecreek and Mayer Camp. On arriving at the assembly centers, the evacuees went through a process of induction (registration, baggage inspection, medical checkup) and were assigned to quarters. Before they really knew what had happened, they were inside the centers, the gates were locked, and the sentries had established their patrols.

In a period of 28 days, army engineers had constructed shelters in assembly centers for 100,000 people, and in a period of 137 days the same number of people had been moved into these centers. By June 8, 1942, the entire movement from points of residence in Military Area No. 1 to assembly centers had been effected; and shortly afterwards those remaining in Military Area No. 2 had likewise been removed. By that date, virtually every Japanese, citizen and alien alike, in the three West Coast states and portions of Arizona was in an assembly center. The only exceptions were Japanese confined to institutions, such as hospitals, prisons, insane asylums, and orphanages. The rapidity and efficiency with which this movement was accomplished represents a major achievement for the Army. Colonel Karl Bendetsen was well within the facts when he said that the entire movement had been effected "without mischance, with minimum hardship, and almost without incident." All observers are in agreement on the proposition that the Army executed the assignment with tact, good judgment, and remarkable efficiency. On June 8, 1942, the assembly-center population totaled 99,700 Japanese.

The efficiency of the Army, however, was matched by the excellent co-operation of the evacuees. No incidents were reported in which the Japanese failed to co-operate; on the contrary, all the evidence points to the fact that they are justly entitled to a major share of the credit for the achievement itself. It requires some measure of discipline, fortitude, and patience, on such short notice, to close out businesses, to wind up affairs, to dispose of homes and furnishings, to take care of the countless details which any move involves, and to report, with a handful of possessions, on time for removal to an unknown destination. Nor did the co-operation of the Japanese end with their arrival in the centers. Many of these centers were not completed when the evacuees began to arrive. The evacuees helped to build them; assisted in making them livable; and quickly assumed major responsibilities in their administration. The construction problem itself was of minor significance when compared with the immediate problem of administration. Some of these assembly centers were good-sized cities (there were 18,000 evacuees in the Santa Anita center). The whole apparatus of municipal facilities — water system, sewer system, hospital, schools, police, post office, stores, recreation, not to mention the detail of feeding 18,000 people three times a day — had to be improvised overnight.

Faced with a problem of this magnitude, the administration would have been completely paralyzed had it not been for the manner in which the evacuees co-operated in the entire undertaking. Imagine moving and relocating 100,000 rank-and-file American citizens — of all classes, ages, and occupations — under similar circumstances! It would have required several army divisions to have accomplished such an assignment and these divisions would probably have had to cope with a new rebellion every fifteen minutes. With no other group of similar size in our population could such a feat have been possible. It is also important to remember that these people were living under great emotional stress: they were fearful, bewildered, distraught. The utmost confusion prevailed. While WCCA had attempted to move entire families and entire communities intact to the same assembly center, it was not possible to do so in all cases. Many of the evacuees were completely alone among total strangers in the strangest world they had ever known. The irritations and inconveniences, major and minor, were legion. In Puyallup, there was one washroom for a hundred families; in Tanforan and Santa Anita thousands of people were housed in stable stalls recently occupied by horses; in Yakima, evacuees were "housed" in an abandoned hop yard. The annoyances of the moment were dwarfed in significance by mounting anxiety and by a growing concern about the future. It is against this general background that the behavior and conduct of the Japanese must be appraised. That they behaved as they did is a remarkable demonstration, in itself, of their loyalty. Mr. Stimson has himself pointed out that "great credit is due our Japanese population for the manner in which they responded to and complied with the orders of exclusion."

6. Economic Consequences

For a variety of reasons, it has been and will continue to be difficult to appraise the economic effect of the removal of the Japanese from the West Coast. The rather boastful statements of California shipper growers to the effect that the removal of the Japanese occasioned no loss in farm production are exceedingly misleading. The figures cited in substantiation of this and similar statements usually have reference to total acreages and not to the volume of production of a particular crop. They also relate to current abnormal price structures which have made possible a temporary shift in acreage from Japanese-controlled to non-Japanese-controlled operations. Asked if the Japanese were necessary factors in agricultural production in California, Mr. Harold Ryan, Agricultural Commissioner of Los Angeles County, recently testified: "Not unless we insist upon having cheap vegetables grown in great quantities on small acreage of land." The qualifications noted in this statement are most significant. Later Mr. Ryan said that "it remains to be seen whether the non-Japanese farmer can continue successfully in the growing of miscellaneous vegetables on small acreages."

It can be definitely stated, however, that the removal of the Japanese has had a most unfortunate effect on production insofar as consumers are concerned. In its annual report for 1942, the Federal-State Market News service stated that Southern California consumers alone paid $10,000,000 more for 10,000 truckloads less of perishable vegetables in 1942, by comparison with 1941.[34] Removal of the Japanese has created a chaotic situation in the wholesale produce markets in Los Angeles. Buyers complain that it is currently either "a feast or a famine"; tomatoes flood the market for a week and the next week cannot be obtained. The deterioration of quality is a self-evident fact to any Southern California consumer. In a report released on January 3, 1944, the State Director of Agriculture accused retailers of fresh fruits and vegetables in the state of charging prices ranging from "higher than necessary" to "wholly unwarranted and exorbitant." In some cases retailers, according to this report, have realized margins of from 50 to 450 per cent above wholesale costs. Independent buyers of produce throughout the state complain that the removal of the Japanese has increased prices unnecessarily and has resulted in a definite consolidation of economic controls and a further extension in the direction of monopolistic price structures. It should be remembered that the removal of the Japanese occurred at a time when prices had begun to rise and when the population of the state was increasing in a most spectacular fashion.

That the Japanese sustained enormous economic losses as a result of evacuation cannot be denied. The whole evacuation program, as it developed, was so uncertain at the outset, and so summary in conclusion, that Japanese did not have time to dispose of their holdings. Their losses must be reckoned in the millions of dollars. Even after evacuation was a foregone conclusion, the federal government failed to set up any satisfactory system of property custodianship. The government agencies that were delegated responsibility in the matter, in most cases, either tried to evade this responsibility or joined in pressuring the Japanese to dispose of their holdings quickly and in a haphazard

[34] *Los Angeles Daily News*, February 17, 1943.

fashion. The grossest imposition was practised upon the Japanese, ranging from petty chiseling to large-scale fraud.

Any number of suits are pending in the California courts today in which local interests are charged with the most serious fraud and, in some cases, with the most flagrant abuse of trust relationships. Considering that some of the individual Japanese holdings were quite large, it is possible to gain some idea of the amount of the stakes that are involved. Naturally the interests charged with fraud are among those most anxious to keep the Japanese from returning to the state. It is quite obvious that if a federal investigation is ever made of the manipulation that has already occurred, it will have the proportions of a national scandal.[35] In Santa Maria – in Santa Barbara County – local interests have been charged with bilking the Japanese out of holdings valued at $500,000.[36] In this instance, the Treasury Department was finally forced to intervene to protect the Japanese against a total dissipation of their holdings; but, as a result of extraordinary pressures brought to bear, the freezing order of the Treasury Department was subsequently lifted.

The creator of the fortune involved in this particular case, H. Y. Minami, Sr., came to California in 1905, to work for the Southern Pacific railroad as a day laborer. He laid the foundation for his considerable fortune by inducing the railroad to lease to him small acreages – then wholly unproductive – along its right-of-way. This is but one of many similar cases. It is out of such a murky background that much of the pressure for the permanent exclusion of the Japanese from the state stems at the present time. Gradually most of the Japanese holdings – urban and rural – are being liquidated. A recent report of their estimated holdings of $5,000,000 in the city of Los Angeles indicates that virtually all of it will have been sold in another year. "It is expected that ultimately there won't be a parcel of Jap-owned real estate in Los Angeles."[37] It should also be remembered that those Japanese still remaining in relocation centers are being steadily

[35] See, for example, the complaint in the matter of *Hiramatsu* vs. *L. R. Phillips et al.* pending in the Superior Court of Santa Barbara County.
[36] See *Santa Barbara News-Press*, October 27, 1943, p. A-2.
[37] *Los Angeles Times*, December 5, 1943.

pauperized. The small amounts that they earn are not sufficient to pay obligations of a fixed character, such as premiums on life-insurance policies and other commitments. As a consequence, it is estimated that the residents of the two centers in Arizona alone are being pauperized at the rate of about $500,000 a year.

The removal of the Japanese has had other and, in some respects, rather amusing aspects. While the race purists of the state have been gloating over the removal of an "unassimilable" minority of around 90,000, the vacuum in the labor market occasioned by the removal of the Japanese is in part responsible for the current influx of Negroes from the Deep South. Approximately 90,000 Japanese have been removed from the state and approximately 150,000 Negroes have been attracted into it. By and large, the Negroes have flooded into the Little Tokyo areas which were left vacant when the Japanese were removed. Little Tokyo in Los Angeles has recently been rechristened as Bronzeville. The influx of Negroes has created special problems of housing, education, and recreation and, at the same time, has contributed to the steadily mounting racial tensions.[38] As a matter of fact, the removal of the Japanese, coming as it did when defense production was increasing by leaps and bounds, artificially stimulated the already extended demand for manpower. What was accomplished, in terms of the war effort, by the removal of the Japanese was the elimination of a wholly theoretical hazard to the detriment of nearly every other aspect of the war.

As long as the Japanese remained on the West Coast, they could only be attacked in rather general terms. For, after all, they were *customers;* they bought and sold; they paid rent and interest; they were good tenants. During the Tolan Committee hearings, many of their competitors remained silent; and most of the witnesses who did appear against them had occasion to pay them compliments of one sort or another. But once they were removed, the tenor of the criticism changed: it became vicious, vitriolic, savage. Their former partners, associates, and

[38] See the report of the San Francisco Grand Jury on conditions in its former Little Tokyo section as reported in the *San Francisco Examiner* of June 15, 18, and 19, 1943.

business colleagues then came forward and began to advance all manner of charges and to urge, in the most strenuous fashion, that the doors should be closed behind them.[39]

7. Hawaii

The "social earthquake" that evacuation precipitated on the West Coast was felt along the entire western rim of the Pacific, from Alaska to Peru, and it had important repercussions in Hawaii.

There were in Hawaii, on December 7, 1941, 159,534 persons of Japanese ancestry, constituting 34.2 per cent of the total population of the islands. Of this group, 35,183 (22 per cent of the total) were aliens with an average period of residence in the islands of something like thirty-five years. Over a period of years, the Japanese had tended to move from the plantations to the cities; from agricultural labor to skilled and semiskilled occupations. At the outset (around 1907), this movement had occasioned some anti-Japanese agitation. But the agitation never reached serious proportions primarily because the economic oligarchy that rules Hawaii did not look with favor upon such a movement (although the same interests actually subsidized anti-Japanese agitation on the Pacific Coast). There is no doubt, as Dr. Andrew W. Lind has observed, that the Japanese in Hawaii clearly surpassed "their cousins in continental United States in the struggle for occupational preferment." They were, by 1941, established in all the major professions; and 15 per cent of the gainfully employed Japanese, in 1940, were employed in preferred professional and proprietary and managerial occupations.

Despite the fact that race relations were much better in Hawaii than on the mainland, the Japanese nevertheless showed much the same tendency there, as on the West Coast, toward internal

[39] On the effect of evacuation in particular areas, see *Pacific Citizen*, April 4, 1943, p. 7; June 3, 1943, p. 6; July 10, 1943, p. 3. As to the extent of their present interests, WRA is currently custodian of 102 markets, 700 hotels and apartments, 32 drygoods stores, 6 newspapers, 56 restaurants, 19 garages, 33 churches, 206 cleaning establishments, 21 floral shops, 230 nurseries, and 75 laundries. Their total holdings were valued, on the West Coast, at around $200,000,000.

solidarity. The Japanese intermarriage rate on the mainland was only 2.3 per cent; in Hawaii it was 4.5 per cent.[40] Japanese was the "second language" of the islands. As late as 1940 some portion of each school day in the lives of 80 per cent of the Japanese children of school age was spent in the 171 Japanese-language schools in the islands. There were twelve newspapers and five magazines published in the Japanese language. Every radio station in the islands carried a regular "Japanese hour." There were two motion-picture theaters which showed Japanese films exclusively.[41] There were the usual number of Shinto shrines and Buddhist temples. Many observers had been impressed, according to Dr. Lind, "by the apparent *slowness* with which the Americanization of the Japanese community in Hawaii had proceeded." I mention these considerations for two reasons: first, as evidence that *external* pressures alone do not account for the internal solidarity of Japanese settlements (which must be accounted for largely in terms of the Japanese cultural pattern itself); and, second, to show that if the character of Japanese settlements on the West Coast was a reason for their removal (and it has been cited as such by the Supreme Court), then the same consideration applied with perhaps greater force in Hawaii.

Yet what measures were taken for the protection of this all-important strategic outpost in the Pacific? In the first place, martial law was immediately proclaimed. Some minor regulations were imposed upon the alien Japanese. Several hundred of them were taken into immediate custody and subsequently removed to the mainland for internment; at a later date, additional Japanese were removed from the islands and distributed in relocation centers on the mainland.[42] Those who were taken into custody immediately subsequent to Pearl Harbor fell within one or another of the following categories: Shinto and Buddhist priests; teachers in the language schools; consular agents; Kibei; organizational leaders having close ties with Japan. There has been no mass evacuation or internment of the Japanese in Hawaii.

[40] See *American Sociological Review*, October, 1943, article by Dr. Leonard Bloom, p. 555.
[41] See "Japan-in-Hawaii" by Ben Henderson, *Survey Graphic*, July, 1942.
[42] *Pacific Citizen*, December 17, 1942.

There are, of course, certain obvious differences between the situation in Hawaii and that which prevailed on the West Coast. In the first place, it would have been practically impossible to have found shipping space to move 160,000 people across 2000 miles of ocean to the mainland. To have done so, if the shipping had been available, would have caused immeasurable damage to the internal economy of the islands. The manpower problem was acute and the Japanese could not be spared. Furthermore, in the islands they have had the "powerful and determined support of the highly centralized business interests of Hawaii." [43] In Hawaii they were supported by the dominant economic interests; on the mainland these interests wanted them evacuated. But a more powerful reason why evacuation was not ordered consists in the fact, pointed out by Dr. Romanzo Adams, that "the race *mores* of Hawaii are or tend to be the *mores* of race equality." Effective interracial solidarity had been established in Hawaii before the war; it had not been established on the mainland. It is not without significance that the *one area* on the western side of the Pacific where the Japanese were permitted to remain undisturbed was the one area where anti-Japanese agitation had never taken root.

To be sure, there was some agitation for their removal from Hawaii. A prominent businessman, Mr. J. A. Balch, published a pamphlet in which he advocated their removal (*Shall the Japanese Be Allowed to Dominate Hawaii?*) and testified before the Dies Committee in favor of their removal. Although he is an official of the Mutual Telephone Company of Hawaii, Mr. Balch does not represent the thinking of the dominant business interests of the islands.

There is still another (and an amusing) reason why the Japanese were not removed from Hawaii: California interests were opposed to their removal! Mr. H. J. McClatchy and Mr. Charles M. Goethe, both officials of the powerful California Joint Immigration Committee, in discussions with Mr. Balch, indicated that they were "*unalterably opposed*" to the removal of any Japanese

[43] In other words, The Big Five — see article of Charles S. Bouslog, *Asia and the Americas*, February, 1943.

from Hawaii either to the West Coast or to other portions of the mainland. While insisting upon the removal of every man, woman, and child of Japanese ancestry from the West Coast — in the name of national security and because of the "strategic importance" of the area — these selfsame individuals were opposed to the removal of *any* Japanese from the far more important strategic area of Hawaii. I know of no more fitting commentary on the motives and objectives of the anti-Japanese forces of California.

It should be pointed out, however, that Hawaii had a very sensible and levelheaded commander in the person of General Delos Emmons. After he had succeeded General Short, General Emmons acted decisively and firmly to prevent the rise of hysteria. He publicly warned that there "must not be indiscriminate displacement of labor"; and stressed that "we must not knowingly and deliberately deny any loyal citizen the opportunity to exercise or demonstrate his loyalty in a concrete way." Hawaii, of course, seethed with rumors of Japanese sabotage after the attack on Pearl Harbor. These rumors were systematically investigated and publicly exposed as unfounded. For the uncontradicted facts are that *no sabotage* occurred in Hawaii on December 7, 1941. This statement can be made today in reliance upon emphatic assurances to this effect issued by the Secretary of War, the Secretary of the Navy, the Honolulu Police Department, the Federal Bureau of Investigation, and the various intelligence services involved.

While General Emmons was careful to inform the people in Hawaii that these rumors were unfounded, no similar precaution was taken by General De Witt on the mainland. General Emmons acted to allay unfounded suspicion and to restore confidence; General De Witt failed to take similar action. On the contrary, it was assumed on the mainland that sabotage had occurred in Hawaii and this assumption still prevails. In a Town Meeting of the Air broadcast from Santa Barbara, on July 15, 1943, my references to undenied proof of the lack of sabotage in Hawaii were greeted, by a reasonably tolerant California audience, with hoots, catcalls, and boos. Long after the facts were known, Warner Brothers made and distributed the box-office success, "Air Force," which depicted Japanese committing acts of sabotage in Hawaii on December 7, 1941. No denial was issued by the Western Defense Command or, so far as I know, by the Office of War Information.[44]

I do not mean, by these comments, to imply that a policy similar to that in Hawaii could have been applied on the mainland. For in the islands, the established mores of the community made such a policy feasible; on the mainland the established mores were such that people automatically *assumed* that all Japanese would be evacuated. In Hawaii, the dominant economic interests supported the policy pursued by General Emmons (and encouraged him to extend this policy); furthermore, he was supported by the press, by local officials, and by most of the stable island institutions. The groundwork had been laid in Hawaii for such a program; it had not been laid on the mainland.

In Hawaii, as on the mainland, the war "brought to a climax stresses and strains" which had long existed in the Japanese communities. The language schools were closed; all but two of the Japanese publications were suspended for the duration (and these two were subject to close censorship). "A house-cleaning of affiliations with Japan has been prosecuted fearlessly and thoroughly, leaving not a disgruntled Japanese population, but a people shocked into appreciation of the land of their adoption or birth and of their rightful position in it." [45] Leadership has tended to pass from the Issei to the Nisei. Despite the presence of large numbers of Filipinos in Hawaii (the likelihood of Filipino-Japanese strife was urged in California as a reason for mass evacuation), no violence has occurred.

The presence of skilled and semiskilled Japanese workmen in Hawaii has made possible the great expansion of our military establishment in the islands. No charges of sabotage have been filed against them; no incidents have occurred to mar their record. In Hawaii, however, the Japanese have been strongly inte-

[44] On the effect of "rumors" in fomenting racial discord and strife, see *Race and Rumors of Race* by Howard W. Odum, 1943.
[45] Article by Stella M. Jones in *Asia and the Americas*, February, 1943.

grated into the trade-union movement.[46] More Japanese civilians were killed by the bombs which fell on and around Honolulu on December 7 than civilians of other ancestry. In Hawaii, Japanese-Americans manned machine guns to fight the Japanese attacking Pearl Harbor; Japanese-American doctors and nurses worked tirelessly to save American lives. They have responded to every appeal; they have contributed generously to every war campaign. When it became possible for them to volunteer for the combat team, the response in Hawaii was overwhelming. They have been repeatedly praised for their conduct by the peoples of the island [47] and have brilliantly justified General Emmons' policy. As a matter of fact, the policy of reopening the armed services to Japanese-Americans for voluntary enlistment was initiated by the Hawaiian-born Nisei.[48]

The war has unquestionably accelerated the process of assimilation in Hawaii insofar as the Japanese are concerned. It has afforded them a chance to demonstrate their loyalty. The extent to which they have gone to sever whatever cultural or other bonds to Japan may have existed is quite amazing. Since Pearl Harbor, over 2400 petitions for change of name have been filed by Japanese-Americans in Hawaii.[49] They are attempting either to Anglicize their names or to adopt short, easily pronounceable names. In most cases, however, they have deemed it sufficient to change their given name. Yoshie becomes Elena; Masao becomes Paul; Toshiyuki becomes Henry; and Chuichi becomes Michael.[50] There is no doubt that the long program of community cooperation and tolerance of cultural differences has stood Hawaii in good stead in this emergency.[51]

One additional comment should be made on the situation in Hawaii. There martial law was immediately proclaimed on December 7, 1941, for the same reason that evacuation was ordered

[46] *Pacific Citizen*, August 28, 1943; see also the interesting series of articles by William Norwood in the *Christian Science Monitor*.

[47] See *Honolulu Star-Bulletin*, May 16, 1943.

[48] See the interesting article by Cecil H. Coggins, *Harper's*, June, 1943.

[49] *Pacific Citizen*, March 11, 1943.

[50] See *Honolulu Star-Bulletin*, November 6, 1942. This issue contained ten such petitions.

[51] On the Hawaiian situation see also *Collier's*, December 11, 1943.

on the West Coast — namely, as a matter of "military necessity." What the military then proceeded to do in Hawaii has been graphically related in two articles written by the Attorney General of Hawaii, Mr. Garner Anthony.[52] A military dictatorship was promptly imposed upon the people of Hawaii of the most exacting, complete, and minute character. The military sought to retain this control long after the danger of "imminent invasion" had passed in the islands. It was only after a headlong collision had occurred betwen the civil authorities and the military that a measure of control was returned to the duly constituted authorities. This phase of the Hawaiian experience alone serves to point out the dangers involved in permitting the military to make their own determination of what constitutes "military necessity."

8. In Alaska

Following the issuance of the general evacuation order on the West Coast, the Japanese were removed from Alaska. About 134 were moved to the Minidoka relocation center in Idaho. Of this group, 45 were of mixed ancestry. In Alaska they lived in native Indian villages, hunted whale and seal. Speaking a jargon of English, Eskimo, Indian, and Japanese, most of these evacuees had never associated with Japanese people in their lives.

9. In South America

From the tip of South America to Alaska, the peoples on the West Coast have usually taken their cue on "the Japanese problem" from the behavior of the Native Sons in California. Canadian groups were affiliated with the Anti-Asiatic League and the residents of British Columbia formed an organization known as the Native Sons of Canada. The identical arguments so carefully developed by V. S. McClatchy in California were echoed in the pamphlets of the Canadian, Tom MacInnes, and in the articles of Salinas Cossio, the South American publicist. Anti-Japanese

[52] See *California Law Review*, Vol. 30, 1942, p. 371; and December, 1943.

legislation, spawned in California, was copied in Canada and in Peru. Riots in California were re-enacted in Vancouver (in September, 1907) and in Peru (May 13, 1940).

Today there are approximately 200,000 Japanese in South America,[53] with important colonies in Peru and Brazil. The stream of Japanese immigration was deflected toward South America after the Gentlemen's Agreement and noticeably after the passage of the 1924 Immigration Act in this country. In Peru, the pattern of settlement and the nature of the colonies follow, in most particulars, the pattern of settlement throughout the West Coast. Brazil presents a somewhat different pattern. The colonies in Brazil represent carefully planned settlement programs, with every detail of colonization being supervised and controlled, first, by so-called colonization companies, and later by the Japanese government itself. The Brazilian pattern of settlement, unlike that on the West Coast, does indicate a deliberate intention of planting "islands of Japan" in the Western Hemisphere, and the location of these colonies would also indicate that they had been selected, in part, with strategic considerations in mind.

From the available evidence, it would seem that the Japanese settlements in South America are even more closely knit than were those on the West Coast. In part, no doubt, this is to be explained by the fact that the South American settlements are more recent in point of time. With the appearance of a large second generation there, the internal solidarity of these settlements will doubtless show signs of disintegration. According to Hubert Herring, there has been little or no assimilation in Argentina, where there is a small colony.[54] Normano and Gerbi make the same observation in reference to the much larger settlements in Brazil and Peru. While there has been a large measure of tolerance shown to the Japanese in South America — they were initially welcomed in Brazil and Peru — anti-Japanese agitation, using the same arguments, the same clichés, the same slogans,

[53] See *The Japanese in South America* by J. F. Normano and Antonello Gerbi, 1943.
[54] *Good Neighbors*, 1941, p. 79.

began to get under way throughout South America after the outbreak of the Sino-Japanese War in 1937. In Brazil a "Yellow Peril" society was formed; anti-Japanese agitation grew by leaps and bounds; and in November, 1937, limitations were placed on further immigration and concessions previously granted on more than 6,000,000 acres of land were canceled. After evacuation from the West Coast had been ordered, Brazil began to take similar action. Dangerous Japanese were interned for the duration and a modified evacuation program was instituted.[55] After the anti-Japanese riots in Peru, in May, 1940, similar action was taken there. The government ordered all Japanese to liquidate their holdings by January 1, 1944.[56]

In some of the Central American republics, where there were small settlements, all Japanese residents were arrested subsequent to Pearl Harbor. Apparently many, if not all, of those arrested in these countries have been sent to the United States for internment.[57] To a very considerable extent, the policy of the American government toward the resident Japanese will doubtless determine the character of the policies to be adopted in South America and Canada. What happens here will most likely determine what happens there.

10. In Canada

The general policy pursued by the Canadian government toward the resident Japanese has been strongly influenced by the policy of the United States. Following the precedent established by our Alien Registration Act of 1940, the Prime Minister appointed a Special Committee on Orientals in British Columbia in October of that year. While the committee found that no evidence of subversive activities existed, it nevertheless recom-

[55] See "Japanese Pincers in Brazil" by John W. White, Saturday Evening Post, June 27, 1942.
[56] See "The Japanese Are Still in Peru" by Manuel Seoane, Asia and the Americas, December, 1943.
[57] See New York Times, February 15, 1943, on the situation in Costa Rica; and a story in Pacific Citizen, November 6, 1943, in which it is stated that 1450 Japanese nationals from Latin-America are interned in this country.

mended that a special registration of aliens be conducted "to help appease the white population." [58] Immediately subsequent to Pearl Harbor, the Royal Mounted Police arrested about 178 "dangerous aliens" and interned them for the duration. Special regulations were invoked; fishing licenses were canceled; curfews were imposed. Following the pattern established on the West Coast, the Japanese-language schools were closed by voluntary agreement with the Japanese; and the press was suspended. At the time of the attack on Pearl Harbor, there were 23,428 Japanese in British Columbia (85 per cent of all in the Dominion). While ineligible to vote in local or provincial elections, they were eligible for Canadian citizenship. Special restrictive legislation had long been in force against them, insofar as certain vocations were concerned; and immigration had been restricted along the lines of our Gentlemen's Agreement.

At a conference called in Ottawa on January 8 and 9, 1942, a proposal for mass evacuation had been rejected as being "not only unnecessary in the interests of national security but highly inadvisable in view of possible retaliation by the Japanese Government on the two thousand Canadian prisoners of war." [59] But the fall of Hong Kong on December 25, 1941, and of Singapore on February 15, and the wild rumors of sabotage in Hawaii, coupled with news of the agitation developing in California, created an alarmist state of mind in British Columbia. Evacuation was finally decided upon on February 21, 1942, "after the British Columbia members of Parliament arrived in Ottawa toward the end of January" and *after* the demand for the removal of all Japanese aliens and persons of Japanese descent had begun to reach serious proportions in British Columbia.

In Canada, as in the United States, the national capitol was inundated with wires, resolutions, and memorials from the West Coast province of British Columbia, and it was this agitation which, as in the United States, forced the federal government to decide upon a policy that, a short time previously, it had rejected as unnecessary and inadvisable. In Canada as in the

[58] See article by Forrest E. LaViolette, *Far Eastern Survey*, July 27, 1942.
[59] See *Minorities of Oriental Race in Canada*, Toronto, 1942, p. 23.

United States, it was more a matter of "political" than of "military" necessity. On March 4, 1942, the British Columbia Security Commission was established to supervise the evacuation of virtually all Japanese from the protected area (defined as British Columbia west of the Cascade Mountains); and a property custodian was appointed. By November, 1942, some 19,867 Japanese had been evacuated from the one-hundred-mile coastal area, and distributed as follows: 11,965 in interior housing projects; 3988 in sugar-beet camps in the interior; 1161 in self-supporting projects in the interior; 1337 released for approved employment; 986 assigned to road camps; and 431 released to certain types of industrial employment.[60]

The temper of the agitation in British Columbia closely parallels that in California. While at least two British Columbia publicists in Vancouver have spoken out consistently for fair treatment — Mr. Elmore Philpot and Mr. Alan Morley — the general tone of the press has been strongly anti-Japanese. Considerable agitation has developed in favor of mass deportation at the end of the war; and the government has apparently been toying with the idea of taking over all Japanese holdings. At the outset, the interior provinces showed the same reluctance to accept Japanese relocatees that interior states had shown in this country. Signs were displayed, for example, in Edmonton, reading: "Keep the Japs Out!" This phase of the matter has considerable importance in Canada since the Japanese could only be relocated in the interior provinces with the consent of these provinces. In most cases, the interior provinces insisted on a guarantee that the relocatees would be returned to British Columbia at the end of the war. They have shown the same reluctance to have British Columbia's "problem people shoved off on them" that other states have shown toward acquiescing in California's determination to oust the Japanese from that state. In general, the relocation program in Canada has followed pretty closely the development of our own program and has been strongly influenced by it. There has been the same clamor in the British Columbia press against "coddling" and "pampering" the Japa-

[60] *Pacific Citizen*, December 24, 1942.

nese that has appeared in the West Coast press in general, and the Canadian government has given serious attention to proposals for mass deportation at the end of the war.

As the program has evolved in Canada, the Nisei there, as here, have come to see that, in the long run, relocation might accelerate assimilation. "The inescapable fact of the matter is," to quote from a recent editorial in the *New Canadian* (published at Kaslo, B. C.), "that prejudice has been crystallized into a tradition in the emotions of many British Columbians. The alternative (to return) is that widely supported by our thinking friends, namely, a widespread dispersion throughout the west of Canada." While admitting that this alternative has its risks and presents its own problems, nevertheless the Canadian Nisei feel that it offers the best hope for the future. Some British Columbia Nisei have relocated as far east as Montreal and have found opportunities there that had long been denied them in British Columbia.[61] "For the major portion of the Japanese," as Dr. LaViolette has observed, "this is their first trip outside of British Columbia. They are beginning to see Canada, and Nisei already report losing their feelings of oppression. If the war continues for several years, they will become rooted into the new communities. Early reports suggest that they are getting along well in their new neighborhoods. Assimilation may in the long run be accelerated by this process, and the Japanese may not want to return to British Columbia." Property losses have been very heavy in Canada as in the United States; and the Japanese-operated produce lands in the areas around Vancouver have, for the most part, gone out of production. These economic losses of the Japanese have been particularly severe because of the marginal position which, in general, they occupied in British Columbia.

The status of the British Columbia Japanese closely approximates that of the Japanese on the West Coast of the United States. While their status had noticeably improved during the last thirty years, still they had never been really absorbed into the community. The social relation between the Japanese and the "whites" has been described by Dr. LaViolette as "a liberalized

[61] See *Pacific Citizen*, March 29, 1943.

quasi-caste system based upon racial differences." These social attitudes, he noted, were the result of *fifty years'* conflict over immigration and related matters. Like California, British Columbia had evolved, out of conflict, a well-established and deeply rooted racial ideology. For many British Columbians the evacuation order was "a realization of a half-century-old desire." It is interesting to note that, in British Columbia as in California, people *seemed to assume* that evacuation would be ordered and were furious when the national government hesitated.[62]

[62] NOTE: Since the above was written, it has been reported that the Dominion government has purchased all Japanese-owned land in the Fraser Valley. See *Time*, February 21, 1944, p. 23.

153

CHAPTER V

Relocation and Segregation

REALIZING that some agency would have to be created to cope with the resettlement program, President Roosevelt, on March 18, 1942, issued Executive Order No. 9102, creating the War Relocation Authority. Broad in scope, the order gave the authority power to formulate and carry into effect a program for the "relocation, maintenance, and supervision" of persons excluded from military areas, and to provide "in so far as feasible and desirable for the employment of such persons at useful work in industry, commerce, agriculture, or public projects, prescribe the terms and conditions of such public employment, and safeguard the public interest in the private employment of such persons." The principal aim behind the creation of the new agency was, in the President's own words, "to relieve the military of the complicated and burdensome job of maintaining and re-establishing a dislocated people." Executive Order No. 9102 did not define a policy — it created an agency authorized, in effect, to work out a policy.

Policy, nevertheless, had to be established within certain obvious limitations. It had to be made in light of the authorizations set forth in Executive Order No. 9102. It had to be made with reference to the war plans of the government. These plans have influenced policy in several respects; they determine, for example, the type of work projects. Also, policy had to be determined within the limitations of the Geneva Convention which provides that enemy aliens cannot be employed on war work. Finally, policy had to be made in collaboration with the War Department and the Department of Justice, each of which retained a measure of jurisdiction over special phases of the program.

Within these limitations, WRA proceeded to improvise a policy and to devise techniques for coping with one of the toughest administrative problems of the war.

On April 7, 1942, the first director of WRA, Mr. Milton Eisenhower, met with a group of Western governors in a conference in Salt Lake City. At the meeting, WRA presented a relocation plan which consisted of three basic points: —

(*a*) establishment of Government-operated centers where some of the evacuees could be quartered and could contribute through work on government projects, to their own support;

(*b*) re-employment of evacuees in private industry or in agriculture outside the evacuated areas;

(*c*) governmental assistance for small groups of evacuees desiring to establish self-supporting colonies of an agricultural character.

The reaction of the assembled governors was "unmistakable." They expressed strong opposition to any type of unsupervised relocation. Following this meeting, WRA was compelled to abandon, momentarily at least, alternatives (*b*) and (*c*), and to concentrate all its efforts upon alternative (*a*). To accomplish this end, WRA worked out a co-operative or joint agreement with the War Department (it is quoted in full in Senate Document No. 96, 78th Congress, 1st Session) whereby, in effect, the War Department agreed to construct the necessary facilities in the centers and WRA assumed full administrative responsibility.

The selection of sites was not an easy problem. All centers had to be located on public land; at a safe distance from strategic areas; capable of providing adequate work opportunities throughout the year; and of such size that a minimum of 5000 evacuees could be assembled in the particular project. Over 300 possible sites were examined and surveyed. In selecting sites, WRA was assisted by the two federal agencies with most experience in the field, namely, the Reclamation Service and the Indian Service. Since most of the development projects contemplated by these two agencies were located in the inter-mountain region, it naturally followed that most of the sites finally selected were in this area. In general, WRA tended to move "in the direction of the 'wilderness' areas — among others, to the desert-type terrain of western Arizona, to the inter-mountain country of Wyoming, and to the delta section of Arkansas only recently reclaimed from periodic floods."[1] By June 5, 1942, sites for ten relocation centers had been selected and construction work at four of them was well under way. By the first of November, 1942, the entire evacuee population had been transferred from assembly centers, or, in some cases, directly from their homes, into relocation centers. The centers and their population as of July 10, 1943, were as follows: —

Topaz, Utah	7,287
Poston, Arizona	15,530
Rivers, Arizona	12,355
Amache, Colorado	6,170
Heart Mountain, Wyoming	9,292
Denson, Arkansas	7,767
Manzanar, California	8,716
Hunt, Idaho	7,548
Relocation, Arkansas	7,616
Newell, California (Tule Lake)	13,422
Total	95,703

Into these centers were also moved a small group of Japanese from Alaska; approximately 1073 Japanese from Hawaii; 1300 Japanese paroled from the internment camps; and a small number of Japanese who, although living outside the Western Defense Command, voluntarily moved into the centers for protection.

1. The Relocation Centers

The WRA centers are, in essence, ten government-sponsored Little Tokyos located in isolated regions of the inter-mountain West. The projects, as such, were designed by the army engineers. Only in the imagination of an investigator for the Dies Committee could they be described as "adequate housing." The

[1] Release of WRA, September, 1942.

barracks themselves are merely temporary shelters, hastily constructed, inadequately planned. In the original plan, one room was provided for each family; but this standard has been more honored in the breach than in the observance. Given the monotonous character of the construction itself and the desolate character of the environment, it is not surprising that the centers are such dreary establishments. They are surrounded by barbed-wire fences, with watchtowers and armed guards, and searchlights play upon the area at night. Community washrooms and toilets are established for each block within the area. In huge mess halls within each block the evacuees are fed at a cost to the government of between 34 and 42 cents per person per day. No one has starved in these centers and no one has frozen to death; everyone has shelter and sustenance. But this is about as much as can be said in defense of the centers as housing projects.

During the first weeks and months after its establishment, WRA was primarily concerned with getting the centers ready for occupancy, recruiting personnel, and establishing certain administrative policies. Recruiting a staff for such a unique agency as WRA was a difficult assignment. There were few persons in the field of government service who had had any experience in dealing with the Japanese or who had any knowledge of Japanese culture or language. The distant location of the centers and their isolation were major obstacles in securing personnel. Fortunately, the Indian Service could be tapped, as it was, for a nucleus of experienced administrators around whom a staff was built. By and large, the staff has been, in the words of Dr. Robert Redfield, more than "ordinarily high," including "men and women with devotion to liberal and humanitarian principles." It is to the lasting credit of the administration that men such as Milton Eisenhower and Dillon Myer were selected to head the authority. It is also to the credit of the administration that political considerations have played virtually no part in the selection of the staff. With the exception of a few clerical employees in the Washington office and in the various relocation employment offices, the entire staff is Caucasian. No Japanese or Japanese-Americans occupy posts in the administrative staff as such.

157

"Nothing quite like these relocation centers," observes Dr. Redfield, "has ever appeared before in the history of America." They resemble army camps; they are like Indian reservations; they resemble the FSA resettlement projects, and they are somewhat like the internment camps for dangerous enemy aliens. To call them "concentration camps" after the pattern of Dachau and Oranienburg would be a gross exaggeration. A degree of self-government is permitted in the camps, and, so far as possible, the constitutional rights of the evacuees have been respected. Complete freedom of religious worship has been safeguarded; every 'variety of church service may be found. There is no censorship of mail. Open meetings may be held with the approval of the project director as to time and place, and both English and Japanese may be spoken. Newspapers are published in most of the centers and are certainly outspoken, as an examination of the files will readily show. Obviously, it would be an exaggeration to say that the rights of free speech and of a free press are exercised in the centers with the same freedom from restraint that exists outside. But the point is that these rights have not been wholly suppressed nor altogether restrained.

Through their co-operative organizations, evacuees carry on many important community enterprises in the centers, including such personal services as shoe-repair shops, mending and pressing shops, beauty parlors and barbershops, and the sale of such goods as clothing, confections, toilet goods, stationery, and books and magazines. These enterprises pay WRA a minimum rental for the space they occupy. They have been financed by the evacuees; they are operated by the evacuees; and they are all co-operative nonprofit enterprises. Certain of these co-operatives have accumulated substantial assets.

Evacuees in the relocation centers are governed by three categories of law and regulations: (1) the general law of the United States and the state in which the center is situated; (2) the regulations of the WRA and the project director; and (3) regulations made by the community council under the authority of the project director and with his approval. The maintenance of internal security is a function of WRA; external security is an army function discharged by small detachments of military police. To assist in maintaining law and order within the centers, WRA has established a special detention center in Leupp, Arizona, to which "incorrigibles" — chronic violators of center regulations — are sent on the authority of the project directors (there are about seventy evacuees in the Leupp center).

Approximately 90 per cent of the employable residents of the centers are employed by WRA — in all manner of administrative and work projects, in the offices of mess halls, hospitals, farms, work projects, and so on. These evacuees receive cash allowances of twelve, sixteen, or nineteen dollars a month, according to the nature of their duties. No one seems to know how these rates were determined, except that they were supposed to bear some relation to basic army pay which, at the time the centers were opened, was twenty-one dollars a month. Medical care and hospitalization are furnished without charge; and, to date, health conditions in the centers have been remarkably good. No charge is made for room and board.

Initially, WRA toyed with the idea of creating genuine resettlement projects; but this policy was virtually abandoned by the autumn of 1942. In fact, the idea was abandoned before even the basic policies for the proposed projects could be formulated. Three factors were responsible for this basic shift in policy: (a) the surprising success of the seasonal leave program; (b) strenuous public opposition to competing commercial projects in the centers; and (c) the ever-increasing manpower shortage outside the centers. At the present time, only a restricted works program is carried on in the centers. There are a few small-scale industrial projects, such as the manufacture of camouflage nets for the Army, silk screen posters for the Navy, ship models for the Navy's construction program, and similar projects.

The farming operations are conducted solely for the purpose of supplying the center residents with a portion of the food they consume. Vegetable production, in all the centers, for the year 1943, was valued at $2,750,000. "We are not planning to produce crops for the market at these centers," to quote from Mr. Myer's testimony before the Dies Committee. Since most of the land was raw, undeveloped land, requiring drainage, irrigation, and the construction of extensive canals and laterals, it would have taken an estimated five years to bring 20,000 acres under cultivation. In its current efforts to avoid the "institutionalization" of the evacuees, WRA has deliberately sought to minimize its agricultural and industrial projects.

There are nearly 30,000 Japanese-American youngsters of school age in the centers. Due to the abnormal population pyramid, there is a higher percentage of school-age children among the evacuees than among the total population, and a striking concentration in the number of students of high-school age. Establishing complete school systems in each of the ten centers has been, in itself, a major undertaking. Local school authorities have not been uniformly co-operative. Proposals that evacuee students be admitted to the state colleges and universities in Arkansas (where two of the centers are located) met with emphatic opposition. Requests from the WRA to the University of Arizona for extension courses, library books, and faculty lectures for the evacuees in that state have been consistently denied. In the words of President Alfred Atkinson: "We are at war and *these people* are our enemies." Even the request of WRA to have twelve or fifteen Japanese children admitted to the Oregon School for the Deaf was curtly denied by the local authorities. "This is no time," to quote from their refusal, "to admit Japanese children to the Oregon deaf school, particularly in view of the war."

Despite all of these handicaps, including a serious shortage of teachers, WRA has improvised a makeshift school system. Some centers have much better schools than others. The schools at the Granada (Colorado) Relocation Center are the best that I have seen. In some of the centers, evacuee personnel has been drafted to meet the demand for teachers; thereby creating a serious rift in the teaching staff between the regularly paid Caucasian personnel and the evacuee personnel paid nineteen dollars a month for precisely the same service. The whole atmosphere of the centers is so abnormal that it is debatable whether, given the best in personnel and equipment, much could be done in creating an adequate educational program. Fortunately it has been possible to relocate a good many college and university students in Eastern and Middle Western institutions (largely through the assistance of private organizations).

In some of the centers, excellent adult educational programs have been conducted. At Topaz, for example, 3250 adults are enrolled in 165 different classes: democracy in action, auto mechanics, cabinetmaking, carpentry, co-operatives, radio repairing, American history, American foreign affairs, current events, psychology, English, German, shorthand, public administration, practical electricity, first aid, and so on. Both Issei and Nisei are enrolled in these courses; and, from my own observation, I should say that the Issei evince a greater interest than the Nisei. For the centers as a whole, over 25 per cent of the adult population is currently enrolled in such courses and the two most popular subjects are English and American history. It is unquestionably true that, for some of the Issei, relocation has afforded an opportunity for study and self-improvement previously denied them. Even in the assembly centers, where the circumstances were most unfavorable, a real and active interest was shown in these courses.

By and large, there has been only a slight impairment of the rights of the Nisei as American citizens. On January 28, 1943, they were declared eligible for enlistment in the combat team; still more recently they have been removed from the 4-F classification, for selective service, into which they had been put after Pearl Harbor. Today they are at liberty to leave the centers whenever they wish (subject only to the liberal clearance rules of WRA) and to go wherever they wish, with the exception of those portions of the Western Defense Command (the coastal areas) from which they were excluded. While citizens in the relocation centers cannot qualify as voters in the areas to which they have been removed, since they lack technical "residence" within the meaning of state statutes, nevertheless they may continue to vote by absentee ballot in the communities in which they formerly resided and in which they still retain residence.

Generally speaking, "evacuees preserve all their rights and obligations as citizens of the state where they reside, as well as the United States, except only those rights and obligations which military necessity temporarily requires to be curtailed." [2] The Native Sons of the Golden West sought, in the case of *Regan* vs. *King*, to strike the Nisei from the voting lists in California. Their application was curtly denied by the Ninth Circuit Court of Appeals — by a decision from the bench without submission — and the United States Supreme Court has refused to review the decision. Nisei soldiers are permitted to return to the West Coast on furlough, and since August 6, 1942, "mixed marriage families composed of Caucasian husbands, who are citizens of the United States, Japanese wives and their mixed blood children" are eligible for release and residence within the Western Defense Command area. Certain Nisei, at the time of evacuation, were arbitrarily removed from civil service positions in California: city, county, and state. The State Personnel Board in California and the California legislature have sought, by various expedients, to make it impossible for these employees to obtain redress for their illegal removal. But the whole question, at the present time, is held more or less in *status quo*, because of strong representations that have been made to the California authorities by the State Department.

On June 21, 1943, the Supreme Court handed down its decision in the case of *Gordon Hirabayashi* vs. *United States*. Hirabayashi had been convicted of violating both the curfew and the evacuation orders. While the court held that the curfew regulation was a valid exercise of the war power, it pointedly refused to pass on the question of the constitutionality of the evacuation order. From language contained in the various opinions filed in the matter, it is quite apparent that the Supreme Court entertains the gravest doubts as to the constitutionality of evacuation insofar as the Nisei are concerned. Mr. Justice Murphy, for example, said that the curfew order "goes to the very brink of constitutional power"; and Mr. Justice Douglas, in a significant concurring opinion, said: "Detention for reasonable cause is one thing, detention on account of ancestry is another." The Chief Justice, in the majority opinion, was careful to point out that the Court was limiting its decision to the curfew orders

[2] From an opinion of the solicitor for WRA.

and was not considering the evacuation orders or confinement in a relocation center.

There is, however, some language in the majority opinion that should be of grave concern to all Americans interested in civil liberties. "We cannot close our eyes to the fact," states the Court, "demonstrated by experience, that in time of war residents having *ethnic affiliations* with an invading enemy may be a greater source of danger than those of a *different ancestry*." (Italics mine.) Again, the Court said that the notion that a group of one national extraction might be more dangerous than another "is not to be condemned merely because in other and in most circumstances *racial distinctions* are irrelevant."

In a later case, *Korematsu* vs. *United States*, decided by the Ninth Circuit Court on December 2, 1943, the evacuation order was upheld as constitutional. But, in this case, Mr. Justice Denman filed a vigorous and courageous opinion, concurring in the result but dissenting from the grounds of the majority opinion. His opinion is of exceptional interest because of the thoughtful manner in which he reviews the whole background of anti-Oriental discrimination on the West Coast. The decision in the Hirabayashi case has unquestionably had the effect of accelerating the WRA relocation program. For it would seem that the Supreme Court will probably hold that, while the government had the authority to remove the Japanese from the West Coast, it has no right *to detain* an American citizen who has been removed and against whom no charges have been filed.

2. The Leave Program

Not only had the governors of the Western states (with the exception of Governor Ralph Carr of Colorado) expressed the most vigorous opposition to the resettlement of the evacuees, but some of them had gone further and had refused to accept responsibility for the maintenance of law and order if individual evacuees were released from the centers. Speaking on May 22, 1942, Governor Chase Clark of Idaho, for example, had said: "The Japs live like rats, breed like rats, and act like rats. I don't want them coming into Idaho, and I don't want them taking seats in our university." So strong was this attitude that the Office of Government Reports stated, in May, 1942, that "there exists definite suspicion and antagonism towards Japanese in Arizona, California, Colorado, Kansas, Montana, Nevada, New Mexico, Oregon, South Dakota, Utah, and Washington."

But, beginning in May, 1942, the manpower shortage in agriculture became so acute that counter-pressures were exerted on WRA to release evacuees for farm work, particularly in sugar-beet areas. By August, 1942, the pressure for the release of evacuee farm labor had become, in Mr. Dillon Myer's expression, "terrific." Once the sugar-beet interests got to work, it was amazing to see how quickly the politicians evinced a change of heart toward evacuee labor and how the local press changed its tone. So swiftly did official attitudes change that, by May 15, 1942, WRA was able to conclude an agreement with Governor Sprague of Oregon (who had violently opposed the use of Japanese labor a month or so previously) for the release of evacuees to work in the sugar-beet areas around Malheur. At first WRA proceeded with great caution in releasing evacuees for seasonal work: special safeguards and restrictions were imposed, special regulations invoked. But as the pressures increased, the regulations were gradually relaxed and, on September 29, 1942, WRA announced a liberalized release program.

By the end of 1942, some 9000 evacuees were working in agricultural areas throughout the West and were being enthusiastically praised as model workmen. There is no doubt that they saved the sugar-beet crop in Utah, Idaho, Wyoming, and Montana. "To many responsible farmers," notes Mr. Frank A. Cleland, manager of the American Crystal Sugar Company in Montana, "Japanese labor is a plain means of crop salvage." "If it had not been for Japanese labor," states the *Deseret News* of September 2, 1942, "much of the best crop in Utah and Idaho would have had to be plowed up." In 1942, the evacuees harvested 915,000 tons of sugar beets, enough to produce 265,000,000 pounds of sugar.

California, faced with the same acute farm labor shortage, resolutely refused to accept evacuee labor. But agricultural interests in California succeeded in pressuring the federal government to import, at an enormous expense, 30,000 Mexican nationals for employment in the state. Although the agricultural interests will not admit that the importation of Mexican labor was made necessary by the removal of the Japanese, such is the case. Testifying before a Congressional committee on November 18, 1944, Colonel Burton, of the Office of Labor, War Food Administration, said: "On the West Coast there is a very great need for out-of-state workers which is related to the evacuation of the Japanese, who, in normal times, are used to a large extent in agriculture." Thus, to the staggering cost of the relocation program itself, and to the loss of manpower which it occasioned, must be added, also, a substantial portion of the cost involved in the importation of Mexican labor.

So successful was the seasonal leave program that, in October, 1942, Mr. Myer announced that henceforth relocation outside the centers would be the major goal of WRA policy. As a consequence, agricultural and industrial projects within the centers were sharply curtailed and the entire program was geared toward rapid individual relocation in private employment. Thus, within the space of six months, the emphasis shifted from resettlement in centers to relocation outside the centers; from planned colonization to individual dispersal over a wide area. Early in 1943 employment offices were opened throughout the Middle West and East; the clearance of leave applications was expedited; and every inducement was offered evacuees to leave the centers and to relocate before the war was over. The relocation centers were envisioned thereafter as merely way stations on the route "back to America." Within less than a year, the evacuation program had come to a full circle: evacuation, temporary resettlement, transfer to relocation centers, seasonal leaves, permanent relocation on indefinite leaves. Now that segregation has been completed, all the evacuees, Issei and Nisei alike, are eligible for unconditional release from the centers. Some 19,000 were released, in this fashion, in 1943, 85 per cent of whom were Nisei. In fact, about 50 per cent of the eligible, employable Nisei in the centers have already been released.

This shift in policy has had important consequences. It has meant, in effect, that the centers cannot be made *too attractive*, since WRA is now exerting great pressure on the evacuees to leave. Improvements that might otherwise have been made in living and working conditions in the centers have been abandoned as part of the all-out effort to relocate the evacuees before the war is over. The same shift in policy has buoyed up the hopes of the Nisei and given them a renewed faith in American democracy. At the same time and by the same token it has alarmed and disconcerted the already troubled Issei, who, by the end of 1942, had just begun to feel somewhat "settled" in the relocation centers. When the program was first announced, they feared that the WRA centers would be suddenly closed and that once again they were likely to find themselves abruptly dislocated. But these fears are gradually subsiding and, to a considerable extent, the pressures against relocation have begun to abate.

The problem today is *to induce* the evacuees to leave the centers. It is not a question of finding jobs. A recent issue of the *Granada Pioneer* contained two long columns listing work opportunities in the Chicago area alone; and these offerings were, by no means, all of menial or marginal positions. One current listing in the Granada center contained offers, at good wages, for the following positions: bookkeeper, laboratory technician, stenographer, domestic, beauty operator, assistant shipping clerk, warehouseman, accountant, chemical process machine operator, basketmaking, and technical assistant in anatomy at the University of Nebraska.

There are, of course, real obstacles to relocation in some cases: lack of skills, family complications, the language problem (for the Issei), lack of financial resources, the housing problem, and many similar considerations. The problem of finding housing is most acute: recently the *Chicago Sun* carried a story about Mrs. Haruye Masacka who, with five sons in the United States Army, could not find housing accommodations in Chicago. WRA is trying valiantly to solve these problems. It has arranged with private agencies to establish hostels for the immediate reception of evacuees upon their release; it provides transportation and a grant of fifty dollars in cash to those released; it assists them in finding housing; and it is toying with the idea of assisting small groups of families to relocate in agricultural areas. Despite all these efforts, however, numerous "resistance pressures" are still noted. Evacuees with whom I have discussed the problem in the centers show a tendency to rationalize their reluctance to leave. In some cases, they invent reasons or alibis why they feel that they should remain in the centers. It is amazing to note how quickly large numbers of people can become adjusted to a pattern of institutionalization and how quickly the "reservation mentality" can develop under these circumstances. The whole problem, however, is closely related to the social and psychological consequences of the relocation program itself.

3. Outside the Centers

By and large, the evacuees who have left the centers for outside employment have been well treated. I have before me a stack of letters from evacuees who have left the Granada Relocation Center, written from such communities as Dayton, Ohio; New York; Milwaukee; Baldwin, Kansas; Kansas City; Chicago; Syracuse; North Judson, Indiana; Lincoln, Nebraska; Cincinnati; Lakewood, Ohio; Ann Arbor; Philadelphia; and Rockford, Illinois. With scarcely a single exception, the letters describe the treatment received by the evacuees as being satisfactory. The major difficulty, in most cases, seems to be housing. There have, of course, been a number of unpleasant "incidents" — at Raton, New Mexico; at Marengo, Illinois; at Goshen, Indiana. At Larchmont, New York (June 18, 1943), irate neighbors destroyed the victory garden of a local Japanese-American resident; some evacuees were assaulted by Filipinos in Chicago (July 17, 1943); in Provo, Utah, some young hoodlums fired on evacuee workers.

But the general reception accorded evacuees has been, on the whole, surprisingly good. In communities where the press has been fair-minded, little trouble has developed. In Chicago, for example, both the *Tribune* and the *Sun* have been uniformly tolerant, which is one of the reasons why the area around Chicago has become a favorite relocation area for the evacuees. In states where local officials have spoken out in defense of the evacuees, virtually no trouble has been experienced. Governor Dwight Griswold of Nebraska and Governor Herbert Maw of Utah deserve great credit for the splendid attitude they have shown.

It is undeniable that relocation has opened up new opportunities for many of the Nisei. While some of the positions they have obtained are marginal in character, nevertheless, in many cases, Nisei have obtained a wider variety of employment than would have been possible had they remained on the West Coast. Of major importance is the fact that WRA can impose checks and controls on relocation. If community pressures begin to mount in a city, WRA can stop the flow of evacuees to that particular area. If WRA feels that a particular community has reached the "saturation point," it can divert evacuees to other areas. In other words, dispersion is being carefully planned and directed. The experience itself may be of great value. It might afford, for example, a key to the problem of securing a more typical geographical distribution of other racial minorities.

There is a tendency on the part of both WRA and the evacuees themselves to overstress the importance of dispersal. The theory is that, in the process of relocation, evacuees should be spread out like a small piece of butter on a very large slice of bread — as thinly as possible. To some extent, the theory is mere rationalization, being premised, as it is, on the assumption that race prejudice can be avoided by isolating a few evacuees in a large Caucasian community. Incidents may be avoided and new employment opportunities created by pursuing this policy. But, carried to extremes, the policy may result in the creation of marginal individuals. Toleration is not acceptance. Communities may tolerate a few evacuees in marginal positions (very much as the lone Negro family is tolerated in many Western communities), but they may still refuse social acceptance.

The evacuees themselves are obsessed with the idea that they must make themselves "inconspicuous." "We must avoid forming small cliques," states an editorial in the *Topaz Times* for May 29, 1943; "we are disgustingly conspicuous." I know several evacuees who are attempting, in the most desperate manner, to commit "racial suicide." They will scarcely be seen talking to another Nisei. There is, also, a slight tendency in the contrary direction — namely, for the Little-Tokyo pattern to be repeated on a small scale. But where this tendency has developed it is largely because of the fact that, given the present housing shortage, evacuees have been forced to obtain housing in the same neighborhoods. In some cities, therefore, they are likely to be "bunched" in a particular section, but in such small numbers that there is little likelihood of an economically self-sufficient mono-racial community developing.

The community or colony in New York is, perhaps, indicative of the type of settlement that is arising by reason of relocation. A small colony of Japanese has existed in New York since the turn of the century, but it has never possessed the internal solidarity of the West Coast settlements; in fact, it has been referred to as a community which exists "merely on paper." [3] Many of these New York Japanese originally lived on the West Coast or in Hawaii and gradually migrated eastward. At the present time, the settlement is quite small: 1750 people — 650 Nisei, 1100 Issei. Prior to the freezing of Japanese assets, quite a number of well-to-do "treaty merchants" and "traders" lived in New York. Most of these individuals, however, have been either repatriated or interned.

The New York community is interesting in that about 51 per cent of the marriages of Issei males have been with Caucasian females. There is a good-sized Eurasian population. With the marriage of these Eurasians to Caucasians, virtually all semblance of Japanese influence has disappeared. The Eurasians are reported to be more thoroughly integrated with the American community than the Nisei. [4] In New York, also, the Nisei seem

[3] Article by Turu Matsumoto, *Japanese-American News*, January 1, 1941.
[4] See *A Social Study of the Japanese Population in the Greater New York Area.*

to have acquired a more typical occupational distribution. In addition to commercial activities, they are found in the professions (engineers, teachers, lawyers, dentists) and in numerous trades (machinists, laboratory technicians). The majority are permanently employed by non-Japanese firms. There is no ethnic community in the sense of an economic self-sufficient unit.[5]

4. The Center Experience

Generalization about the social and psychological consequences of relocation, in terms of the evacuees as a group, is an exceedingly precarious undertaking. Almost any general statement that one might make would be subject to important qualifications; and the reverse of the particular proposition might be argued with considerable force. The fact is that evacuation and relocation have not had the same effects or consequences on all evacuees. Not only is this true of the evacuees as a group, but it also is true of special categories of evacuees, such as Issei, Nisei, and Kibei; male and female; rural and urban; old and young. The evacuees are individuals of diverse background, training, experience, and outlook; and while they have all undergone a common experience, they have reacted variously and differently. Furthermore, relocation has been a dynamic process and the attitudes of the evacuees have changed as the program itself has changed. No two of the centers are exactly alike: in personnel, program, center population, or administration. What one might say about center attitudes in Topaz, in November, 1942, might not be true of center attitudes in Minidoka for the same period or for Topaz in November, 1943. Even in a particular center, program changes, personnel changes, evacuees come and go. All that is said in this section on the subject must, therefore, be taken as purely tentative.

To begin with, the centers are not normal communities; they

[5] NOTE: There are several other such pre-Pearl-Harbor "colonies" in areas outside the West Coast, for there were 20,000 persons of Japanese descent who resided outside the Western Defense Command and were never involved in the evacuation and relocation program.

are institutions, of a sort, and they breed a type of "prison complex." The evacuees who were suddenly moved by the thousands into these large, ghetto-like, segregated, geographically isolated Little Tokyos were not in a normal state of mind on their arrival. They had but recently undergone a profoundly disconcerting experience. For to the vast majority of the evacuees evacuation was interpreted as "a wholesale rejection by other Americans." [6] "The indiscriminate inclusion of American citizens and the mass nature of the evacuation left them suspicious of the motives prompting the measure. They were quick to equate this with earlier attacks against them as a racial group." They felt, too, that the breach which evacuation had caused might be widened still further. By the time they arrived in the centers, they were filled with feelings of insecurity and their apprehensions multiplied as they heard of renewed attacks against them in the West Coast press.

A study made in the Tule Lake center, in 1942, listed certain apprehensions that prevailed in the center. The dominant fear of the people, the one which most strongly influenced their behavior, was "the concern about their livelihood in the postwar period." There was also the fear of financial dependency; of unfavorable postwar treatment outside the center; of immediate needs, such as fear of food shortages, clothing shortages, winter shelter and fuel; fear of fire, of violence, of disease; parental fears relating to the education, manners, morals, and conduct of children; personal fears, such as fear of immobilization ("God, I'm getting tired of this place"); fear of the consequences of relocation, of stagnation, of further relocation, of strangers, of sectional feeling; and a general fear of the outside. In some cases, center residents were fearful of other evacuees. "The fears catalogued," states the report, "are by no means all the fears that exist in the community or will exist." The general feeling of insecurity unquestionably accounts for the extraordinary manner in which rumors sweep through centers like wildfire. This tendency is related, in turn, to the manner in which wild rumors about

[6] See *Annals, American Academy of Political and Social Science*, September, 1943, p. 151.

the centers sweep through the communities in the areas in which the centers are located. Wholly irresponsible stories circulate in these communities about the "luxurious ease" enjoyed by the center residents. Outside communities give credence to such stories as that the shortage of milk (an assumed fact) or of meat is occasioned by the demand for milk and meat in the centers; that WRA is grabbing all the available teachers, and so forth.

There were important social cleavages in the Little Tokyo communities prior to evacuation; and, in general, evacuation and relocation have deepened some of these cleavages and created still new ones. The gap between first and second generation was, in most cases, widened. Disagreement and strife, over all manner of issues, split the evacuees into factions and tended to bring about a disintegration of the tightly knit Japanese family. The Nisei blamed the Issei; the Issei blamed the Nisei. Factional struggles which had existed in pre-evacuation days were renewed and intensified in the centers. "Mutual suspicion became a destructive force and there were widespread rumors that every community had Japanese informers who turned in lists of innocent names in order to make money and ingratiate themselves with the authorities." [7] Old feuds and grudges came to life again. Evacuees who were suspected or accused of having imposed on other evacuees, such as, for example, trafficking in property transactions during the troubled period preceding evacuation, were hunted out for punishment and retaliation. "Resentment against Nisei Uncle Toms," writes Eddie Shimano, "flared up again in the centers with an over-intensification of racial hyper-sensitivity." [8]

Evacuees were divided into pro-administration and anti-administration groups and this division was, by no means, identical wth the pro-Japan and anti-Japan grouping. At the outset, WRA aggravated this internal strife by its failure to encourage the young pro-American Nisei leadership. These elements, as a consequence, felt badly let down, deflated, discouraged. Outside agencies, such as the church groups, sometimes stimulated the divisive tendencies by their "Oh-the-poor-Japanese" missionary approach. The

[7] *The Annals*, p. 154.
[8] *Common Ground*, Summer, 1943, p. 83.

frustration which confinement in relocation centers necessarily engendered found outlet, not infrequently, in race baiting on the part of the evacuees themselves. A situation where, as John Embree has pointed out, one racial group does the administrating and another is administered "leads inevitably to a caste distinction." [9] The fact that the Caucasian personnel in the centers have better housing and living accommodations, that they are sharply set apart from the evacuees themselves, creates a basic cleavage. It results, also, in an irrational tendency on the part of the evacuees to blame all of the annoyances and irritations which they experience — all of their problems in fact — upon the administration.

Each and all of these tendencies have been aggravated by the housing situation: the overcrowding, the enforced intimacy, the lack of privacy, the community toilets, the mess halls. "The whole housing situation," as John Embree notes, "has had a demoralizing effect on family standards of living and on family controls over children's behavior." Because of the housing situation, the disorganizing effect of evacuation, and the heterogeneous mixture of elements in the centers (rural and urban, simple and sophisticated, poet and farmer all thrown together), the usual community and family controls on behavior have tended to break down. The usual incentives are lacking. Juvenile delinquency has tended to increase; gang behavior develops; "hooliganism" and "hoodlumism" are reported.[10] Pre-existing parental and cultural conflicts become more pronounced. The longer the evacuees stay in the centers, the more their meager assets are dissipated, the greater the degree of dependency. On the eve of the evacuation, family ties seemed momentarily to be strengthened; the number of marriages, for example, showed a sharp increase just prior to evacuation. But most observers agree that, in the centers, the family structure itself has tended to disintegrate. A striking fact about the evacuees in the centers is the manner in which they magnify minor issues and see only what is close at hand. To some extent, this was true of the Nisei prior

[9] *Journal of the Washington Academy of Sciences*, August 15, 1943, p. 241; see also article by Dr. Robert Redfield, *American Society in Wartime*, 1943, p. 155.
[10] See *Manzanar Free Press*, August 12, 1942.

to evacuation, for Little Tokyo was itself a small world. The relocation centers, however, are still smaller. As their assets dwindle, the wardship or reservation complex becomes more pronounced; they become increasingly dependent upon WRA, elaborate their grievances, and daydream about their postwar claims against the government.

The geographical isolation of the centers and the loss of contact with majority groups have tended to reduce contacts with American culture, and to slow down, if not altogether to retard, the process of assimilation. The Japanese were somewhat isolated and segregated prior to evacuation, but the relocation process served to make total what had previously been partial. If their opportunities for acculturation were limited prior to evacuation, they have been almost wholly restricted since relocation. "Each center," writes John Embree, "houses 6,000 to 17,000 people, all of Japanese ancestry. In fact, this ancestry is the only thing common to the whole group. . . . One of the effects of this situation was the increase in the use of Japanese language and also an increase of the influence of older Japanese. In California, before the war, young Americans, 18 to 20 years old, were gradually becoming independent of their parents and following American patterns of life. In the relocation centers the only older people to guide them were the Japanese, and because of the breakdown of various social and community organizations, the average person was thrown back to a greater dependency on his family as the only stable group left."

These observations, however, cannot be taken as true of the entire group or as true for the entire period of relocation. Influences have waxed and waned in the centers; and have produced, in many cases, diametrically opposite tendencies. For example, I think it is extremely doubtful that the long-range effect of evacuation has been to retard assimilation. Doubtless assimilation was momentarily retarded; but in the long run the experience has probably accelerated the process *for many individuals*. It has created, at least potentially, better opportunities for assimilation and acculturation, by loosening certain ties and removing certain restrictions. The general effect, despite the existence of a contrary tendency with some groups, has been to weaken the Japanese family structure. Those who feel that this particular type of family system was a potent force for the creation of good citizens and the development of valuable personality types [11] naturally deplore the consequences of relocation. But it is my personal belief that this particular family system was, on the whole, a reactionary, retarding influence and that its modification is not necessarily a disastrous consequence.

Similarly, observers have said that the relocation program has resulted in disillusioning the Nisei, in weakening if not destroying their faith in American democracy. It is probably true that evacuation and relocation have orientated several thousand Nisei toward Japan; that they have become bitterly anti-American; and that they will carry with them, when they go to Japan, a hatred of all things American. This would be true of some — a few — of the Nisei in the Tule Lake center. On the other hand, I believe that the entire experience has actually strengthened the faith of a majority of the Nisei in American democracy. From passive deference to democratic ideals they have moved to militant advocacy, *as it has become apparent to them* that democracy corrects its mistakes and that they stand a chance to win final acceptance as full-fledged American citizens.

While the indirect and unintentional consequences of evacuation and relocation may, as I have tried to suggest, contain an important democratic potential, nevertheless nothing can be said in defense of the continuance of the WRA centers themselves. As long as they exist, we, as a nation, will be in an equivocal and, in some respects, paradoxical position: attempting to instill a respect for democracy behind barbed-wire fences; advocating principles that we fear to trust in action; endeavoring to administer democratically a program that produces, in the centers themselves, anti-democratic crosscurrents and tendencies. The atmosphere, in some of the centers, is indeed very bad. One Nisei girl, who recently "escaped" from the Jerome center, writes: "The place has a foreboding air. There's a constant tension of imminent horrors to happen. It made me cringe — I could not feel

[11] See *Annals*, p. 156.

relaxed and at peace for a single moment. Everybody with any courage or undistorted vision is attempting to get out. The ones that will be left are those without any guts or with a twisted sense of values or those unable to leave because they can't get leave clearance through suspected loyalty. Then there's that other large group unable to leave because they aren't employable — the old and infirm and the children."

5. The Manzanar and Poston Incidents

Two incidents which occurred in the fall of 1942 have had a far-reaching influence upon WRA policy and upon West Coast and national public opinion toward the evacuees. These incidents — one at Poston, the other at Manzanar — were a natural and, in a sense, inevitable consequence of the center experience itself. The year 1942 was so taken up with the whole relocation effort that little opportunity was afforded, until late in the year, for these accumulating tensions to find expression. Once these "explosions" or "blowoffs" had occurred, an opportunity was provided the West Coast die-hards to resume the agitation which evacuation had momentarily curtailed.

Preoccupied with a host of problems of the most complex and urgent variety, WRA had neglected the problem of internal policy within the centers. As a matter of fact, WRA did not acquire jurisdiction of the entire center population until mid-August, 1942. It really had not had time to formulate definite policies before the Poston and Manzanar incidents occurred. Initially WRA made the mistake of ignoring the fact that we are in the midst of a world-wide revolution — a revolution which rages inside relocation centers as well as throughout the world. WRA adopted what might be described as a "hands-off" attitude insofar as social and political differences were concerned. It sought to treat all center residents alike and to minimize, wherever possible, both actual and latent cleavages. Such a policy of "non-intervention," here as elsewhere, actually aided the fascist elements. The pro-American Nisei elements felt let-down and defeated by their own government. On the other hand, the Issei

176

felt disgruntled because they were excluded from the elective positions on the center councils. While two thirds of the population belonged to the Nisei or citizen category, many of them were minors and the others were immature and inexperienced. The dearth of people in the age category from thirty to forty had created a leadership vacuum. Furthermore, the active and more energetic Nisei began to leave the centers in the fall of 1942 on seasonal work-permits, thereby accentuating the problem of leadership.

The population within the centers constituted, at best, merely the raw material out of which communities might have been created. But a community is not created by suddenly dumping 10,000 people (the average center population) together. While these residents are racially homogeneous, they are certainly not culturally homogeneous. While they may look alike to the uninformed, they are torn apart by various social, economic, cultural, and political differences. The 1378 high-school students at Manzanar came from 205 different schools, all the way from Seattle to San Diego. Center residents are from rural and urban communities; from backward and progressive environments; and from every variety of economic grouping. These varied groups were, moreover, drawn together under highly exceptional circumstances, under great emotional stress. In the centers, they were compelled to live in semi-communal fashion under the most exasperating conditions. Facilities were primitive; overcrowding was common; and the enforced intimacy created literally limitless possibilities for friction and irritation.

Neither Poston, on the Colorado River, nor Manzanar, in the Owens Valley, is located in a particularly congenial environment. In the summer and early fall, the temperature at Poston rises to 120 degrees nearly every day, and in the winter the nights are bitterly cold. Somewhat similar conditions prevail at Manzanar. Neither center was completely constructed when the evacuees began to arrive by the thousand. Dust clouds billowed about the centers; it was hot; the confusion was intense. Good drinking water was not available. People were crowded into small apartments with several families living in the same unit without partitions, and all of the residents of each block eating in one mess hall. Manzanar was the only relocation center which had been constructed and used as an assembly center. Mistakes were made there which were avoided in some of the other centers. In Manzanar were the families from Terminal Island who had been evacuated under extremely harsh circumstances and whose resentments were still raw and acute.

Not only were both centers made up largely of California evacuees, but one was located in California and the other near the California-Arizona border. It has been noted that evacuees from California "seem to be peculiarly inclined to settle accounts through violent means; evacuees from other sections of the Pacific Coast are not so bellicose." [12] In the Manzanar, Poston, and Tule Lake centers (Tule Lake is also in California), most of the evacuees read the Pacific Coast newspapers, particularly the *Los Angeles Examiner* and the *Los Angeles Times*.[13] The residents of these three centers were quite well aware of the fact that, by the fall of 1942, an agitation had developed in California, sponsored by many public officials, and supported by the press, for their eventual deportation to Japan. Under these circumstances, the most normal individuals can develop "relocation fever." Slight injustices are magnified into outlandish wrongs; minor inconveniences assume major proportions.

The future, as one observer noted, "appears to them as a dark cloud of uncertain but threatening possibilities, and on all sides they perceive that others in America look on them as dangerous enemies exactly as if they were all nationals of Japan and had started the war. . . . The stigma most of our Japanese feel over their evacuation from the Pacific Coast, their bitterness over loss of property, of lifetime savings, of income; their fear over the swift, sudden, silent FBI raids and roundups following Pearl Harbor; the continual emotional and cultural conflicts between Issei parents and Nisei children," all tend to be disturbing factors. The red tape is vexatious; the regulations are annoying; the surveillance hard to bear (Manzanar, for example, was more

[12] *Pacific Citizen*, January 7, 1943.
[13] *Ibid.*, May 13, 1943, and August 21, 1943.

heavily guarded than the other centers). Residents become disappointed and disillusioned when promised improvements are not forthcoming on schedule. The very isolation of the centers, in time and in space, creates a type of claustrophobia. There is time for gossip and intrigue. Dissident elements find explosive possibilities in the very nature of center life. Political disputes, simmering in pre-evacuation days, are fanned into overt hostility. Personal disputes break out into acts of physical violence. The fear of insecurity, of postwar reprisals, of gnawing anxiety; the endless talk and gossip and rumor-mongering — all these tend to upset the residents. It is interesting to note that British and American prisoners in Japanese internment camps were similarly affected by precisely these same factors.[14]

Once in relocation centers, a definite rivalry for power developed between groups that had long been at loggerheads with each other. There was, for example, a small group of militant anti-fascists anxious to assume leadership of the centers. Then there was another Nisei group made up of fairly prosperous middle-class elements, definitely pro-American and unquestionably loyal, but essentially conservative and strongly inclined to "red-bait" the anti-fascists. Lastly, there was a small but compact group of politically conscious fascists, fanatically loyal to Japan, and determined to make trouble in the centers. None of these groups really commanded the allegiance of the people; none of them really represented the people. An exceedingly well-informed Nisei resident of Manzanar has told me that 95 per cent of the 10,000 center residents were "curious, fearful, somewhat bewildered spectators" of the struggle going on in the center between the groups mentioned. The anti-fascists were isolated from the people in the centers just as they had been in pre-evacuation days. They were courageous, intelligent, but very lonely voices in a wilderness.

Karl Yoneda, a former longshoreman, a man who has fought fascism in Japan and on the San Francisco waterfront for years, was severely beaten at Manzanar and his life was threatened. He

[14] See "City in Prison" by Joseph Alsop, *Saturday Evening Post*, January 9 and 16, 1943.

circulated a petition in the center calling for the opening of a second front in Europe and promptly volunteered for service when enlistment was made possible (he is today serving in the Southwest Pacific). These anti-fascists were called "Aka" or reds and denounced as trouble-makers; and the middle-class pro-American groups were vilified as sneaks, informers, and appeasers. Also in the Poston, Manzanar, and Tule Lake centers was a small hoodlum element, troublesome, anxious for a fight politically unconscious of what was going on. When the anti-fascist and loyal middle-class elements were removed from these centers, for their own safety, it had the effect of leaving the fascists in possession of the field.

These were the factors that throughout 1942 were building toward a climax. In the fall of 1942, the explosions occurred first at Poston, and then at Manzanar. (Nearly every center however, had a somewhat similar blowoff or "incident.") From November 14 to November 25, the center residents at Poston were on strike, protesting the arrest of two persons charged with having beaten an alleged informer. The protest was orderly enough (there was no rioting); but the incident which precipitated the protest was not its real cause. The causes were to be found in all of the tensions, resentments, and frictions that I have mentioned. Similarly, on the eve of the anniversary of Pearl Harbor, December 6, 1942, a riot occurred at Manzanar. Here, too, the ostensible cause of the incident was the arrest of a center resident; but the incident was merely the result of antecedent tensions. In both cases, the bulk of the center residents were not directly involved and were spectators rather than participants. Both incidents were widely and sensationally reported in the West Coast press and contributed to the wild outburst of agitation that developed during 1943.

6. Segregation and the Tule Lake Incident

As a result, first of the Manzanar and Poston incidents, and second of the demand of the West Coast Congressional delegation, WRA determined to segregate the loyal from the disloyal elements in all the centers and to concentrate all the "disloyal segregants" in one center. While plans for segregation were being considered, the President announced on January 28, 1943, that the Army had decided to form a Japanese-American combat team on a volunteer basis. "It is the inherent right of every faithful citizen," the President stated, "regardless of ancestry, to bear arms in the nation's battle." Since the Army proposed to send a recruiting team to each of the centers, and to circulate a selective-service questionnaire, WRA decided to conduct, at the same time, a general registration of all persons in the centers seventeen years of age and older. The registration was conducted on extremely short notice; and with virtually no advance preparation. The personnel of the centers were not clear as to the purpose of the registration and could not, therefore, answer perfectly pertinent questions raised by the evacuees. Registration was conducted during February and March, 1943, and came, at Poston and Manzanar, almost immediately after both centers had been profoundly disturbed by the incidents previously described. The timing of the registration was, therefore, extremely bad. Psychologically, it is unfortunate that the registration should have been conducted at the same time that a call was being made for volunteers.

It is extremely important to keep in mind that *only* those center residents seventeen years of age or older were asked to fill out the registration form. The registration form itself was in part devised for the purpose of securing information that might aid in finding employment for the evacuees. Question 28 was the so-called loyalty question. All male United States citizens were asked: —

> Will you swear unqualified allegiance to the United States of America and faithfuly defend the United States from any or all attack by foreign or domestic forces, and foreswear any form of allegiance or obedience to the Japanese emperor, or any other foreign government, power, or organization?

Citizen females, seventeen years of age and over, were required to fill out a form which contained these two questions: —

> *Question 27:* If the opportunity presents itself and you are found qualified, would you be willing to volunteer for the Army Nurse Corps or the WAAC?

Question 28: Will you swear unqualified allegiance to the United States of America and foreswear any form of allegiance or obedience to the Japanese emperor, or any other foreign government, power, or organization?

Aliens, both male and female, over seventeen years of age, were also asked to answer Question 28 as it appeared in the questionnaire for citizen females. While the registration was being conducted, Question No. 28 was changed insofar as aliens were concerned. They were then asked to answer this substitute question: —

Will you swear to abide by the laws of the United States and to take no action which would in any way interfere with the war effort of the United States?

At the Manzanar center, registration had already proceeded so far that the Project Director concluded that it would merely confuse matters to use the substitute question for the aliens. For reasons not clear to me, the project director at Manzanar had, in fact, devised a substitute question which was *asked only* the aliens in that center. It read: —

Are you sympathetic to the United States of America and do you faithfully agree to defend the United States from any or all attack by either foreign or domestic forces?

This procedure calls for specific comment. In the first place it is extremely doubtful whether the complex question of loyalty under the most ideal conditions, can be determined on the verbalistic basis of "yes" or "no" answers to questions. A Japanese agent, for example, citizen or alien, would not be inclined to avow *disloyalty* when, by merely answering the question affirmatively, he might pass as loyal. The proper basis of the segregation procedure should have been much the same as that followed in the internment centers — namely, individual hearings before a formally constituted hearing board.[15]

[15] See *The Internment of Aliens* by F. LaFitte, London, 1940; also the article by Lieutenant Commander Ringle, *Harper's*, October, 1942; and my own testimony before the Tolan Committee.

Few persons realize that "loyalty" is a complex, and not a simple, issue to determine. Even the well-trained lawyers who have served on the Department of Justice boards (set up to hear the cases of those Japanese arrested on Presidential warrants) have confessed that their task has not been an easy one. "It is a difficult question," writes one of them, "to try to determine the loyalty to this country of a man who comes before you and who cannot speak your language, who is a native of a country with which we are at war, who may have relatives in Japan, whose children are citizens of this country and perhaps whose sons are in the army of this country, whose record discloses some ties with Japan, contributing to Japanese army relief during the Chinese-Japanese War, membership in some society now considered detrimental to the security of this country, who expresses the view that as his own country and his children's country are at war, he cannot give the board any statement which will help them in determining the case. He may have a wife and minor children who will be deprived of the support and comfort of the husband and father if the ruling is internment." [16] This difficulty might have been resolved, insofar as the aliens were concerned, by posing, not the question of loyalty, but, as Lieutenant Commander Ringle suggested, *the degree of probable menace.* The question of "loyalty" is a question for psychologists and philosophers to debate; the degree of probable menace is a juridical issue.

Not only was the procedure inherently faulty, but the questions themselves were objectionable. It should be remembered that Japanese aliens were and are ineligible to American citizenship. To answer question No. 28 as originally phrased, in the affirmative, meant that they would automatically divest themselves of the only citizenship they possessed, particularly as they were not offered the alternative of becoming American citizens. Many of them had relatives in Japan and naturally feared reprisals. Furthermore, they were well aware of the fact that Californians were advocating their deportation to Japan. If they were

[16] See article by Mr. Stephen M. Farrand, *Los Angeles Bar Bulletin*, May, 1947

to be deported to Japan, then it would certainly be very unwise for them to answer this question in the affirmative.

The question used at Manzanar was very confusing to the aliens since there is no Japanese character, apparently, by which the words "to defend" can be literally translated. As translated, it carried the connotation of "taking up arms to defend." The final question, or rather the substitute question asked the aliens, was a proper question. But before the problem could be straightened out, the confusion in the centers was waist-high. The question asked the Nisei or citizen group was capable of a rather insulting interpretation. It could be interpreted as implying that they were citizens of Japan or that they had previously acknowledged their allegiance to Japan. It was argued, for example, that an affirmative answer implied or acknowledged the existence of prior dual citizenship.

The recruitment campaign and the registration program afforded the trouble-makers in the centers a magnificent opportunity for rabble rousing. They came to the meetings, at which both matters were discussed, with carefully prepared arguments, a well-thought-out strategy, functioning as a well-organized fraction. They grabbed the microphone and monopolized the discussion; they heckled other speakers; they interrupted patriotic demonstrations. They objected to the Special Combat Team because it was a "segregated Jim Crow" unit; they harped upon the wrongs and injustices of evacuation and relocation. They baited the Nisei by shouting: "So you're an American citizen? Well, let's see you walk out of this center." Some well-meaning and quite innocent Nisei, losing all sense of perspective or proportion, fell for this line. They had become so intensely preoccupied with their "civil rights" that they could not see any other considerations. Some of them expressly refused to answer the loyalty question unless: (a) their full rights were restored; and (b) until the ban on their return to the West Coast was lifted. In most of the centers, the meetings were tumultuous and disorderly, with the disloyal elements taking full advantage of the chaos that prevailed. There was, also, considerable direct intimidation and coercion. Twenty-seven evacuees were arrested or acts of violence in the Gila center; nearly sixty were arrested at Tule Lake; Dr. T. T. Yatabe was severely beaten in the Jerome center; Saburo Kido, president of the Japanese-American Citizens League, was savagely attacked at Poston; Professor Obata and the Reverend Taro Goto were beaten at Topaz.

The worst phase of the mess was this: once the parents had determined to answer the question "no," the pressure on the children (over seventeen) became intolerable. If they answered "yes" it meant permanent separation from their parents. The facts, in particular cases, were hopelessly complicated. I know of one case involving an Issei widower. He had four children — two Nisei sons now serving with our armed forces and two Nisei daughters (eleven and thirteen years of age) living with relatives in Japan. Is this man to be branded as disloyal because he felt that his primary duty was to join his daughters in Japan? It is also grossly unfair to brand a Nisei as disloyal because, for example, he felt that his duty was to remain with aged parents who had expressed a desire for repatriation. I know of one case in the Topaz center where a fourteen-year-old boy held out against his parents and against his brothers and sisters, all of whom were being sent to Tule Lake. The boy insisted on remaining in Topaz. One week after his parents and family left for Tule Lake, he was in the hospital suffering from a complete nervous and spiritual breakdown. In literally hundreds of cases, the registration issue cut families apart, precipitated the most intense personal crises, and resulted in starkly tragic situations. In other cases, this all-important determination was premised upon the most trivial considerations. In one instance, an Issei couple insisted on repatriation because their Nisei daughter was in love with a young man they disliked. I know the couple and it would never occur to me to regard them as "disloyal," yet they have branded themselves as such, and for extremely inadequate reasons. But human beings have an unfortunate propensity for making foolish decisions and for doing all sorts of things with little or no reason.

In Hawaii, the Army called for 2500 volunteers for the combat team: nearly 10,000 volunteered. In the relocation centers, due to the mess that was made of the procedure itself, the results were somewhat disappointing: 1200 evacuees volunteered for service. There are in the Army today approximately 8000 Japanese-American citizens (4500 were in the Army on December 7, 1941). It is interesting to note that the proposal to form a combat team of volunteers met with instant opposition in California from the American Legion, the Native Sons of the Golden West, and the California Grange. Representative Rankin of Mississippi took the floor in Congress to denounce the proposal. All persons of Japanese descent, he said, should be put in labor battalions. He was particularly upset by the response shown by the Nisei in Hawaii, who, he charged, had "aided in fifth-column activity," despite conclusive evidence that no acts of sabotage were reported. At the same time, he recommended that the United States deport all persons of Japanese descent at the end of the war and that the government buy their property holdings, valued at $200,000,000. Interestingly enough, he suggested that the South would be happy to co-operate with the West in its efforts to "wipe out the Japanese menace." [17] Senator Chandler, of Kentucky, has also spoken out in favor of a racial alliance between the South and the West.[18]

The male citizens answered Question 28 as follows: 15,011, "yes"; 340, "qualified yes"; 4414, "no"; 375, "qualified no"; 128 made no reply. In other words, 73.7 per cent answered affirmatively; 21.7 per cent answered negatively. Of the female citizens, 15,671 answered "yes"; 376 "qualified yes"; 1919 "no"; 210 "qualified no"; 226 "no reply" — 85 per cent affirmatively, 10.4 per cent negatively. Of the male aliens, 20,197 answered "yes"; 137 "no" (96.4 per cent affirmative, 0.7 per cent negative). Of the female aliens, 14,712 (96.5 per cent) answered "yes"; 263 (1.8 per cent) "no." Considering the entire group, citizens and aliens alike, and before any changes were made in the replies given, 65,079 (87.4 per cent) answered "yes"; 6733 (9 per cent) answered "no." In considering these answers, two factors must

[17] *San Francisco Examiner*, February 1, 1943.
[18] See *Arkansas Democrat*, March 28, 1943.

be remembered: first, many evacuees feared that WRA, in circulating the registration form, was preparing to close the centers. They thought, therefore, that an affirmative answer might mean another compulsory dislocation. Second, it should be noted that of the Nisei who answered the question, 25 per cent were between the ages of seventeen and twenty; three fifths were under twenty-five; and less than 10 per cent were in their late thirties and forties. Being quite young as a group, they were influenced, in many cases, by the stated wishes of their parents.

Once the returns to the questionnaire were tabulated, it was announced (May 25, 1943) that the "disloyal" evacuees would be transferred to Tule Lake center and the loyal elements in Tule Lake would be distributed among the other centers. This transfer was effected between September 15 and October 15, 1943. The adoption by the Senate, on July 6, 1943, of Senator Downey's resolution, which called for a policy of segregation, prompted this decision (although I am sure that WRA officials would be the first to admit that the registration technique did not constitute a proper basis for segregation). Segregation involved the transfer of approximately 9000 people to the Tule Lake center and the transportation of approximately the same number of people from Tule Lake to the other centers: an exchange of loyal for "disloyal" evacuees.

The basis of segregation, as finally determined, was as follows: (1) all persons were automatically sent to Tule Lake who had requested repatriation; (2) the "no-nos," that is, those who had answered the loyalty question negatively, were sent to Tule Lake after a hearing in the center at which they were given a chance to explain, qualify, or change their answer; (3) all evacuees to whom the director of WRA had denied leave clearances were also sent to Tule Lake; and (4) close relatives of persons in the foregoing categories who expressed a preference to remain with the segregants rather than to disrupt family ties.[19] After the exchange was effected, the total number of "disloyal" segregants in Tule Lake was 13,540, divided into the following categories: —

[19] Statement of Mr. Dillon Myer, November 14, 1943.

Repatriates and expatriates 5,127
Registration segregants 4,222
Other segregants 4,191

Since the segregation was effected, all of these people in Tule Lake have been labeled by the press as "disloyal." Personally, I doubt if more than 25 per cent of the total can, by any fair test, be regarded as "disloyal." Of those who requested repatriation, family considerations, in nearly 90 per cent of the cases, were the determining factor (that is, the presence in Japan of near relatives — wives, husbands, children). Political considerations, insofar as those requesting repatriation are concerned, were wholly negligible. Of those leaving Manzanar for Tule Lake, *28 per cent were children under sixteen years of age whose loyalty has never been questioned and who did not fill out the registration form.* Of this same group from Manzanar, 483 or 22 per cent actually answered "yes" to Question 28 and are going to Tule Lake as "family members" and solely to preserve family ties. Thus, 176 "no" answers have been found to involve 731 "yes" individuals and family members. In the Manzanar group, 80 per cent of these who requested repatriation had actually answered the loyalty question in the affirmative. Of this same group, *35 per cent of those going to Tule Lake are minors.* These percentages, which I was able to obtain for the Manzanar group, would, I am sure, apply to those who went to Tule Lake from the other centers.

I witnessed the departure of the segregants from some of the centers for Tule Lake and it was my most fervent wish that the entire membership of the Native Sons of the Golden West might have been present to see for themselves the anguish, the grief, the bottomless sorrow that this separation occasioned. They might then have been convinced — although I doubt that even these scenes would have convinced them — that the Japanese are not an inscrutable, unemotional, stoical, or mysterious people. The evacuees realized that those who were going to Tule Lake were destined to be deported, some day, to Japan; and that this was a final separation, a fateful farewell. Parents were being separated from children and children from parents; brother from brother, sister from sister. In these scenes was the stuff of timeless tragedy and excellent documentation for the one immortal theme: man's inhumanity to man.

I also witnessed the arrival in the Topaz and Granada centers of the Tule Lake contingents. Mothers were running around in a dazed and distraught manner, trying to find children, to corral possessions, to locate relatives, to find some means of heating the baby's formula or some place to wash out a diaper. When several hundred new families move into a center overnight the whole community is turned upside down. The new arrivals want to live in the same barracks with friends and relatives. The whole center becomes a madhouse, and even the best trained administrators appear to be slightly insane. The exchange was not, however, without its amusing sidelights. There is a story current in the centers about the two trains passing in Wyoming; one carrying segregants to Tule Lake, one moving east with loyal evacuees. As the two trains passed, a group of east-bound Sansei yelled at a group of west-bound youngsters: "Go on back to Tokyo, you Jap bastards!"

Anyone familiar with the background of the relocation program might have anticipated the trouble that subsequently developed at Tule Lake. With the arrival of 9000 new residents, the usual battle for power ensued. As in the Poston and Manzanar incidents, the same compact clique of trouble-makers began to take advantage of the situation. On October 15, 1943, an accident occurred at the center in which some 29 evacuees were injured and one was killed. On the day following, no evacuees reported for work. The strike or protest lasted for about two weeks. During this time, the real trouble-makers raised a very serious legal issue. Prior to segregation, it could be argued that the evacuees were not "prisoners of war" and that they were, therefore, not protected by the provisions of the Geneva Convention. But the moment segregation was effected, a different situation arose. WRA had been careful to call those sent to Tule Lake "segregants" and not "prisoners." But Tule Lake is not a relocation center: it is a concentration camp. There is a much larger detachment of troops on hand; the camp is carefully guarded; a double barbed-wire fence encloses the camp; and a military censorship prevails. Residents of Tule Lake are not, of course, eligible for either seasonal or permanent leaves. Unquestionably, their liberties have been restricted in a sense that was never true of those in the other centers. As a consequence, the Tule Lake agitators raised the issue that all residents of the center were, in fact, prisoners of war, and entitled to treatment as such. It must be admitted that the issue is a very close one: the distinction between a "segregant" and a "prisoner" is largely a matter of semantics.

Demonstrations occurred at the Tule Lake center on November 1, and on November 4 the Army assumed full control. During these demonstrations a doctor was beaten, some property was damaged, and some of the resident personnel were moved outside the center for a few days. The evidence indicates, however, that the demonstrations, with the exception of the acts noted, were conducted in an orderly fashion and that their subsequent characterization as "riots" was wholly unjustified. As in the Poston and Manzanar incidents, the vast majority of the residents were not directly involved and were merely spectators: some were friendly, some were partially hostile, some were laughing good-naturedly. Children were present in large numbers at the demonstrations. Major General David McCoach subsequently announced that the Army had no difficulty in handling the situation; that only a "small group of evacuees" were involved in the disorders; and that no firearms or explosives had been found. On January 14, 1944, control of the center was restored to WRA.

CHAPTER VI

One Nation, Indivisible . . .

NOT ONLY has the relocation program been a vast experiment in planned resettlement — challenging in the unprecedented demands it has made on available techniques and resources — but it has also been a stupendous human drama. The time has not yet arrived when this story can be told in full. It will have to be told in retrospect by an evacuee, someone who actually saw, felt, and was a part of this amazing adventure. The adventure itself involved highly diverse types and an infinite variety of individuals, from aged farm laborers to sophisticated artists, from shopkeepers to professors. The impact of the experience naturally varied with the type of individual involved. For some it has meant nothing but bitter disappointment and defeat; for others it has promised liberation and new opportunities. Regardless of its varying impact on particular individuals, it has profoundly affected the lives of every individual involved. Having witnessed this drama at close range, I feel wholly inadequate to convey even the vaguest impression of its magnitude and dimensions. Yet no account of the relocation program would be even tolerably complete that failed to convey at least an inkling of the feelings and emotions it has precipitated among the people themselves.

I have sought to resolve this difficulty by including a variety of quotations, selected more or less at random, from letters and documents that have been sent to me by the evacuees or taken from documents gathered by WRA. Wherever possible, I have selected documents written by children, for they seem to have the best eye for detail. Obviously my selection is incomplete; but it may suggest the enormous drama of relocation. In this section, then, the evacuees speak for themselves.

1. Before Evacuation

"My father," writes a seventh-grade youngster, "said it would be nice to go for a little ride around San Francisco. The front door opened and I saw my father coming out of the house. Just as he entered the car we heard the telephone ringing and my father ran and opened the door. He didn't come out for about ten minutes or so and my mother went into the house to see what was keeping my father. . . . My mother didn't return; so I put on the radio and was listening . . . suddenly the music was out and there was a flash. I was listening with all my might. He started to say something and said Japan has attacked Pearl Harbor. I ran into the house to tell my folks. My father said that my uncle had told him that war has been declared between Japan and America. I couldn't go for the ride. . . ." "We were coming back from Golden Gate Park," writes another child, "and I noticed the headline of the *San Francisco Chronicle*. It read WAR! It was written in black print and covered about half the front page. Before long every paper had the headline WAR!" . . . "As soon as I heard the news," writes one child, "I ran out to get a newspaper. Just then the man next door told me to come in. I was kind of scared but I went in. He said, 'I don't want you to worry about what occurred and I want you to feel just the same as if this war hadn't started.' " . . . "At school the next day I found most of my friends treating me as if nothing had happened. I was glad of this because I knew they were my friends, no matter what happened." . . . "I went to school," writes another, "feeling like I would get picked on. When I entered the school, my school mates were very nice to me. Some of the boys gave me a dirty look and said bad things about me. I did not feel too bad because I knew that I was an American citizen and I would always be. This always gave me courage after that." . . . "One of the kids popped up and said, 'Say, how did you kids feel when the teacher started to talk about war?' 'Funny!' we all agreed. We had a little talk about it, and before I knew it, the subject was changed and we were talking about something else."

As the weeks passed, the shadow of evacuation deepened. What had seemed a remote possibility began to loom large as a very real eventuality. "It just didn't seem true!" writes one school-age Nisei. "Moving from the place I was born, raised and half-educated. Moving from friends, not just ordinary friends, but life-long, dear friends. This also meant moving from the city we loved and everything about and around it. All of these things added up to losing something of very great importance which we dreaded to lose. We tried to grasp the meaning of it. Some people said, 'Just a rumor.' Some said, 'Indeed it's true.' But way deep in our hearts we knew it was no rumor, it was no matter that should be considered lightly, that it was something very important that would leave an impression for the rest of our lives. Although I was just a child I knew and could sense the terror of evacuation in my mother and father's eyes. It was worse enough to go but when we found out that we were the first contingent, that was quite depressing news. Our friends and relatives all gathered to see us off and when they whispered words of encouragement we realized there and then that this was one means of showing patriotism to our country."

Preparing to leave for an assembly center, Kenny Murase, a brilliant young Nisei, wrote these lines: —

A lot of you have felt the same way — you get an aw-fully funny feeling, knowing that in a few days you are going to be living in a world so unbelievably strange and different. You never thought such a thing could happen to you, but it has. And you feel all tangled up inside because you do not quite see the logic of having to surrender free-dom in a country that you sincerely believe is fighting for freedom. It hurts especially because you were just begin-ning to know what freedom really means to you, as an indi-vidual, but more so, as one of 130,000,000 other Americans who are also beginning to know the meaning of freedom. You are upset about it but you are not mad, though there was a time when you were furious and you wanted to shout from the house-top that you thought it was an out-and-out fascist decree, and that this was America, a democracy, and you wanted to know what's the Big Idea. . . . You think you know something about the background of evacuation — about California's long anti-Oriental history — and it helps you to understand why it was so, but it still does not ease a disturbed conscience that is trying to seek an explanation consistent with a deep-seated faith in the workings of American democracy. You start off on another line of reasoning, and you think you are getting closer to an attitude that will keep you from turning sour and cynical. You begin to see democracy is something tremendously alive, an organic thing, composed of human beings and behaving like human beings; and therefore imperfect and likely to take steps in the wrong direction. You see that democracy is still young, untried and inexperienced, but always in the process of growing and growing towards higher levels of perfection. And because you realize that democracy is a process, a means towards better ends, you now see that it is not precisely the failure of democracy that produces undemocratic practices. You know that you cannot say democracy has failed because truthfully we have not attained a level of democracy that can be fairly tested. You are not going to judge democracy on the basis of what you have found it to be, but rather upon the basis of what you think it is capable of. . . . You are aware that discrimination against racial, religious and political minorities, attacks on the rights of labor, suppression of the press and radio, and all the rest of the undemocratic practices in America today are *not* the products of the free will of the people; but rather the actions of powerful minorities who stand to gain economically and politically by such measures. . . . As you prepare to entrain for a distant resettlement camp, you think you have some objectives pretty well established in your mind. You are not going to camp because of "military necessity" — you know that such a reason is groundless. You are going because groups of native American fascists were able to mislead an uninformed American public, and this partly because you yourself were uninformed and unaware of your responsibility as one integral part of the democratic process.

Up in the state of Washington, Yuri Tashima and another Nisei girl attempted to leave the West Coast area voluntarily in order

194

to resume their college studies in another university. An over-vigilant sheriff picked them up in Idaho and lodged them in jail, needless to say without a warrant and without cause. Miss Tashima writes: —

On an April night in 1942 I sat on a hard bunk bed covered with cheap new blankets, and scribbled on a sheet torn out of a notebook, a sheet which I had headed, "Notes on a Night in Jail." The occasion, as I expressed it in my notes, was "demagogues having a field day," with us as their objects of attention. It was difficult to be objective about a situation like this, although, as a student of the social sciences, I was trying hard. All we wanted, was to be allowed to continue quietly our interrupted education. At that moment, however, my companion and I were only two frightened girls trying to keep our equilibrium, she by knitting furiously on a sweater and smoking, I by resorting to my usual outlet, writing out my confused thoughts in an attempt to formulate a clearer picture of what it all meant. The past week had been like a bad dream — a hostilely curious small town, recurrent threats of mob violence floating up from the saloon gangs downtown, a ranting sheriff refusing protection in event of actual danger, the shock of encountering in an American setting some of the worst fascistic elements we were supposed to be fighting, and now this, the necessity of hiding behind barred windows and locked doors to avoid possible "accidents." The kindness of those faculty members who had taken us in and the unspoken trust of a few other educated townspeople stood us in good stead. We were grateful, too, for the indignant protests of students who saw in the refusal of their president to admit us to their institution a weak toadying to the powers that held the political strings. Our stay in the cell and in the town itself was a brief one, but I will never forget it. The reception we received was too vivid. Events since then have proved that it was not a typical reception. And perhaps it was of value in itself, to me as an American citizen. I am more convinced than ever that the fight for freedom and equality must be carried on in *all* the corners of the earth.

2. White Papers on Posts

"I didn't live on Terminal Island," writes Hiro Kusudo, "but one morning in March my boss told me to take a truck to Terminal Island and help the women and children there. The able-bodied men had been taken to internment camps because they were fishermen and lived near the navy base. Those left were told by the army they wouldn't be evacuated, but the navy came in and told them to get out within 24 hours. No one talked much, everybody was too busy. The women cried awful. That was one thing about the whole evacuation that was terrible, the way the women cried — so hard and they couldn't stop. The evacuation of Terminal Island was long before the rest of us were evacuated, so I've seen a lot of crying. Men came out to the Island to buy the stuff the people couldn't take with them and had to sell, as most of them rented houses. Some of them smashed their stuff, broke it up, right before the buyers eyes because they offered such ridiculous prices."

"I ran home," writes one youngster, "to tell my father they had put white papers on the post, so my father went to see what it was. I read one part and it said after May 1st no Japanese people are allowed to come into the white zone." . . . "We were told," writes Dave Misakami, "that if we voluntarily evacuated Zone 1, we'd be all right. So we did, right away, leaving our places, our crops, and got an 80 acre place in the so-called White Free Zone, which we cleared and planted with tomatoes. They were just coming along nice when the Army pushed us all in relocation camps. I didn't have to go to an Assembly Center being out of Zone 1. I went right to Poston, but I'll never forget that ride. We left Lindsay at 7 P.M. We hadn't had any supper and we were given a dried out apple butter sandwich, an orange, a piece of cake and ½ pint of milk. The next morning we were given the same thing for breakfast and that was funny — everybody — all together — threw their apple butter sandwiches out the windows."

"We were on the back seat of the greyhound bus," writes an

eighth-grader, "with crowds of people outside bidding us good-bye. As the bus started to move, I caught a last glimpse of our pink house. How I wished then, that I could stay. . . . I was not happy, nor were my parents. But my little sister and brother were overjoyed since it was their first ride on a greyhound bus. They didn't know why they were moving, they just thought that they were moving to another place. My mother was not happy. She was smiling but I could tell by her face that she was thinking of the hardships ahead of her. When we came near the City Hall almost everyone in the bus looked out to see it, because they knew that it would be a long time before they saw it again. Soon the bus started to slow down and I looked out the window and saw rows of little houses. We had reached the gate of Tanforan."

"My cousin's dog," writes another youngster, "was a big colly. He knew something was wrong because my cousin said we will be back soon. He said we're going shopping, but somehow the colly knew it was not so and he also knew that he wanted to go with us. He suspected because we were carrying our suitcases. When we were going down our garden, the dog followed us. I told him to go home. He just sat and howled. My cousin and I got mad at him but we love him almost as if he were a human being. He seemed to be one that day because he seemed to understand what we were saying to him. I got down to the sidewalk (I was the last one) and looked back and I could see him but he was still following me. His name was Spruce. The lady that rented our house said she would take good care of him. When we drove away from the front of the house, he was sitting inside the fence looking out."

"The first time I have ever been among so many Japanese," writes another, "was on the day of May 1st, when we arrived at Tanforan. There were only three in our family so we had to have a horse stable for our apartment. Thinking it was about time for supper, we set off for the messhall. The road was very muddy. On the way I saw many people, who had just come in. They were all dressed in their best. Many of them had no umbrellas and were soaking wet. Children and babies were crying.

Men were all carrying heavy baggage, and the women had tears in their eyes, making their way through the mud. I thought it must be very discouraging for them, getting their good shoes muddy, mud getting splashed on their clothes, and then finding that they were to live in a horse stall where it still smelled." . . . "When they have roll calls," wrote another, "the sirens ring. I get so scared that I sometimes scream and some people get scared of me instead of the siren. I run home as fast as I can and then we wait about five minutes and then the inspector comes to check to see that we are all home. I hate roll call because it scares you too much."

"The soldiers that guarded Tanforan," to quote from another document, "were all very nice. They would joke around with us. Once when we were playing baseball, a soldier shouted from his watch tower: 'Come On! Make a Homer!' One night we had a festival. We dressed like the people from the South Sea Islands (at least we tried to). The boys wore sarongs. Everybody had leis to wear. We carried signs, too. The people that won were from Recreation Hall No. 2. Their theme was 'Sultan Takes a Holiday.' They were very good. I often get homesick for Tanforan. There was so much doing there but there isn't a thing to do here." The novelty and excitement of life in an assembly center did tend to offset the crowded living conditions and the turmoil and the tangled scheme of things. "When I first came I thought this place was really going to be fun and exciting," writes one Nisei. Some groups had come to the centers with plans already prepared for social, educational, and cultural activities. But these bright hopes did not long survive the distractions, the petty irritations, the innumerable inconveniences of assembly center life.

"Already a year and a half have gone," writes Paul Asano from a beet field in Utah, "since that memorable day when we Japanese, citizens and aliens alike, packed our meager belongings and sadly trudged to registration halls where we were tagged, counted, put in busses, and sent away to what was virtually a concentration camp. We departed bidding tearful farewell to lifelong friends and looking back with mingled feelings to see all that we had left behind: friends, homes, churches, much that had been built by a lifetime of labor, sacrifices and love. Yes, it was almost like a dream until the gates clanged shut behind us in the Assembly Centers and we stood inside looking out to life and home while between us stood barbed wire fences and patrolling sentries who shot and killed. There, certainly every one of us felt extreme bitterness."

"It would be quite impossible," writes Togo Tanaka, "to describe how I felt on that dusty, dismal day of April 28th, 1942, when suddenly I found myself and my little family staring out at the world from behind a barbed wire fence. . . . Let me try to tell you something about how my wife and I felt, as we sat in the misery of a Manzanar dust storm one rather gloomy afternoon, with thick clouds of dust practically billowing in our barrack room. It was mostly in such moments as these, when our eyes became bloodshot with the fine dust, our throats parched, and I suppose our reason a little obtuse, that we fell into the common practice of trying to figure out just how in the world we would find our way out of this little man-made hell. Why were we here? What had happened to us? Was this the America we knew, had known?" They all asked the same question. "Why," wrote Kiyoshi Hamanaka, "why did it have to be me? What did I do to deserve this? what rhyme or reason is there? I don't know why . . . I guess I'll never know all the reasons, all the causes."

Gordon Hirabayashi, who refused to comply with the order for evacuation, wrote some interesting reflections in jail. "Sometimes," he wrote, "I think about evacuation and its various implications. The reaction is usually one of deep disappointment. At other times I am overcome with callousness and think, 'if I were only born of Caucasian parents . . .' Yet I am quite aware that these feelings will not achieve the things which I desire. I try to understand why it has happened. . . . Why? Why? . . . Lin Yutang once wrote: 'the causality of events is such that every little happening is conditioned by a thousand antecedents.' This evacuation, then, came as a result of the various experiences of the various persons who encouraged it, perhaps. Some may have learned race prejudice in their homes; others may have had unpleasant experiences with the Japanese; still others learned to consider that business came first; then there are many who have lost on the battle front close relatives. Add to these the things which whip up hysteria. Could these and a few other incidents have been some of the 'antecedents'? Could I through thoughtfulness and study come to understand some of these actions and thereby not only learn the why of it but also get an insight into how to overcome it? It seems to me that a lot of these little things have turned out to be significant things."

3. The Trek Begins

No sooner had the evacuees become partially adjusted to life in an assembly center (usually a fairground or race track or pavilion converted overnight into a city accommodating thousands of people) than they were moved again. This time they were moved from California to center cities that had been hastily built in the inter-mountain "wilderness" areas, in Utah, in Idaho, in Wyoming, in Arizona, in Colorado. Most of the evacuees, needless to say, had never been outside the West Coast states in their lives.

"One afternoon," writes a youngster, "I saw on the bulletin board a note saying we were going to Utah." Again the rush to get suitcases packed; to be checked and counted; to bid farewell to friends; to get children dressed, tagged, and in their places. "There were miles and miles of desert, sagebrush, and mountains," writes one Nisei; and "then we came to Delta, Utah, where soldiers put us on the busses for Topaz. We traveled a long time. And then some barracks came in sight. We came closer and saw some people. Most of the people were sort of dark. We then heard music which was off tune a bit and we learned later that it was played by the welcome band. We finally got out. As I stepped on the ground, the dust came up in my face. This was Topaz! We had a hard time to find our home for the barracks were all alike. Topaz looked so big, so enormous to us. It made me feel like an ant. The dust gets in our hair. Every place we go we cannot escape the dust. Inside of our houses, in the laundry, in the latrines, in the mess halls, dust and more dust, dust everywhere. . . . I wonder who found this desert and why they put us in a place like this, but I hear it is a good place to live for the duration of a long war."

"Sometimes I wonder," writes another young Nisei, "how the garden in our home in San Francisco is coming along. Whether the plants withered and died and weeds cover the garden or the house was torn down and the sign that says — 'Real Estate — call so and so on so and so street to buy this place' — covers the front while among the weeds which cover the lot bloom roses and violets. I wonder which is better — dying from lack of care or blooming among the weeds every year. Maybe someone moved into the house (although it isn't very likely because the house is sort of old) and tended the garden with care and planted a victory garden among the flowers." Those who left the centers for occasional visits, on special passes, to near-by towns and cities felt like strangers in a world they had almost forgotten. "In the morning I woke up in our hotel room," writes one youngster, "and it felt good to hear the horns of automobiles and everything you hear in the city. I thought, for a moment, I was back in San Francisco and the whole evacuation was just a dream, but it was not a dream and I was only visiting Salt Lake City for a few days."

"It is exactly a year ago today," writes Mrs. Mary Tsukamoto, "that we came to Arkansas. I remember we were tired but eager to get our first glimpse of our new home. Then, we saw the black rows of regimented, one story barracks surrounded by dust. I felt only tears and inarticulate words choked me. . . . Then, I remember the cold of our first winter, the fuel shortage! The Arkansas mud! We dug ditches, women and children too, to fix the paths in the blocks so that we no longer waded through the impossible mud. There were great lessons to be learned in every block, barrack, and apartment. None of us were ever so closely confined. Doctors, scholars, wealthy business men, humble farmers, we were all thrown together, and for the first time, forced to live closely and intimately with each other. Ugly traits were forced to the fore. We were unhappy. We were bitter. We were afraid. All these intensified our difficulty to make adjustments."

For the evacuees, the "gate" at the relocation center is the symbol of hope and despair; it is also the scene of endless departures and arrivals, of welcomes and farewells. New evacuees arrive as old ones depart; visitors come and go; seasonal workers leave in groups for the sugar-beet fields and are welcomed "home" with much fanfare; Nisei soldiers, on furlough, pass in and out; volunteers depart for the army as "disloyal segregants" leave for Tule Lake (and perhaps for Japan); "repatriates" leave to meet the *Gripsholm* bound for Japan as new evacuees arrive from Hawaii. "Incorrigible trouble makers" are taken through the gate on their way to the special detention center in Leupp, Arizona, as young Nisei leave to take jobs in Boston and Chicago, Kansas City and Baltimore. Young Nisei girls, in the uniform of the WAC, arrive to visit parents who are leaving for Tule Lake. And, through the gate, comes a constant stream of "investigators": gimlet-eyed amateur sleuths from California legislative committees anxious to believe that muddy pools in the canals are "luxurious swimming plunges"; that the fare in the mess halls is the equivalent of the Santa Barbara Biltmore; and that the "white" personnel sleep every night with a new batch of Japanese girls. Through the gate come California legislators breathing death, damnation, and destruction; reporters from the Hearst press seeking to take a few "angled" photographs; pious missionaries to pray with the people; wide-eyed social workers to "deplore" and "survey." Every center has had its "blowoff" — its "incident." And in every center registration and segregation were major events.

Writes Mrs. Tsukamoto: —

The darkest days since Pearl Harbor, I remember now, to be those oppressive, stifling days of registration. We were afraid to breathe. There was a tenseness in the air. Bewilderment and confusion was at its height. People walked the roads, tears streaming down their troubled faces, silent and suffering. There were young people stunned and dazed. The little apartments were not big enough for the tremendous battle that waged in practically every room: between parents and children, between America and Japan, between those that were hurt and frustrated, but desperately trying to keep faith in America and those who were tired and old and hurt and disillusioned. Then, there was a strange hush, something was sure to snap. Then a few were attacked! We wanted to run away. There were rumors, gangs, prowlers. The outside world seemed hostile; we were falling apart within, with no where to turn! It is hard to believe that we are still living in the same camp. We all feel and look years older. We've had tears to shed every week through the spring and summer. Friends were leaving for freedom. The new friends we grew to admire and love. Then, too, there was the echo that followed registration. Over 1600 from our camp left for Tule Lake. They were ridiculed, they were cowards and quitters, they were ungrateful to this country. No, not all, only a few out of that great number were disloyal. Many had been here for over forty years. Many had never been to Japan. They haven't seen the new terrible Japan. Many were going only because there were leaders that swayed their decision. Many were forfeiting the future of their American children. There were so many fine young people that suffered, more than we will ever know, because they could not break up the family. They sacrificed this time for their parents who had sacrificed all these years for their children. Then, there were a few courageous youth, a shining symbol of true loyalty and love for this country. They endured beatings, but they were determined. There are not a few who are remaining alone, not even of age, but certain that they belong to America, and America alone. So, they parted from their family, to start life alone. . . . I will never forget the children. There was one boy, 17, who did not want to accompany his family to Tule Lake. The truck came for the family. He refused to get on the truck. He walked behind it to the train. He hugged his favorite high school teacher and refused to let her go. Finally, he said, "I'm going to return, I am an American." The train pulled out . . . how long is this nightmare to last?

For the old people, the Issei, relocation has not been as trying an experience as for the young. "The life of most of us Issei," writes Akana Imamura, "is now well spent. We stand in the evening of life where there is no hope — the hope attributed to the Phoenix which brings a new vibrant life out of the ashes of the old. We are told and encouraged to relocate again into the world as a stranger in strange communities! We now have lost all security. WRA urges readjustment, relocating outside. Where shall we go? What shall we do at the twilight of the evening of our lives?"

"I know an old man," writes Kiyoshi Okamoto from the Heart Mountain Relocation Center, "who started as a railroad laborer forty years ago. He pioneered in the fish canneries in Alaska; he contributed his mite toward the development of Imperial Valley. Then, because of an increasing family and failing health, he bought a stall in Little Tokyo and established himself as a vendor. Shortly afterwards, he underwent a major operation. . . . His fortitude and his wife's loyalty enabled them to maintain their self-respect and to contribute towards their children's education. His efforts are only one portion of a hundred and thirty million hopes and aspirations that contributed toward the commonwealth of this nation. . . . Today, he is sick in bed. He admits that he may not live until spring. He visualizes the little cemetery on the bleak hillside back of our camp, where a small dozen have already preceded him. Despite his stoicism, there is something that bothers him. He was pauperized at the time of evacuation; his children are still minors; his wife cannot earn a living. What is to become of them after this winter?"

One old Issei bachelor, James Hatsuaki Wakasa, on April 11, 1943, left his barrack at the Topaz center, and started walking toward the barbed-wire fence which surrounds the area. The soldier in the watchtower ordered him to stop; but he kept right on walking toward the fence. He was unarmed, alone; he seemed in a daze. Again he was ordered to halt; but he seemed not to hear or to understand. He was shot and killed by the sentry. There are old bachelors like that in the centers; men who have been broken by a lifetime of hard labor, utterly indifferent to what goes on around them, insensitive to pleasure or pain, not caring what goes on, not minding what happens. . . .

"This is my second evacuation," an old Issei woman told Toshiko Imamura. "You see, we lived in Yakima, Washington, for twenty-three years. We leased 160 acres of sagebrush land which we cleared and turned into green tillable acres where we raised potatoes known as Yakima Beauties. But during 1923, when the Alien Land Act was passed, we got into an awful predicament and we were done up. They threatened to blast our farmhouses and camps with dynamite. We were all tied up — we couldn't buy or sell. So we finally decided, reluctantly, to take the last step and evacuate by stealth. My husband took our four children and me with a few suitcases one day, and we came to California, leaving behind us the house, all our furniture, farm implements, sixteen domestic animals, and over three thousand tons of potatoes that were kept under the ground in an old-fashioned way of storage. We started all over again in Arroyo Grande. Nine years ago we bought twelve acres of land, but no sooner had my husband signed the paper one day when he passed away the next. There was no savings nor deposits in our account. Fear and worry overcame me and I took to bed. I lay there for days like one to whom life's cord seemed nearly snapped. I got up one morning. I felt an irresistible feeling surge within me which made me feel as strong as a man. After that time, I got up nearly every day at four o'clock in the morning, put up breakfast for my children and saw to it that they got to school. Then I went out to the field, to oversee my Filipino workers and drove the team myself, plowing and cultivating. There was always so much to do in the field, usually it was dark when I came back to the house. I made it my business to plan out what I should plant next. To do this I devoted a good deal of my time and thought. Literally, I worked hard, like a horse, and thank God, I have this year paid off the balance on the land. Two children had finished the junior college. The oldest girl got married. I began to see my way again. I had made up my mind to take a long-expected voyage back to Japan, to see my old parents and friends . . . now I am an evacuee. But this time, my second exodus was not so miserable as that of the first. I have leased my land and my personal property is in safekeeping."

4. Life in a Relocation Center

No two impressions of life in a relocation center, from the evacuee's point of view, would be the same. The centers themselves differ each from the other. Minidoka in Idaho, Topaz in Utah, and Granada in Colorado — in the order named — are "the cream of the lot." Minidoka rates highest, on all counts, and there are at least a dozen explanations of the fact. The Minidoka evacuees are better adjusted; there has been virtually no trouble. One reason suggested is that most of the evacuees in Minidoka came from Portland where they were fairly well integrated in the community prior to evacuation. The theorizing about Minidoka is fancy and profuse. Topaz has its partisans and Granada insists that it is the best of all possible centers. It is difficult, therefore, to select, from the material I have collected, documents that might be said to be typical of the reaction of the evacuees to center life. I have, however, selected two. The first was written by a Caucasian observer about the Heart Mountain Relocation Center in Wyoming. It gives the "dark side" of the story. The other document was written by a Nisei friend of mine, S. J. Oki. It refers to the Topaz center, in Utah, and is the most objective document of the kind that I have seen. First, then, the story from Wyoming: —

As the first light breaks the darkness, the roosters of a concentration camp suddenly come to life. First one, then another, then a chorus of dishpans rattle and clatter the call to breakfast. It is partly clouded, and the deep pink in the Eastern sky suddenly gives way as the whole heavens blaze. The eyes are pulled up and up, above the drab barracks and the drab countryside, to this spectacle of the Great Plains. The color dies as quickly as it had lived. For a moment the whole world is gray, and then the sun catches the snow on the mountains to the southeast.

Inside the black barracks the people stir. Some groan and

206

roll over. Others push back the covers and slip quickly into their clothes. Grabbing towel and toothbrush, they go outdoors where the bits of snow and ice crunch under their feet. "Cold," they say to one another, and hurry towards the warmth of the latrines. Soon they are lining up to get their breakfast: grapefruit, cold cereal, french toast, coffee.

As the sunlight reaches the camp, a bell on one of the barracks starts ringing and the kids come down to school. Lacking a schoolhouse, they sit in barracks all day, many on benches without backs, sharing textbooks because there aren't enough to go around. The teachers try to get along under the primitive conditions, finding their classes noisy because the partitions separating the rooms are flimsy and don't go up to the roof.

Over in the Administration Building the block administrators get together for their daily meeting. Appointed by the WRA, this group is all-Nisei. It carries out the minor functions of government, takes the complaints of the people to the Administration. Like any governing body that doesn't have much power, its members sit and smoke and appoint committees. The Issei, who are not eligible to be block administrators, serve on a block council. And the people laugh, and call the block administrators stooges and the block council blockheads, for they know who really runs the government.

Out in a corridor two Caucasian members of the Administration talk with each other about the colonists. Unlike the Army which ordered the evacuation, most of the WRA staff want to see the Japanese really relocated. One of these men is from Washington and tells how well former colonists who have gone out under student relocation have fared. He hopes the WRA will work on public opinion so that more and more colonists can go out. And the Administrators are tall, clean-cut, Caucasians who are rather embarrassed because they know as well as any one the difference between voluntary partnership and coercion.

And two of the people overhear a snatch of their conversation as they pass, and one mutters: "Colonists! Jesus Christ! I wonder if they call tigers pussy cats?"

As the morning goes on, the sun becomes warmer and

now it falls full on the ground which forms the streets and the spaces between the barracks. The puddles of water which have been frozen hard all night long begin to melt. When a boot lands on them, they crack and break, and muddy water spurts up over the toe of the boot. Then the millions of little frozen water particles in the earth that had been holding the ground firm and hard, these too begin to melt, and the ground softens. As the sun continues to shine on it and the people to walk over it, it becomes muddy. The people's feet get wet and dirty whenever they step outside a building.

Two Nisei girls walking across the camp jump and slide in the mud, and try to keep in the shade of the barracks where the ground is still firm. They are social workers. Social workers in a place like this? What does a social worker do to prevent juvenile delinquency when kids are suddenly jerked from normal life to this? Recreation? When there's no item in the budget for recreational material and the recreation halls are even used as offices? Education? When they promise us school buildings and good equipment and we don't get them? Worthwhile work? When the majority of the jobs they give us are so meaningless that most of the kids act as if they were doing time?

How can you teach democracy in a concentration camp? Or praise American labor standards where people get $4 for a 44-hour week, and nothing for overtime? Or talk about racial equality when the Caucasians on the WRA staff are setting up a whole Jim Crow system of their own? Lookit these little boys. They used to worship football players. Remember when you were a little kid, how every little boy had a hero? Now they follow the toughest gang leaders, and the gangs get tougher and fight one another and steal lumber. New gangs are formed, and they look at the girls more often . . . lookit that girl, most gregarious damn person I ever saw. But even she needs to be off alone sometimes — but she never can. We're not individuals here, but cogs that eat and sleep and work and live all alike. Lookit that Mother — she used to be the core of her family, providing the meals, training her children, those little things that build a family unity. Now other people throw food at us, the kids no longer

208

eat with the parents, but learn their manners from the rough-necks, run wild most of the time.

I read in a paper how a minister said we oughta be satisfied because we are being well-fed and housed and given a chance to work. Is that all living means to that guy? Is life just getting your belly filled and a hoe put in your hands? Betcha that same fellow talks a lot about liberty and spiritual values when he's thinking about Hitler. . . .

The people have learned to laugh at the things that hurt them most. Whenever anyone mentions that they may stay here permanently, "like Indians on a reservation," everyone always laughs. But they do not think the subject of Indian reservations is funny.

And they tell me about the two washrooms at the Pomona center. Over the big washroom was a sign which read: "Caucasian Administrative Staff Only" and over the little washroom, "Japanese Administrative Staff Only."

Then there's the story about the Caucasian history teacher who told her class: "Today we will study the Constitution." And the class laughed and tittered so that they never did.

And the people who have been hurt make cracks about the number of Jews on the WRA staff, and they say to one another: "Did you see the two new Hebes who are here?" And they make disparaging remarks about Negroes, and point to the economic degradation of the Mexicans.

In the afternoon many persons crowd into the "Court-house" for a public forum. The Niseis who run it have hope-fully hung a sign which proclaims Voltaire's famous statement about free speech. Toward the end of the speech a Caucasian walks in, and one woman whispers to another: "Here comes an administrative stooge. Now we can't say anything." But the other, sizing the newcomer up, disagrees: "Naw, he's only a kid high school teacher."

The discussion begins, and the chairman is nervous. He wants it to be a frank discussion to satisfy the people, but is scared of future censorship if it gets out of hand. A tall, lean fellow with a goatee rises again and again. "Are you going to participate in this camp government? Do you still think you're citizens of this country? Do you have the rights of citizens? Isn't the government just going to coddle you and make you into another bunch of people on an Indian reservation? Or will they ship you all back to Japan? What sort of jobs could you get if you could go outside? What are you, citizens or Japs? Or, are you donkeys?"

The fears that lurk in the people have been touched, and they stir nervously. The chairman raps for order. A block administrative officer jumps up: "I read in a novel once where Kathleen Norris or someone said a man and his wife with chickens could live on the prairie happily as in New York City. We've got plenty of prairie here. All we need is the chickens!"

The crowd roars, the chairman relaxes a little, the talk goes on and the Niseis ask each other about Nisei problems and discuss "Japanese-American Salvation" as if the Japanese-American problem was the only problem in an otherwise unimportant world.

It is Hallowe'en evening, and across the camp are many parties. In the mess-halls, gay streamers enliven the walls, and the people crowd together as the orchestra comes in. Ten Nisei boys, each wearing a red-and-black checked flannel shirt, and a girl at the piano, start to play remarkably good music. But no one dances. Finally a boy says to a girl: "Hell! Let's dance!" The ice is broken, and the floor is suddenly jammed with couples dancing or watching a hot jitterbug exhibition. People laugh and joke and a boy says to a girl he is dancing with: "I almost forgot where I am!" "I never do," the girl replies, as the smile goes from her face.

What will these camps produce? Out of them can come great leaders and prophets. Men and women of great faith and great patience, blazing new paths in overcoming racial prejudice. Will hardship burn and temper their faith and make it strong?

The people do not know. In one of the barracks, a late bull session is going on around the warm stove. "It's too easy," said one boy. "We get food, there's no rent to pay, the routine is deadening. Everything leads to a degenerative life instead of an invigorating one. Everyone is grabbing for himself. We grab the coal, grab bits of wood lying around, grab for clothing allotments, grab our food. No wonder the little kids are getting so that they do it too, and think only of themselves. No wonder we're apathetic and ingrown."

The people walk quickly home through the sharp cold of the night. The ground is hard under their feet along the brightly-lighted streets and alleys. From a thousand chimneys the harsh coal smoke tries to rise, curls under the weight of the cold air, and settles like a blanket close to the ground. A train whistle sounds in the darkness. Music comes from a guard tower where a bored soldier listens to the radio. From the floodlights an arc of light surrounds the camp.[1]

S. J. Oki, who wrote the following statement, is a "premature anti-fascist." I have known him for years, long prior to evacuation. A young man, he is at present serving in the language school at Boulder, Colorado. The following statement was written while he was at the Topaz Relocation Center. It is entitled "Notes on What They Think."

Objectively, and on the whole, life in a relocation center is not unbearable. There are dust-storms and mud. Housing is inadequate, with families of six living in single rooms in many cases. Food is below the standard set for prisoners of war. In some of the camps hospitals are at times understaffed and supplies meager, as in many ordinary communities. Yet while Mr. Ata, former San Francisco importer, complains of the low quality of the food, Mrs. Baito, widow of a San Joaquin farmer, is grateful for what the United States government is doing to make life as comfortable as possible for the evacuees. In short, no one is pampered and at the same time no one is starving or sick because of neglect on the part of the War Relocation Authority.

What is not so bearable lies much deeper than the physical make-up of a center. It is seen in the face of Mr. Yokida, 65, a Montebello farmer. It is seen in the face of Mrs. Wata, 50, a grocer's widow from Long Beach. It is seen in the face of little John Zendo, 9, son of an Oakland restaurant owner. It is seen in the face of Mary Uchido, former sophomore from UCLA and the daughter of a Little Tokyo merchant.

[1] NOTE: This document is dated November 6, 1942.

It is seen in the face of Sus Tana, young *kibei* who had been an employee in a vegetable stand in Hollywood.

Their faces look bewildered as they stare at the barbed-wire fences and sentry towers that surround the camp. Their eyes ask: Why? Why? What is all this?

Kats Ento, serious-looking ex-farmer from Norwalk, has made up his mind. He says: "I am an American citizen. I was born and brought up in California. I have never been outside the United States, and I don't know Japan or what Japan stands for. But because my parents weren't considerate enough to give me blue eyes, reddish hair, and a high nose, I am here, in camp, interned without the formality of a charge, to say nothing of a trial. Does the Constitution say that only white men are created equal? Put me down as disloyal, if you will, but I'm going where I won't have to live the rest of my life on the wrong side of the tracks just because my face is yellow. Keep me in camp for the duration. I will find my future in the Orient."

Mrs. Jones, elementary school teacher appointed by the WRA, sighs as she looks towards the little children in shabby but clean clothes. "To be frank with you, it embarrasses me to teach them the flag salute. *Is* our nation indivisible? Does it stand for justice for all? Those questions come up to my mind constantly."

Mr. Yokida, technically an enemy alien after forty years' continuous residence in California, appears tired. "For forty years I worked in central and southern California. I remember when Los Angeles was only a small town compared to San Francisco. This country never gave me citizenship, but I never went back to Japan and I have no interests there. The evacuation has worked a hardship on me and my family, but I suppose in time of war you have to stand for a lot of hardships. Don't ask me what I think of Japan or about the incident at Pearl Harbor. I don't know. What I know is that this is my country, and I have given my only son to its army. I wrote him just the other day, telling him to obey his commander-in-chief without reserve. I have worked as long as anyone and I am satisfied. The only thing I think about is my son. I hope that he will make good in the army. I hope that he will come back to me as a captain, at least."

"I have a son in the army too," says Mrs. Wata. "Besides, my daughter has volunteered to join the WAACS. I am an alien, and being an alien I have nothing to say about evacuation or about having to live in camp, although it would have been so nice to have spent the last winter in Long Beach. It was so cold here, and the stove in my apartment never gave out enough heat. I do wish, though, that they would let my children go back to California on furloughs. They have so many friends out there, and they miss them."

John Zendo, 9, is always talking about his friends, too, says his mother. "He was a pretty popular boy in the neighborhood," she smiles reminiscently as she speaks. "He talks about them all the time, and asks me when we can go back to them. When we were in Oakland, Johnny used to bring all his friends to our restaurant — Mexicans, Chinese, and white children — and my husband used to give each of them a dish of ice cream. Poor Johnny, he talks about such things every day."

"I keep on thinking about Los Angeles and the people I know," says Mary Uchido, an attractive girl of twenty. "My girl friend writes me and tells me all about the changes that have taken place since evacuation. How the Little Tokyo has been left unoccupied, how some of our Chinese and Korean friends are working in airplane factories, things like that. But I don't want to go back there any more, except perhaps for a visit. Yes, my father is in internment, but I don't think about him much. Maybe he will go to Japan the next time there is a boat, but I am going to stay here. We will try to relocate, of course. Maybe I will try to get a domestic job or something, because I can't possibly hope to continue my education. I would join the WAACS if they would put us in an ordinary unit instead of an all-Japanese unit."

Sus Tana, 32, is a volunteer for the special Japanese-American combat team. He smiles broadly and seems jolly, but his dark eyebrows betray an uneasiness which is concealed somewhat behind his sunburned forehead. "I am a kibei and a Young Democrat. I lived and worked in Los Angeles nine years after my return from Japan. I never made over a hundred dollars a month, mostly seventy-five to eighty, and I could never save enough money to buy anything. So when evacuation came, I had nothing to lose. I do miss my friends among the Young Democrats, though. They were such a fine bunch. You forgot you were a Jap when you were with them; you were just an American fighting for the President and the New Deal. I do wish I could be back there now. Maybe I could get a defense job and do what I can. But I am glad that we are going to have a combat unit. Maybe I can show the reactionaries in California that a Japanese-American can be just as good a soldier as any American — if not better."

Tana's best friend is Mr. Osaka, 40. He, too, is a kibei, but his English is good. They call him a Red, because he is an anti-fascist. He has been against Japanese imperialism for years, and for that reason he led a poverty-stricken life for twenty years among the Japanese-American communities in California where the Japanese consuls and fascist-minded officials of the Japanese chambers of commerce held a dominant position until the outbreak of the war. Osaka is a man of few words, except when he is aroused by a challenging topic. And now he speaks out: "They call me a Red, but I am only a democrat with a small *d*. In fact I am quite opposed to the way in which Communists seem to be doing things, and I have tried to make it clear a number of times. Yet there are people here, even people in administrative positions, who resort to name-calling in order to defend their 19th-century opinions against progressive ideas. While they denounce anti-Japanese racism, they themselves are anti-Semitic, anti-Negro, and anti-Mexican. What do I think of evacuation? I don't believe there is a single right-minded Japanese-American who didn't feel the necessity of evacuating some, though I personally think the government could have saved a tremendous sum of money and much manpower if they had tried selective evacuation. Post-war? If we can win the war for democracy, then we Japanese-Americans will be in a very fortunate and unique position of being able to choose one of the two courses for our future: remain in a fully democratized America or go to a defeated but popularly-controlled Japan to help construct a democratic Japan. There is no use talking about compensation. Wars require sacrifices.

Draftees don't talk about the constitutionality of the draft act, and they don't complain when they are 'evacuated' from their homes into army camps. Everything must be concentrated on winning the war if we are to see the race-caste system destroyed in America as well as elsewhere."

Mr. Osaka smiles as he reads this passage from a pamphlet: "The color of one's skin is a permanent, immutable characteristic, while habits of dress, speech, or action can be modified and outgrown. An Americanized foreigner with an adopted name can pass completely into the dominant society as long as his skin is white and his features are not pronounced. An American of a different color is always apart. . . ."

Always apart?

"No, not always," says Mr. Osaka.

5. To the Beet Fields

Beginning in the fall of 1942, hundreds and later thousands of evacuees were released, on seasonal leaves, to relieve the manpower shortage in agriculture, particularly in the sugar-beet areas of the inter-mountain West. The experience represented, for the evacuees involved, their first taste of "freedom" in long months — although they were subject to certain restrictions. "I can't make much money," writes one sugar-beet worker, "but the idea of being a 'free' man and eating the things you like — the way you like them — is mighty fine." While they were paid the prevailing wages for the different types of work involved, the evacuees nevertheless realized that they were in effect on parole. "We are aware," writes one, "that we must not do or say anything or go anywhere that might incite antagonism. Therefore we are avoiding public places, such as restaurants, bowling alleys, and theaters. We are avoiding being obvious. For our responsibility is to pave the way for those to come." The universal praise that they evoked from employers, the fact that no "incidents" resulted and that the seasonal-leave program involved 15,000 or 16,000 evacuees, are tributes to their ability to make themselves inconspicuous and to their tact and good judgment.

I have before me a stack of reports, written by evacuees,

about their experiences while on seasonal leaves. They are written from beet fields, from potato fields, from carrot fields, from turkey farms, and from many types of camps. They describe very bad working conditions, tolerable working conditions, and good working conditions. The variety of impressions encountered makes generalization impossible. Many letters testify to the kindliness of the Mormon people in Utah. "The people are very friendly," writes one evacuee. "They seem to be our kind of people." . . . "The people are very polite and amiable," writes another (also from Utah); "for the first time in a long while I had a sense of freedom. To walk and to look at the streets of an American town — that was quite a feeling." In the main, I believe the seasonal-leave program built up, in most of the evacuees, a sense of self-confidence; it made them feel, once again, part of America. It encouraged thousands of them to apply for permanent leaves. Obviously working in the sugar-beet fields is no lark. "Our living quarters," writes one evacuee, "are very primitive; oil-lamp, wood-burning stove, no bath or shower, an old bed with hay mattress and a broken leg; and a stinking outhouse filled with dried hay." Working in the frosty mornings, in the heat of midday, in the whipping winds of evening that tear across the inter-mountain flatlands, they managed to average not more than $3.00 to $4.50 a day. But to most of them the experience seems to have been a profound relief from the monotony of life in a relocation center. "As we got up this chilly morning," one of them writes, "we noticed the quiet, serene atmosphere of this valley community. A typical rural community with large barns stacked high with golden hay. The valley is bounded on all sides by high green hills as though to shelter it from the outside world. Our little shack is surrounded by tall poplars and cedars with leaves turning yellow in the autumn sun. The hills on the east are tinted by yellowing leaves of the Box Elder, reddening leaves of the Maple, and the golden colors of the Sarsaparilla. As we three slowly hiked toward the fields, countless grasshoppers sprayed the ground before us. We followed the winding irrigation canal, just day-dreaming along. My mind is much clearer and my appetite has grown quite ravenous. I give my personal recommendation that this valley will cure nervous breakdowns and other mental ailments that center people are susceptible to or have incurred through long confinement and boredom." There is no doubt that the psychological success of the seasonal-leave program, as well as its admitted economic success, encouraged WRA to go forward with the program for permanent relocation.

6. California Interlude

Not many evacuees have returned to California since they were removed. Some Nisei soldiers on furlough have returned; and a few have been permitted to return for short business trips or to attend sessions of court. Mrs. Cecil Itano returned to Los Angeles in October, 1943, to survey the damage caused when vandals broke into the Nichiren Church in Los Angeles and wantonly destroyed personal property which the evacuees had stored in the church. "As we neared Los Angeles," she writes, "many familiar landmarks brought faint nostalgia of former happier occasions. After registering at the hotel, I had a chance to glance around. The Los Angeles that I knew is no more. Everything has changed. On October 11th, 1943, we went out to view the Nichiren Church. The catastrophe before my eyes was a hopeless mass of deliberate destruction. Everything was a conglomeration of unrecoverable damaged things. Nothing was untouched, sewing machines were ruined, furniture broken, mirrors smashed to smithereens, broken glass from breakable articles, household goods scattered helter-skelter, trunks broken beyond repair, albums, pictures, precious only to the respective owners, thrown to the four winds. It had been like a dream, returning to the California that is so dear to my heart. Standing among this debris of disreverent damage, I thought, could this unwarrantable plundering have been averted if we had not been slandered by a propaganda depicting us as a despicable and undesirable race? My only hope is that such pilfering will be stopped before malice gnaws too deeply in our hearts."

7. From a Nisei Soldier

Not all of the Nisei in our armed services are in the special combat team. Quite a few are serving with other units. I have a letter from one of these. Although he spent one or two years in Japan, this man is not considered a Kibei by the authorities. He enlisted in the Army immediately after Pearl Harbor. "I was taken to a camp in California," he writes, "for my basic training. I spent a few months there, and then came evacuation. There weren't more than a dozen or so Nisei in our camp. We were kept there until April, 1942, when we were all gathered together and brought here, to Camp X. There are a couple of hundred Nisei here, all brought from different states. Shortly after we arrived, we were disarmed; we turned in our guns and were assigned to service jobs, mess hall details and such. I suppose they think we are not exactly to be trusted. Remember the time President Roosevelt went around to different camps for inspection? He came to our place, too, and that morning, a short time before his arrival, they put us Nisei in a garage, surrounded us with machine guns and armed officers, and kept us there under guard until he left. That's when our morale really went down. If we are dangerous, why don't they tell us we are dangerous? Why don't they courtmartial us or something? Why don't they discharge us? I'll never forget that it was *after* this evacuation rumpus in California that I was segregated from the rest of the American soldiers. I don't want any part of California as long as I live. I'd rather be in a country where nobody talks about democracy or dictatorship or anything, where people just work to make a living. Of course, I'd like to stay here. I like America better than any country. But how can I ever change my face? Tell me that."

8. Two Trains

During the period of segregation, when the "disloyal" segregants were being taken to Tule Lake and the loyal Tuleans were being distributed among the other centers, I received many interesting comments from residents in the centers. None of these comments, however, is as graphic as this brief note which appeared in the *Minidoka Irrigator:*—

The train that came from Tule met the train going to Tule at a junction. The occupants looked at each other, but no conversation was possible. They were patterned from the same genus, skin and hair color. Many of them were Japanese-Americans. They shared typical American lives, knew the love for slang, coke and hamburgers. The Issei nursed the earth, they did their bit in the making of the United States into one of the greatest industrial nations in the world. They lived, loved, and laughed in the cosmopolitanism that is America.

But yet a Himalayan wall of psychological difference placed the groups in two tragically distinctive categories.

One group, a tragic picture of lost faith, had bowed to the desire to walk down a metropolitan street and see faces with the same structure and color; they had swayed to a longing to walk through life free of prejudiced glances. But all of them had left their lives strewn in memorable bits around the country they loved. In the rusting plow in the barn back on the Coast, in the baby willow planted on the river bank, in the carved initials on the drug store counter at Bill's, in the basketball championship trophy displayed at the High with the lone Japanese name inscribed on it, in the waving apple orchard in the dip of the valley. . . .

The other group chose to go back to that drug store counter, to urge on once more the plow, to add another name to the trophy, to nurse the willow to be a stalwart bulwark. They heard and answered defiantly the challenge in every doubting look of other Americans. They chose to fight and extinguish the ugly red light of discrimination. They chose to fight until democracy was real.

9. On the Relocation Centers

While generally endorsing the program of WRA and commending its policies, the evacuees *as a group* feel the relocation experience itself is irredeemably bad. Even those who, for a variety of reasons, are opposed to individual relocation outside the centers (for the duration of the war) echo the same sentiments about the centers. "In the relocation centers," writes Franklyn Sugiyama, "the people are like fish dynamited — they are helplessly stunned, floating belly up on the stream of life." . . . "The most terrible factor concerning camp life," writes Frank Watanabe, "is the havoc this uneasy, restricted and enclosed life is working upon the young people's character and personality. Many of the youngsters are growing up in this environment knowing very little about the outside. Consequently, their ideas, their outlook upon life have changed greatly. Many are bitter towards the outside society while others are just indifferent. It's just not an ordinary healthy environment. Parent-child relationships are broken down in many cases. Discipline is neglected because the parents in many cases have lost faith in themselves as well as in this country. Initiative, individual assurance and the will to succeed have been lost in the desert sands just as water evaporates in its intense heat. Even educated men and women in a few cases have gotten this 'devil-may-care' attitude and it sure hasn't helped matters very much." Those who have remained in the centers are becoming overcautious, more timid, highly race-conscious. Their world tends to grow smaller, not larger; and it was a small airless world to begin with. They lose perspective; they become Rip Van Winkles, out of touch with the world, with the nation, with the people.

"The shock that we sustained," writes Hanna Kozasa, "and the bitterness that overwhelmed us was most trying. The barbed wire fences, the armed sentries, the observation towers, increased our sense of frustration to the point that many have not been able to regain a proper perspective. The most alarming aspect of life in the centers is the demoralization it is working in the people. It is sapping their initiative in a frightening manner. The forced labor, with its low pay, indecent housing, inadequate food, the insecurity of their position in a post-war America, have contributed to a deterioration of family life that is beginning to show in a sharply increased juvenile delinquency — this among a people that had the lowest crime rate of any group in the United States." . . . "Evacuation," writes Howard Imazeki, "distorted the life philosophy of the Japanese-Americans and their parents. It completely warped the perspective of the majority of the Nisei in its earlier stage. They are, however, slowly recovering from this initial impact." . . . "The wounds both physical and spiritual," writes an Issei woman, "caused by the tragic evacuation have begun to heal. Some are beginning to have vision enough to think about the future."

As the relocation program itself has moved forward, more and more of the evacuees (a clear majority of the Nisei) are inclined to regard evacuation itself as "past history." Letter after letter speaks of "evacuation as a thing of the past." Had it not been for the prompt adoption by WRA of the present release or relocation program, I am convinced that little or nothing could have been salvaged from the program itself. The moment the possibility of relocation was offered the evacuees, "the tragedy of evacuation" began to recede. If WRA is permitted to continue this program, evacuation will soon become merely a memory for most of them. One observation should, however, be made on this score: not more than one per cent of the evacuees believe or have ever believed that evacuation was ordered as a matter of military necessity or that it was, in fact, justified. The only Nisei who have taken the position that the measure was justified are a handful of individuals holding pronounced anti-fascist views. With scarcely a single exception, the Nisei believe that evacuation was brought about by race bigots in California and that they were singled out for removal by reason of the color of their skins and the slant of their eyes. This is a factor which must be taken into account in any appraisal of the entire program. In the eyes of the evacuees, however, as expressed by Joe Koide, "the very boldness with which the American government has endeavored to rectify this wrong *while the war is still going on* is a tribute to American democracy." More is involved in the relocation program than the economic and social rehabilitation of

100,000 people. It is equally important to see that they are psychologically rehabilitated and that their somewhat shaken faith in American democracy is fully restored.

There were about 20,000 Japanese who resided outside the Western Defense Command and who were never involved in the relocation program. Needless to say, they have watched this program with the most intense interest. Typical of their attitude toward evacuation is this excerpt from a letter which I received from Tsuyoski Matsumoto: —

Fortunately, I had left the Pacific coast before the outbreak of the war and was elsewhere when the mass evacuation took place. Therefore, I have gone through this historic event only vicariously. To me, the evacuation came as a shock, a sobering eye-opener of the blind worshipper of America that I had been, a wound in the heart. I was shocked because America failed to live up to her professed principles of democracy, and the decent and humane manner in which the authorities carried out the evacuation does not in my mind erase the blunder the nation at large committed against the Japanese immigrants and their descendants. I am made to feel like a fool before 100,000,000 Japanese subjects in Japan who now have a good reason to question the sincerity and moral integrity of this Republic. This is a wound in my heart, because I love this country for what she is. I still love her.

I am being comforted by the fact that, despite the blunder, the government of the United States has been quick to correct its own mistakes and is sincere in trying to bring justice to all people. I have fully recovered from the initial shock and can now proudly point to my fellow slave-like brethren in the world outside and say that a democracy like the United States of America is not perfect in the sight of God but is surely better than any other form of government man has ever known or tried. As for the future of the Japanese-Americans in this country, I have no doubt that both they and their fellow citizens of Caucasian blood can work out a democratic solution. If not, I will be damned!

10. Back to America

Today most of the talk in the centers is about "relocation." "Relocation," as one evacuee phrases it, "is in the air." For most of them, the past year has been largely given over to a debate — to relocate or not to relocate; but thousands are now preparing to leave. They are making plans now for their return to normal society; for their return, as they phrase it, "back to America." They are quite clearheaded about the risks they will run; about the unforeseeable factors involved. But some are leaving the centers every day and others are packing their belongings, once again, for still another phase in this curious cross-country trek. You are likely to see them on the trains; inclined to be shy, highly self-conscious, and endeavoring to "make themselves inconspicuous." The first leg of the journey, they report, is the most trying. It is that initial experience on the train that they fear most. Rather to their astonishment, they quickly discover that few questions are asked; few incidents arise, few people stare. Soon they begin to feel, as one of them writes, "like a human being. You begin to forget that you are of Japanese ancestry, or any other ancestry, and remember only that you are an American." They are stepping from trains and buses, throughout America, "leaving the dust of relocation centers behind," as Larry Tajiri writes, "and returning to the broad boulevards, the movie palaces and the sky-scrapers of America. From Topaz and Minidoka, from Rivers and Poston, from Heart Mountain and Granada, from the California and Arizona camps, from all the giant 'Little Tokyos' of war relocation, the exiles of evacuation are returning to the free lives of ordinary Americans."

They are not coming back into the stream of American life with any unseen chips on their shoulders; nor are they harboring any grudges against their fellow Americans. Most of them sincerely *want* to forget about the entire experience of evacuation. All they ask, as George Yasukochi writes, "is to be treated as individuals — as fellow Americans and not as problem children to be cried over and pitied. They are willing to be judged on individual merit — whether the Japanese-American unit fighting on Italian terrain covers itself with glory, or whether the Tule Lake segregants riot in shame — for as individuals they are then judged on what they are. They wish to be grouped with Tojo no more than LaGuardia would with Mussolini. Unfortunately a large number of Americans simply cannot digest the idea that a person with dissimilar physical characteristics may speak perfect English, may possess American ideologies and yearnings, and be an ordinary human being." They are not inclined to regard themselves self-pityingly as "victims of injustice." "Evacuation," writes Eddie Shimano, "is no more important than the poll tax in its denial of American rights. Only the theatrical suddenness and the immediate personal tragedies of it, together with the fact that it was the Federal government which decreed it, plus its relation to the war, make it seem so important. The denial of Constitutional rights in the practice of the poll tax affects more American citizens than did the evacuation."

"The Nisei," to quote again from a letter by George Yasu-kochi, "are ahead of their first generation parents in American ways and thought and speech. And even in wartime America, the Nisei face more favorable public opinion than their parents did three decades ago, as far as the country east of the Sierras is concerned. So long as the Nisei do not attempt to entrench themselves economically in conspicuous fashion, they will avoid the treacherous attacks of jealous reactionary groups. The Nisei thus must forge ahead as individuals rather than as a group so that they will be assimilated into the main stream of American society — continuing to offer whatever cultural gifts and understanding they can transmit from the Oriental to the Occidental civilization. The Nisei can be Americans pure and simple and discard the Nisei label." (They are already doing this in their determined effort to avoid being called "American-Japanese" or "Japanese-Americans," referring to themselves frequently as "AJ's" or "AJA's.") "An imperative 'must' for the Nisei is to realize that their own problem is but a back scratch in the great problem of American democracy — to unite peaceably all people of different races, backgrounds, creeds and ideologies in a progressive society. The Nisei should give full support to all publications and all organizations working on behalf of democracy — political, social and economic — for all. They must fight the insidious press that tries to use them as scapegoats, as they will protest the grossly unfair action of the Navy in closing educational institutions to the Nisei while its left hand recruits the same Nisei to teach language to its cadets in those institutions. But they must defend with equal vigor attacks upon the rights of the Negroes, Catholics or Labor. The complacent pleasures of their own society are not to serve as sands into which the Nisei may duck their heads ostrich-like, nor is the sight of their own problem to blind them into thinking the universe revolves about them. The Nisei, like everyone else in the country today, must be thinking how to promote the democratic well being of America."

"Several months ago," writes Robert Hosokawa from Independence, Missouri, "my wife and I were permitted to leave a WRA center and to pursue the normal life with freedom and responsibility which waited beyond the barbed wire and watchtowers of the mono-racial wartime community. We have settled in a suburban community close to one of the great Midwest cities. We have tried to be honest and diligent. We have tried to carry our loads as Americans, who want foremost to help win the war. We have made friends and have established ourselves fairly well. We are hopeful of the future and we will jealously fight for the perpetuation of true American ideals, opposing all the pseudo-democrats. During the months of confinement, our minds lived in the future — not in the past — hoping, planning, dreaming and thinking. The freedom we had always taken for granted — as most Americans still do — began to take on deep meaning when we had been deprived of it. There were times when we began to lose faith in ourselves and our ability to take it. Life in the camps was not easy. It was inadequate and morale-killing. But never in those months did we lose faith in America. Sometimes we were bitterly disappointed and enraged when we read the lies, distortions and testimony of un-American politicians and false patriots. If the government gives genuine backing to make a success of the plan for widespread resettlement, then the heartaches, losses and hardships will be partly compensated. If this fails, if Americans with Japanese faces are cast aside as unassimilables, as creatures to be shipped across to the land of their ancestors, despite their citizenship, then American democracy may as well throw in the towel. For what happens to one minority group will happen to another and the four freedoms will be enjoyed by only those powerful enough to keep it from the others. Now the Nisei are knocking at the door, asking to be admitted."

11. The Sansei

In the centers is a group of American citizens that not even the Dies Committee has honored with much attention. This group is made up of the Sansei, or third generation, American-born of American-born parents (there is also a small *fourth* generation). There are several thousand of these youngsters in the centers; many of them have now spent two years in the "giant Little Tokyos" that are the relocation centers — attending school with other dark-skinned, black-haired youngsters, associating exclusively with Japanese and Japanese-Americans, and becoming highly conscious of their racial ancestry. Several hundred of them have been born in relocation centers. It was to one of these Sansei, her son in fact, that Ellen Kiskiyama wrote these lines: —

TO MY SON, ARTHUR

Listen my son, now that you are older, Mother wants you to understand why your only friends are the sanseis and why your only home is the barrack — why you eat in the mess halls and why you don't ride the street cars, busses and automobiles.

When Dad and Mother found out you were coming to live with us, we started making big plans for a most hearty welcome. Like most new parents, we looked forward to your arrival and talked to our friends about you.

One Sunday we were, as usual, enjoying a late breakfast

and listening to the radio. All of a sudden, unbelievably, we heard the tragic news of Pearl Harbor. Even to this day, Mother can vividly recall that day when our Caucasian friends dropped in to assure us of their friendship and to tell us not to worry.

And so we began changing our plans. We sacrificed the new car, the lovely gas range, the refrigerator, the vacuum cleaner, the rugs, sofa and all the rest of the household furnishings. Dad had a wonderful collection of rare tropical fish, complete with electric motor for light and filtering and we used to talk about how much you would enjoy watching the Angel Fish, the gapies, Black Molly, Scavenger and snails. But we had to leave it all behind. Mother, too, had more than forty dolls collected from China, Korea, Manchuria, Hawaii, etc. Little by little our home was broken up and all the fancy dreams we planned for you had to be altered.

The well-established business had to be left behind. We had also planned for you to have a good college education, so we began laying aside a definite sum. Each week Mother went to the bank and bought war bonds until one day in May, 1942, when we were moved to the Pomona Assembly Center.

Preparations for moving added to worry and anxiety somehow taxed your Mother's burden and ten days after we were inducted in the center you, my son, came so unexpectedly that we caused the Center Hospital Staff quite some excitement. "First Jap Baby Swells Center Population" was the headline in the Pomona newspapers.

Two weeks later we were back in the screenless, dusty barrack. We were so afraid to even handle you, for you didn't weigh more than four pounds. After three months of California sunshine, the whole camp was moved still further inland — this time to Wyoming.

Being a camp baby, we had no baby picture of you until a news photographer snapped one on your 100th day — and that is the only picture we have of you.

Listen, son, did you know you have an Uncle who is serving in the United States Army? He is the one who keeps you supplied with toys. And you have never met your cousins who are in camps in Manzanar, Poston, Gila, and Minidoka.

Some day soon, we hope, we will all be able to get together for a grand reunion.

Your first Christmas was observed in camp, and Mother took you to see the nice Santa Claus and the colored lights and the prettily decorated tree. You with your tiny friends had a merry time and received your gift from Santa.

And so each day rolled into weeks and weeks into months and months into years —

You look tired and sleepy now, my son. Go to sleep and dream of the glorious future we will plan together. Good night, my son, Arthur.

Arthur is a "camp baby" living in a center; but Joyce is the six-year-old daughter of a Nisei couple living in Boulder, Colorado. "The other day," her father writes, "Joyce came home from school and said: 'Mommy, I want to be a real American.' When she was assured that she is an American, she repeated: 'But I want to be a real one.' The implication is clear. If Joyce were much older than she is now I'm confident that I could reason with her and give her consolation, not of course an apology for her having Japanese blood, but in terms of humanity and the universe and Americanism. I might perhaps point out the cultural heritage of her race and the country of her birth. But all these things are beyond her imagination now. If you were in my shoes, how would you explain this deep and disturbing question to your daughter?"

12. A Young Patriot Writes Mr. Stimson

February 4, 1943

SECRETARY OF WAR STIMSON
WASHINGTON, D.C.

DEAR MR. STIMSON:

I know you are a very busy man and I hate to bother you like this when you are busy in more important matters.

This is just a simple plea that comes from within my heart, crying for someone to listen.

I was very happy when I read your announcement that

Nisei Americans would be given a chance to volunteer for active combat duty. But at the same time I was sad — sad because under your present laws I am an enemy alien. I am a 22-year old boy, American in thought, American in act, as American as any other citizen. I was born in Japan. My parents brought me to America when I was only two years old. Since coming to America as an infant, my whole life was spent in New Mexico. My only friends were Caucasian boys.

At Pearl Harbor, my pal Curly Moppins was killed outright without a chance to fight back when the Japanese planes swooped down in a treacherous attack. And Dickie Harrell and other boys from my home town came back maimed for life. Then more of my classmates volunteered — Bud Henderson, Bob and Jack Aldridge, and many others; they were last heard of as missing in the Philippines. It tears my heart out to think that I could not avenge their deaths.

The law of this country bars me from citizenship — because I am an Oriental — because my skin is yellow. This is not a good law and bad laws could be changed.

But this is not what I want to bring up at this time. As you well know, this is a people's war. The fate of the free people all over the world hangs in the balance. I only ask that I be given a chance to fight to preserve the principles that I have been brought up on and which I will not sacrifice at any cost. Please give me a chance to serve in your armed forces.

In volunteering for active combat duty, my conscience will be clear and I can proudly say to myself that I wasn't sitting around, doing nothing when the fate of the free people was at stake.

Any of my Caucasian friends would vouch for my loyalty and sincerity. Even now some of them may be sleeping an eternal sleep in a lonely grave far away from home, dying for the principles they loved and sincerely believed.

I am not asking for any favors or sympathy. I only ask that I be given a chance — a chance to enlist for active combat duty. How can a democratic nation allow a technicality of birthplace to stand in the way when the nation is fighting . . . to preserve the rights of free men?

The high governmental officials have ofttimes stated that this is a people's struggle — regardless of race or color. Could it be a people's struggle if you bar a person who sincerely believes in the very principles we are all fighting for from taking part?

I beg you to take my plea and give it your careful consideration.

I have also sent a copy of this same letter to President Roosevelt in hopes that some action will be taken in my case.

Sincerely,

HENRY H. EBIHARA

TOPAZ, UTAH

230

CHAPTER VII

The Manufacture of Prejudice

FROM 1900 to 1924, the anti-Japanese forces in California conducted an unrelenting campaign for the exclusion of Japanese immigration. After this major goal was achieved, a momentary lull ensued. But when an emergency developed after December 7, 1941, these same forces, taking advantage of the situation, began to urge evacuation of all resident Japanese from the West Coast. Mass removal of the Japanese was merely the logical end-result of the earlier campaign for exclusion: first exclusion; then, at the earliest opportune date, removal. Once evacuation had been achieved, the next logical step was taken: the launching of a large-scale campaign to prevent the return of the evacuees. But the eventual goal that these forces have in mind, and toward which they are now bending every effort, is the deportation of every man, woman, and child in the United States of Japanese ancestry — old and young, citizen and alien, first, second, third, and fourth generations.

It was not the failure or mismanagement of the relocation program, but rather the likelihood of its being successful, that served as a match to light a keg of dynamite. During 1942 there was relatively little agitation in California. All of the Japanese were in either assembly or relocation centers; there was no immediate issue that could serve as the basis for a renewal of the 1941 agitation. But by the end of 1942, WRA policy had begun to assume definite form. Over 9000 evacuees had left the centers on seasonal work-permits; and a number of employment offices had been opened throughout the Middle West and a number of permanent leaves had been granted. Early in 1943, WRA announced that, perhaps, 25,000 evacuees might be released during 1943. On October 12, 1942, the Attorney General had lifted the "enemy alien" restrictions on Italian nationals; and, on December 12, 1942, General De Witt had, in effect, removed the restrictions on German nationals on the West Coast. At the same time, Japanese were granted permission to re-enter Military Area No. 2 (being the eastern part of Oregon and Washington), while the prohibition against their return to Military Area No. 1 and the California portion of Military Area No. 2 was retained. A Gallup poll, taken in January, 1943, indicated that 54 per cent of those interviewed in the Pacific Coast states were favorable to the return of the Japanese after the war (some would permit only citizens to return, others would permit all to return). The Poston and Manzanar incidents in 1942 had merely given additional impetus to the relocation policy, since the public began to demand segregation of the disloyal (which implied that the loyal would, and should, be released). By the end of 1942, WRA was wholly committed to the policy of getting as many of the evacuees out of the centers as possible. Noting all of these developments, the "anti" forces in California decided that the time had arrived for the final — the big — push.

There were, however, other motives that served to inspire this 1943 campaign. An extremely important Presidential election was approaching in 1944 and past experience had amply demonstrated the effectiveness of anti-Japanese agitation. The WRA could be denounced as another absurd New Deal agency; the administration could be accused of "pampering" the evacuees; in short, the relocation program could be effectively used as a means of "smearing" the administration in power. A renewal of anti-Japanese agitation would serve to divert public attention from the real issues of the campaign; and it could be used to "smear" the liberal and progressive movement in California. Lastly, it could be used to frighten the people and to shift public opinion in general to the right.

These same forces also realized that the WRA program stood an excellent chance to succeed. In urging mass evacuation they had never, for one moment, contemplated that the evacuees might be released. They had assumed that all evacuees would be interned for the duration. Once they realized that the evacuees might be released before the war was over (thereby making it possible for some of them to return to the West Coast the moment the ban was lifted and also serving as an important break on eventual deportation), they decided to renew the attack. An important objective of this strategy was to interfere with — to disrupt if possible — the entire relocation program. If necessary the agitation could be carried to Congress with the possibility that it might become a national issue. If successful, they might even succeed in driving the evacuees back to the centers. Once this was accomplished, the campaign for deportation could be accelerated. For obviously deportation could be urged with greater effectiveness if, at the end of the war, all the evacuees were conveniently assembled for shipment to Japan.

It is not necessary to infer such an intention in the resumption of agitation, for it has been expressly avowed. Shortly after January 1, 1943, Senator Ward of Santa Barbara County, representing the anti-Japanese forces in the state, toured California outlining the tactics and strategy of the campaign. This tour represented the first attempt *to organize* a state-wide agitation against the return of the Japanese. At one of these meetings, Mr. C. L. Preisker (for thirty years chairman of the Board of Supervisors of Santa Barbara County) stated the objectives of the campaign: "We should strike now, while the sentiment over the country is right. The feeling of the East will grow more bitter before the war is over and if we begin *now* to try to shut out the Japanese after the war, we have a chance of accomplishing something. Now that all the treaties between the two nations have been abrogated by Japan's war on the United States, Congress is under no treaty obligation and it could easily pass an act ordering all nationals of Japan to return after the peace and forbidding the immigration of others after the war. This would at least relieve us of part of the problem. Maybe the return of the aliens would mean that some of the American-born relatives would follow them. I think the state legislature should memorialize Congress for action. We don't want to see the time return when we have to compete with the Japanese again in this valley." [1] During this

[1] *Pacific Citizen*, February 18, 1943.

tour, Senator Ward repeatedly stated that this was a problem *peace would not solve*.

The implication of this statement is best read in the light of an editorial which appeared in Mr. Hearst's *San Francisco Examiner* of January 25, 1943: —

Bad as the situation is in Europe, the war there is between European Occidental nations, *between white races*. Antagonisms, hatreds and jealousies, no matter how violent, cannot obscure the fact that the warring nations of Europe stem from common *racial*, cultural, linguistic and social roots. *It is a family affair*, in which the possibility of ultimate agreement and constructive harmony has not been dismissed even by the most determined opponents. [Italics mine.]

Such has been the consistent policy pursued by the Hearst newspapers. "The war in the Pacific," to quote from the *Los Angeles Examiner* of March 23, 1943, "is the World War, the War of Oriental Races against Occidental Races for the Domination of the World."

One other important factor was behind the renewal of agitation in 1943 — namely, the relocation program had operated so successfully that Californians were becoming *indifferent* to the entire question. If they lost all interest in the problem, reactionary forces in the state would be robbed of one of their favorite and most effective political weapons — a weapon as effective to them as anti-Semitism to Hitler. As late as December 3, 1943, the *Los Angeles Examiner* complained bitterly that "there is an amazing lack of public interest" in the problem. The Gallup poll of January, 1943, showed a much fairer attitude on the West Coast than one might have expected. The anti-Japanese forces really do not represent the people of the West Coast, not even in the state of California. My own appraisal of the situation is that 30 per cent of the California public is poisonously anti-Japanese (that is, *anti-evacuee*); 30 per cent are moderately anti-evacuee; and 40 per cent are indifferent or inclined to be fair. While the press, as a whole, is vicious (there are exceptions, notably the *Santa Barbara News-Press* and the *Tidings* — the Catholic publication in Los Angeles), many individual columnists and reporters are conspicuously fair. For example, Mr. Chester Rowell, the dean of California journalists, has consistently denounced the current agitation in his column in the *San Francisco Chronicle;* and, on the *Los Angeles Times*, the columnists Bill Henry and Lee Shippey and the reporter Chester Hanson have been notably fair-minded. Public opinion in California would not present a problem if the issue were not constantly agitated in the most unscrupulous fashion.

There was a time in California when everyone hated the Chinese. Today there is no hatred whatever of the Chinese (although the professional anti-Oriental organizations retain their traditional position). The famous *Daily Alta* (June 15, 1853) summarized the widely prevalent view of Californians of the time, when it said that the Chinese were "lower than the beasts that prey upon the flesh of inferior animals." The explanation for the disappearance of anti-Chinese feeling is simple: there has been no anti-Chinese agitation in the state for nearly twenty-five years. For nearly a decade prior to 1940, there was very little anti-Japanese feeling (and for the same reason — namely, that agitation had abated). Writing in 1935, Harry Carr, for years the ace reporter and columnist for the *Los Angeles Times*, correctly stated the fact when he said: "There is very little anti-Japanese feeling in Los Angeles." [2] Race prejudice is not indigenous in California: it is manufactured there. As one observer has said: "people have to *work hard* in California to keep race hatred alive." Just who are some of these individuals and organizations?

1. Dramatis Personae

In the present as in the past, organizing race hatred has been a fairly lucrative business in California. Japanese-baiting, in particular, has always paid high political dividends. It is not surprising, therefore, to discover that organized groups, of the "fringe" variety, have been actively needling the Californians since mass evacuation was ordered. It is fervently to be hoped that some

[2] *Los Angeles: City of Dreams*, 1935, p. 241.

day the searchlight of a Congressional committee of inquiry will be thrown upon certain of these groups, organizations, and individuals.

One such group is the Americanism Educational League (838 South Grand Avenue, Los Angeles). Incorporated under the laws of California, this organization is really the alter ego of an interesting character, Dr. John R. Lechner, M.A., LL.D. — a former clergyman. It is interesting to note that Dr. Lechner, at the outset, could not make up his mind whether he opposed or favored mass evacuation of the Japanese from the Coast. Speaking in Los Angeles he said that mass evacuation "would only cause hardship both to the Japanese and to the other residents of the state." [3] Shortly after this speech was given, the editor of *Rafu Shimpo*, a Los Angeles Japanese-American newspaper, received a letter from Dr. Lechner, enclosing a clipping of the speech and suggesting that the *Rafu Shimpo* might do some printing, gratis. Not long after the incident mentioned, he published a pamphlet entitled *Playing With Dynamite*, full of the usual bedtime stories about the Japanese.

Dr. Lechner has not only been extremely active in organizing anti-Japanese sentiment in California (by speaking at meetings throughout Southern California), but he has had a hand in organizing two recent "investigations" into "the problem" conducted by committees of the California legislature. On December 14, 1943, he addressed a mass meeting in Phoenix, Arizona, which was widely advertised by "newspaper ads, handbills, and announcements on local radio stations," [4] at which he inveighed against the Japanese in his by now familiar and inimitable style. A great many of the anti-Japanese resolutions adopted by California service clubs, civic organizations, and similar groups emanate from Dr. Lechner's organization. He recently testified that his organization had sent out some 900 letters containing copies of the "stock resolution" for concurrence. It is also apparent from his testimony that he has long worked in the closest collaboration with the "white-American" interests in the

[3] *Los Angeles Daily News*, January 21, 1942.
[4] *Pacific Citizen*, December 25, 1943.

floral industry in Southern California. A prominent figure in the industry — Mr. T. H. Wright — is a director of the Americanism Educational League. Under date of October 15, 1943, Senator Jack B. Tenney of Los Angeles County (a would-be Martin Dies of Southern California) addressed a letter to all members of the Los Angeles Bar, on the letterhead of the Americanism Educational League, requesting these lawyers to join in an "investigation" of the Japanese problem. Several of the so-called "front" names, or sponsors of the organization, knew nothing of the letter and had not authorized its issuance. Shortly prior to the issuance of this appeal, the Right Reverend Joseph T. McGucken, of the Catholic Church, resigned as a sponsor of the organization. Recently Dr. Lechner made a trip to Washington, during which he interviewed various Congressmen and officials "as a representative of the American Legion." In its issue of January 15, 1944, the *California Legionnaire*, official publication of the California Department of the Legion, not only repudiated any connection with the gentleman, but characterized his action as being in "flagrant violation of written notice from our Department Commander."

Another interesting "anti" organization is the Home Front Commandos, Inc., of 607 Nicolaus Building, Sacramento, California. The president of the organization is Mr. A. J. Harder, a Sacramento lawyer. In sponsoring a mass meeting in Sacramento on June 20, 1943, dedicated to "Ousting the Japs" (all Japanese had, of course, been removed from the state for over a year), the Home Front Commandos issued a handbill which contained these stirring exhortations: —

> Come and hear the facts — Lend your help to Deport the Japs — If you can't trust a Jap, you won't want him as a neighbor — Any good man can become an American citizen, but a Jap is and always will be a Stabber-in-the-Back gangster; rebel. After the war, ship them back to their Rising Sun Empire.

A recently issued pamphlet urges all patriotic Californians to "Slap the Jap Rat." Prominently featured on the pamphlet is a list of the characteristics of all Japanese: "treacherous, faithless, untrustworthy, irresponsible, inhuman, depraved, ungodly, soulless, disloyal," which is coupled with the generally benign statement that "No Jap Is Fit to Associate with Human Beings." The organization issues bulletins, pamphlets, and throwaways; and conducts a continuing agitation against the return of any Japanese to the West Coast. It is also responsible for the adoption of many resolutions and has circulated numerous petitions.

The financial angel of this organization is Mr. C. M. Goethe, a Sacramento millionaire, who, however, is unwilling to be listed as a sponsor. His reluctance to join an organization that he did not hesitate to subsidize is probably to be explained by reason of the fact that he was one of the founders of the Church Council of Sacramento County, extremely active in the Northern California Council of Churches, and a pioneer in the work of the Federal Council of Churches. Formerly chairman of the Immigration Committee of the Commonwealth Club of San Francisco, Mr. Goethe is also treasurer of the California Joint Immigration Committee.

One of the interesting things about him is that, ideologically speaking, he is a direct and self-acknowledged heir of Mr. Madison Grant. For years he has been the director, and the sole motivating force, in the Eugenics Society of Northern California, which has issued a stream of pamphlets, documents, and press releases devoted to eugenics but which also show a constant preoccupation with the doctrine of "racial integrity." In the rather weird vocabulary of these pamphlets, society is said to be made up of the "high-powers" — that is, the energetic, ambitious, industrious Anglo-Saxons — and the "morons." Since "about 1870," it seems that the "high-powers" have been committing "race suicide," while the "morons" and "near-morons" have actually accelerated their birth rate. They tend to "breed like rabbits." The Old New Englander or the Virginian is constantly praised, in these pamphlets, to the detriment of the "Sicilian black-hander" and the "Mexican peon." In Eugenics Pamphlet No. 12, which carries the code number "O-W23 VSNC 538," one finds this interesting statement: —

. . . Since Hitler had become Fuehrer, he had made eugenics an applied science. Germany has set up hundreds of Eugenics courts. These try German social inadequates as to their fitness for parenthood. Please do not think these trials are based on race hatreds. Whatever else may happen in the Reich, the eugenics trials proceed with fully as much caution as if they were held in the United States. Germany has cross-card-indexed her people until she has located all her probable weaklings. Available food supplies considered, her population is at the saturation point. Her plan is: Eliminate all low-powers to make room for high-powers. And thereby ALSO SAVE TAXES!

It is also worthy of note that not even in "Superior" — that is, Northern California — where the native sons are most numerous, have the Home Front Commandos been able to secure volunteer workers. For the organization has run the following advertisement in many editions of the *Sacramento Bee:* —

> Out with the Japs. Men and women wanted to solicit membership in the Home Front Commandos, an organization whose objective is to deport the Japs after the war. Workers will be compensated for their time. Write for appointment, give references, age, and occupation, telephone number. Address Home Front Commandos, 1020 8th Street, Sacramento, California. Help organize a Chapter in your county.

It should be pointed out, parenthetically, that Mr. Goethe is not the only Californian to have swallowed the Hitler line on eugenics. I had occasion, in a series of articles written in 1935, to point out that the Human Betterment Foundation, of Pasadena, was giving wide currency to Nazi doctrines on eugenics. As a matter of fact, the *Los Angeles Times* actually carried the propaganda of Dr. K. Burchardi, at that time a resident of Southern California.[5]

Still another "anti" group is the Pacific Coast Japanese Problem League (112 West Ninth Street, Los Angeles). Formed on July 13, 1943, the purpose of the League is to "co-ordinate" the efforts

[5] See *Los Angeles Times*, Magazine Section, August 11, 1935.

of all groups on the West Coast interested in the "Japanese menace." Its incorporators include two prominent officials of the Native Sons of the Golden West, an American Legion Official, the president of the Junior Chamber of Commerce of California, a former Mayor of Los Angeles, and a number of ambitious local politicians. This organization boasts that it was responsible for at least one legislative investigation of the "Japanese menace" during 1943. It circulates petitions and obtains numberless resolutions. The executive director of the organization, Dr. John Carruthers, is an interesting personage. Presbyterian minister, graduate of Princeton, one-time professor of religious history at Occidental College, for five years assistant to the President of the University of Southern California, Dr. Carruthers is also a politician and, at this writing, a candidate for the state legislature. His testimony before a committee of the California State Senate on October 19, 1943, represents a fancy and incoherent flight of racist theorizing.

"It is our Christian duty," he says, "to keep the Japanese out of this western world of Christian civilization. . . . Let's get up and be counted," he said, "and let's help the helpless, disturbed, confused people of the coast to feel that it is the moral obligation of the Christian civilization to preserve what it has against its own deterioration, and its external penetrations" — whatever that may mean. Before testifying, he had bowed his head "in the privacy of that precious American heritage, the Christian home in a Christian city in a Christian land of freedom. . . . I prayed," he said, "at this altar of my dining room where my silent typewriter rested on the freshly garnished breakfast table." As a result of this prayer session, he had come before the committee to urge "the deportation, if possible, by every means possible, of all the Japanese from the American continent." The Japanese-Americans should not object, he said, if they were Christians, since, as Christians, "they ought to be glad to be shoved out anywhere that they can bear witness to the Kingdom of Christ." It is interesting to note that, like Dr. Lechner, Dr. Carruthers has not *always* been anti-Japanese. During the years 1924–1926, he was a director of the Council of International Relations in

Los Angeles which had been created primarily to combat anti-Oriental prejudice on the West Coast.

But there are still other groups, such as the California Citizens Association of Santa Barbara, formed on February 25, 1943 (after a speech by Senator Ward). Included among the incorporators of this group appear such sterling old-stock American names as Giorgi, Ardantz, and Fernini. Still another organization is the California Citizens Council (416 West 8th Street, Los Angeles), formed on October 11, 1943, by two ambitious local politicians. This organization began to circulate petitions for the "ouster of the Japanese from California forever," at the very moment Congress was considering the bill to place the Chinese on a quota basis. Its slogan is: "Remember a Jap is a Jap," and its members are urged to put this sticker on the windshield of their automobiles. The sticker contains a picture of a rat with a Japanese face. Still another organization is the American Foundation for the Exclusion of the Japanese, incorporated on December 16, 1943, by a group of Los Angeles citizens. And yet another incorporated anti-Japanese group is No Japs, Incorporated, formed by a group of San Diegoans on August 16, 1943.

It is significant that virtually all of the resolutions concerning the Japanese that have been adopted in California during the last year are identical in text and that, almost without exception, they are circulated by organized groups. I have examined scores of these resolutions, memorials, and petitions and have yet to find one that gives evidence of having arisen spontaneously within the ranks of the particular organization. Taken at their face value, these resolutions would indicate that the people of the state are about 95 per cent opposed to the return of any Japanese after the war. I doubt, however, if more than 35 per cent of the citizens of the state actually hold this view. The presentation of such a resolution to a civic group for concurrence smacks of intimidation, for the group, as such, will be somewhat reluctant not to concur. Its members, moreover, hesitate to oppose such a resolution, although, in private conversation, they freely admit that the whole procedure is so much hokum.

Certain of these actively "anti" groups in California are spreading the virus of race hatred throughout the United States. The Salinas Chamber of Commerce (a California community dominated by shipper-grower interests) recently sent its secretary Mr. Fred S. McCargar, on a nation-wide speaking tour, for the purpose of "warning Eastern residents" against the "dangers of Japanese-American relocation." Speaking before the secretaries of all the Western Chambers of Commerce in Denver, Mr. McCargar stated that California was opposed to the return of any Japanese after the war but was ready to co-operate with other communities in finding some "way to settle the Jap problem." The next day a committee was appointed to explore the various possibilities for a solution of the problem satisfactory to California's interests. Thus a program has doubtless been evolved which will ultimately reach every Chamber of Commerce in the inter-mountain West. Speaking in Pittsburgh, the Salinas spokesman emphasized the "racial undesirability" of the Japanese. In the wake of this tour, numerous Western committees began to pass anti-Japanese resolutions and to explore the possibilities of adopting restrictive clauses in property deeds.[6] If these California groups were honestly concerned with keeping the Japanese out of the state, then logic would compel them to support the relocation program. For the greater the number of Japanese who can be satisfactorily relocated outside the state before the war is over, the fewer there will be who will want to return to the West Coast.

Some of these organizations, however, are distinctly of the "fringe" or "crackpot" variety: they represent no one but the original incorporators and the paid organizers. The most effective organizations are the groups that originally initiated anti-Japanese agitation in the state and have consistently worked at the problem ever since: the California Joint Immigration Committee (currently directed by Mr. H. J. McClatchy); the Native Sons of the Golden West; the American Legion (not quite as rabid as it used to be); the State Grange; and the Associated Farmers. The State Federation of Labor is still nominally a sponsor of the California Joint Immigration Committee, but it has not taken

[6] See *Pacific Citizen*, November 6, 1943.

an active part in the current agitation. The California Joint Immigration Committee, created by V. S. McClatchy, is the real force behind the current agitation.

2. The Campaign Begins

The current campaign was opened early in December, 1942, when the Executive Committee of the American Legion, California Department, announced the creation of a special five-member committee to conduct an "impartial investigation of all Japanese Relocation Areas in the State of California."[7] Appointed as members of this committee were Harper L. Knowles (who figured prominently in the La Follette Committee investigation of antilabor activities in California); H. J. McClatchy (of the California Joint Immigration Committee); and Senator Jack Tenney of Los Angeles County (chairman of the state legislature's "Little Dies" Committee). Actually this committee made no investigation: its work was promptly taken over by the Little Dies Committee, headed by Senator Tenney.

Throughout 1943, the committee held numerous hearings on the Japanese problem; detailed its investigators to visit relocation centers, in collaboration with the Dies Committee; and late in 1943 issued, in red covers, a volume entitled *Un-American Activities in California*. Containing much lush material of the pulp-magazine variety on "the Japanese problem," the volume is chiefly remarkable for the illiteracies that are embalmed in its turgid pages. The principal witness, at all hearings of the committee on the Japanese problem, was Dr. John Lechner. Before this committee had held any hearings on the relocation program, local posts of the American Legion, in January, 1943, began to pass resolutions urging the deportation of all Japanese, citizens and aliens alike. The moment the original American Legion committee was appointed, resolutions and memorials began to flow from California; grand juries throughout the state began to adopt resolutions asking for the permanent exclusion of the evacuees; city councils, boards of supervisors, public officials, and lay

[7] *California Legionnaire*, May 1, 1943.

groups began to take similar action. All of this activity occurred nearly a year before the Little Dies Committee had concluded its so-called investigation. With scarcely a single exception, these protests, resolutions, and memorials are identical in character and in most cases the same printed forms appear.

Within a space of two months (January 1 to March 1, 1943) literally hundreds of organizations in the state had "gone on record." In addition to adopting the form resolutions, they began to contrive fancy and contradictory demands of their own. The Supervisors Association of the State of California, for example, went on record in favor of the proposition that "the teaching of the Japanese language should be forever barred in the United States" (with the Army and Navy clamoring for translators and interpreters!); the Native Sons of the Golden West and the California Grange opposed the formation of the Japanese-American combat team (which was the first unit to storm the beaches at Salerno); the city of Gardena omitted, from its honor roll of citizens in the service, the names of seventeen Japanese-Americans from that area; and on December 10, 1942, the American Legion suspended the charters of the Townsend Harris and Commodore Perry posts (made up exclusively of persons of Japanese ancestry who had served in the First World War). In Portland, Oregon, the American Legion protested against local citizens caring for the local Japanese-American cemetery. Vigilante groups were formed in Salinas "to prevent the return of any Japanese." The California Federation of Women's Clubs expressed grave anxiety for their "sisters" in the East and Middle West, into whose communities the evacuees were being released. Miss Hedda Hopper, movie columnist for the Los Angeles Times, did not want to be accused of "implying anything"; at the same time, however, she called her readers' attention to the fact that "we've had more than our share of explosions, train wrecks, fires and serious accidents since the evacuees were relocated." While in San Francisco, Elsie Robinson, the Hearst columnist, said that she would "cut the throats" of any evacuees who returned to the West Coast (in 1938 she was attempting to drive the Okies out of California).

"California," wrote David Starr Jordan, "is emphatically one of 'earth's male lands.' " "It is not apparently in the nature of the average Californian," wrote Julian Street, "to go at things in a moderate way. He likes antagonism. He feels the need of it. He must have something to combat — to neutralize — the everlasting sunshine and the cloying sweetness of the orange-blossoms and roses." Everyone certainly had his say during this melodramatic free-for-all. All the organizations "spoke out," including the California Society of the Sons of the American Revolution, the San Jose Knights of the Round Table, and the Grand Court of California of Foresters of America. By seizing upon this inspired activity, the press managed to convey the impression that the entire state was just one step removed from open rebellion and that it might probably secede from the Union if so much as a single Japanese-American were to set foot in California.

The moment the California legislature convened on January 6, 1943, a spate of anti-evacuee bills, resolutions, and memorials were immediately introduced. In the debate on these measures, as during all of the preceding excitement, it is interesting to note that a new twist had suddenly been given the Japanese problem. The fact that the federal government had ordered evacuation was cited *as proof* of the undesirable traits of the Japanese *as a race* and *as proof* of their disloyalty as a group. The *Pacific Citizen* (official publication of the Japanese-American Citizens League) correctly analyzed the situation when it stated editorially on December 24, 1942, that "there is every reason to believe that a deliberate campaign is being conducted to keep the 'Japanese' issue alive in California. . . . The function of these antidemocratic campaigns seems to be the maintenance of a public opinion which will make difficult any reassimilation of the evacuated people. The stress and continuance of these campaigns make it increasingly evident that military necessity alone was not the only catalyst in activating evacuation." This campaign convinced most of the evacuees, in fact, that they had been manipulated out of California for economic and political reasons. As Bill Hosokawa pointed out: "These attacks that *persist* against us are more sinister [than evacuation], for now it is no longer possible to say that our persecutors are motivated by an honest if misguided patriotism. There has been plenty of time now to ascertain the facts. There is no reason after all these months for anyone to be morally honest and yet base his charges against us on misinformation." [8] Most emphatically, this campaign was *not* launched to prevent the return of the Japanese to California (although it was represented as such to the public). Its real objective was to prevent the release of any further evacuees from the centers and to drive back into relocation centers all those who had been released and relocated in the Middle West.

Since no one was urging (least of all the WRA) that the evacuees be permitted to return to California, this initial campaign began to fall apart. An issue had to be found and, since none existed, the anti-forces invented one. Consequently an inflammatory campaign was launched in the California press in January over the question of "idle" Japanese-owned farm machinery and equipment. Not only was the amount of this machinery inflated out of all relation to the facts, but news stories implied (and public officials were quoted to the effect) that thousands of acres of tomatoes were in jeopardy because of the "willful" refusal of the evacuees to "co-operate." The McClatchy newspapers (*Fresno Bee* and *Sacramento Bee*) on January 28, 1943, charged that the tires on 25,000 Japanese-owned trucks and automobiles were rotting in storage and "that is the way the Japanese want them," implying in the most unequivocal fashion that the evacuees were interfering with the war effort. The campaign took on increasingly fantastic proportions. A sports writer for the *San Francisco Chronicle* on February 7, 1943, argued that California should seize, for "home defense, all firearms stored by the evacuees. Vast quantities of mighty expensive rifles and pistols," it seems, had been acquired by the Japanese prior to evacuation. No proof whatever was cited in support of this provocative statement. Senator Tenney's committee announced that it "would ferret out" the concealed farm machinery if it took all year. This agitation continued throughout January, February, and March, 1943. As late as April,

[8] *Pacific Citizen*, January 28, 1943.

246

responsible state officials were still implying that as much as 80 per cent of the tomato crop might be lost because of the failure of the evacuees to turn over idle farm machinery. These same stories implied that WRA was being "obstinate" and "stubborn" about the matter. Long after the WRA had punctured this bogus balloon, the stories kept appearing. By April the agitation began gradually to disappear from the newspapers. The public, however, was left with the definite impression that the evacuees had been guilty of a discreet but effective type of sabotage.

3. "An Almost Sensational Report"

The "idle farm machinery" ballyhoo was a satisfactory issue to keep the Japanese problem alive in California; but obviously the nation could not be expected to froth at the mouth over such an issue. Something bigger and better had to be devised. Early in January, Senator Wallgren (from Washington) and Congressman Leroy Johnson (from California) introduced resolutions in Congress calling for a transfer of control from WRA to the Army (despite the fact that the Army insisted then and still insists that it does not want to be burdened with this additional assignment). Accompanying the introduction of these resolutions, much comment began to appear about the "coddling" and "pampering" of the evacuees. Since the fight had now been carried by West Coast agitators to Congress, the whole question began to assume national proportions and the national press began to show some interest in the matter.

The Senate resolution (No. 444), introduced by two West Coast Senators (Wallgren and Holman), was referred to a subcommittee of the Senate Committee on Military Affairs, consisting of Messrs. Chandler, Wallgren, Holman, Gurney, and O'Mahoney. It should be noted that Senator Holman had previously introduced a bill to strip the Nisei of their American citizenship. Senator Chandler, chairman of the subcommittee, obviously thought of the investigation as part of his "Lick-Japan-First" campaign. Newspaper reports indicate that he actively sought the chairmanship of the subcommittee. "There has been a persistent rumor around Washington," commented Helen Fuller in the *New Republic* (on May 1, 1943), "that at an early stage of his own personal 'Pacific-consciousness,' Chandler received overtures from Hearst representatives, keen on strengthening their traditional yellow-scare editorial policy, who offered him nationwide publicity and backing for a national office in return for constant harping on the Japs-First and Yellow-Peril-at-Home tunes. Regardless of the truth of the rumor, large hunks of Hearst front pages have recently been devoted to Chandler's 'exposés' of Japanese relocation centers, and a Hearst correspondent in Washington, Ray Richards of the *Los Angeles Examiner*, is most often the one who floats Chandler's atrocity stories about the recent methods the War Relocation Authority has used in handling our Japanese-American evacuees." Throughout 1943, as a matter of fact, Ray Richards, assisted by Warren Francis of the *Los Angeles Times*, directed, steered, and manipulated the "anti-Japanese" campaign.[9]

The committee hearings opened in Washington, with Mr. Dillon Meyer and former Ambassador Joseph Grew as the chief witnesses. Ambassador Grew testified that, in his opinion, it was altogether possible to segregate the loyal from the disloyal elements among the Japanese. His statement scarcely received mention in the West Coast press. Then Senator Chandler set out on a tour of the relocation centers, announcing that he was momentarily prepared to submit "an almost sensational report," and releasing press statements from time to time en route. His first announcements stated that he had discovered that 60 per cent of the residents of one center were disloyal (with no further explanation of how he had arrived at this determination); he then proceeded to state that "in my mind there is no question that thousands of these fellows were armed and prepared to help Japanese troops invade the West Coast right after Pearl Har-

[9] NOTE: At the same time, Representative Henry M. Jackson, from Washington, introduced a resolution for the appointment of a standing Congressional committee "to review the intricate web of subversive activity which Japan wove over this country by means of business representatives." (*San Francisco Examiner*, February 9, 1943.)

bor." [10] The Senator's investigations were, to put it mildly, brief. Observers noted that his technique was to breeze into a center, ask a few questions with the rapidity of a quarterback calling football signals, and then depart. Great prominence was given the Senator's hurried inspection by feature stories written for the Hearst press by Mr. Ray Richards. As a direct consequence of Senator Chandler's visits to Arkansas and Arizona, local groups became excited and agitation was renewed against the WRA centers in these areas. It is significant that anti-Japanese legislation was introduced in the legislatures of both states at about the time of the Senator's flying visits.

The general upshot of these alleged investigations was a report, the recommendations of which had little relation to the sensational stories written by Ray Richards. For, after all this fuss and fury, the committee recommended: (1) that the Nisei be reclassified so that they might be drafted for service in the Army; (2) that the disloyal elements be held in detention camps for the duration; and (3) that the rest of the evacuees be placed in private employment. One explanation for the mildness of the report is that Senator Wallgren, about this time, began to receive a barrage of letters from his liberal constituents protesting that he was playing the fascist game. The Senator suddenly became very conciliatory and began to "clarify" his position.

During the course of these hearings, the consequences of the agitation in California began to be apparent. Governor Osborn of Arizona, for example, told the committee that "California was attempting to close its back doors to the Japanese." If the West Coast states persisted in this position, he explained, then Arizona would have to appeal to Congress for "protection," since, at the end of the war, it would be left with a disproportionate number of Japanese on its hands. Shortly afterwards WRA was forced to declare Arizona "out of bounds" for relocation purposes. The net result of such action is, of course, to build a *cordon sanitaire* around the West Coast and to force the evacuees farther east. Noticing the policy of California, several Congressmen began to ask questions. Representative Karl Mundt, of South Dakota, a

[10] *Washington Post*, March 9, 1943.

member of the Dies Committee, asked a question which, to this day, has not been answered. "If the Japanese were, in fact, a menace to the defense industries of the West Coast, and were removed for this reason, why aren't they an equal menace in Omaha, Nebraska, or Kansas City, Missouri?"

While the West Coast anti-Japanese forces did not get all that they had anticipated out of Senator Chandler's excursion into the Japanese problem, nevertheless the hearings served their purpose. For the effect of the hearings, and of the carefully planned newspaper campaign conducted by the Hearst press, was to make Middle Western, Eastern, and Southern communities Japanese-conscious. By starting a campaign "to prevent the return of the Japanese," California implied that the evacuees were collectively and individually an undesirable lot. Since California refused to accept any of these evacuees, other states began to feel that there was no reason why they should. Arizona passed a memorial protesting the admission of Japanese-Americans to its colleges and universities and a bill to restrict the liberties of released evacuees (this was before the state was declared out-of-bounds). Wyoming passed a bill making it impossible for the evacuees at the Heart Mountain center to qualify as voters in the state; Arkansas sought to close the doors of its public schools to "members of the Mongolian race"; communities in Michigan and Indiana protested against the employment of evacuees in their localities; the *Denver Post*, on February 14, 1943, launched a vicious series of articles aimed at making the position of the evacuees in Colorado untenable; the movement for deportation gained definite momentum in California; petitions and resolutions from various state legislatures and California citizen groups against the student relocation program and the induction of Japanese-Americans into the services were presented to Congress; Arkansas passed a bill making it illegal for a person of Japanese ancestry to own land in the state; Arizona passed a statute making it virtually impossible for anyone to conduct business transactions with a person whose liberties had been "restricted"; mass meetings were held in Wisconsin protesting the employment of evacuees; "unreceptive attitudes" towards evacuees were reported from points as distant from the West Coast as Alexandria, Virginia, Toledo, Ohio, and West Virginia. (All between January 1 and May 1, 1943.)

4. "Once a Jap, Always a Jap"

On April 19, 1943, General J. L. De Witt issued Public Proclamation No. 17 which, by its terms, authorized Japanese-American soldiers, serving with our forces, to return to the West Coast while on furlough or on leave. There is every reason to believe that General De Witt signed this proclamation not on his own initiative, but pursuant to instructions from the War Department. For on April 13, testifying in San Francisco before the House Naval Affairs Subcommittee, he had volunteered this information:

> "There is developing a sentiment on the part of certain individuals to get the Japanese back to the Coast. I am opposing it with every means at my disposal. . . . A Jap's a Jap. They are a dangerous element, whether loyal or not. There is no way to determine their loyalty. . . . It makes no difference whether he is an American; theoretically he is still a Japanese and you can't change him. . . . You can't change him by giving him a piece of paper."

He was not worried, he said, about German or Italian nationals; "but the Japs we will be worried about all the time until they are wiped off the face of the map." [11] In response to this statement, which was volunteered by the General and not given in response to a question, two California members of the Congressional committee gave vent to their own lawless sentiments by saying: "If you send any Japs back here we're going to bury them." A little later, rumors began to circulate on the West Coast that General De Witt was to be replaced by General Delos Emmons, commander of the Hawaiian Department. These two events — the granting of permission to furloughed soldiers to return to the Coast, and the rumor of General De Witt's replacement — were

[11] See *Los Angeles Times*, April 14 and 19, 1943.

widely interpreted on the coast, in the light of General De Witt's testimony already quoted, as indicating the existence of a plot in the War Department to lift the ban altogether and to permit the return of the loyal Japanese to their former homes.

The reaction was instantaneous and violent. Several California Congressmen opposed the proclamation granting permission to furloughed soldiers to return to the Coast and indicated they would oppose any attempt to replace General De Witt;[12] the Los Angeles Chamber of Commerce immediately sent its representatives to Washington to confer with Assistant Secretary of War McCloy;[13] and the editorial Big Berthas were at once brought into action. Denouncing the "current soft-headed agitation for the return of loyal Japanese" as "stupid and dangerous," the Los Angeles Times proceeded to rest the opposition on strictly racial grounds. "As a race," it stated in an editorial of April 22, 1943, "the Japanese have made for themselves a record for conscienceless treachery unsurpassed in history." Ergo, all resident Japanese, including the American-born, must per se be treacherous. This agitation, moreover, occurred at a time [14] when the newspapers carried sensational headlines about the barbarous execution of American fliers in Tokyo.

For weeks on end, the West Coast newspapers were full of a torrid denunciation of everything Japanese with, curiously enough, the resident Japanese (who had quickly denounced the Tokyo executions as "a barbaric defiance of the Geneva Convention")[15] becoming the principal targets for the public's wrath. Mayor Fletcher Bowron — an able and honest public official, reform mayor of Los Angeles — completely lost his head, bombarded Washington with protests against the return of the Japanese, and proceeded to advocate measures to deprive the American-born of their citizenship.[16] The orgy of Jap baiting that swept the West Coast press was not limited to protests against the return of the Japanese to California, but began to

[12] Los Angeles Times, May 6, 1943.
[13] Ibid., April 23, 1943.
[14] April 22, 1943.
[15] Los Angeles Times, April 23, 1943.
[16] Los Angeles Daily News, May 26, 1943.

assume the form of a protest against the release of *any* Japanese from the centers to go *anywhere*.[17]

Because they suspected a "plot" to lift the ban on the Japanese returning to the West Coast, California groups sent a hurry-up call to the Dies Committee to conduct still another "investigation." Arriving in Los Angeles before the committee hearings had even been prepared, Representative J. Parnell Thomas of New Jersey (a member of the Dies Committee) registered at the Biltmore Hotel and began to issue press releases at regular intervals to meet the demands of the local newspapers for more anti-Japanese headlines. At this time, the Dies Committee had conducted no hearings and Representative Thomas had not so much as visited or been within a hundred miles of a single relocation center. Yet bloodcurdling press releases literally flowed from his headquarters at the Biltmore Hotel, as the headlines burgeoned hourly. "Stop Freeing Interned Japs!" screamed the *Los Angeles Herald-Express* on May 19, 1943; "Dies Prober Charges Whole Relocation Plan Is Farce." "Rep. J. P. Thomas Reveals Jap Army in L. A." ranted another headline (May 13, 1943).

Knowing full well that only three types of Japanese were permitted in the state — namely, soldiers on furlough or leave, those in public institutions, and Japanese women married to Caucasians who had children (about twenty in all Los Angeles County) — the newspapers nevertheless steadily insinuated the notion that Japanese were being allowed to return to the Coast. Groups that must certainly have known the true facts, such as the San Joaquin Council of the State Chamber of Commerce, passed resolutions demanding the *"re-evacuation* of those who have moved back into the state." [18]

5. The Dies Treatment

The antics of Representative Thomas — advance triggerman for the Dies Committee — would constitute the subject matter of high-grade farce were the implications not so serious in terms

[17] See *Los Angeles Herald-Express*, May 19, 1943.
[18] *Los Angeles Times*, June 11, 1943.

of the well-being of thousands of American citizens. Shouting in the press that "fat-waisted Japs are being released while our American boys on Guadalcanal are barely receiving enough food with which to keep alive," Representative Thomas, on May 25, 1943, released the following statements to the press (see *San Francisco Examiner* of that date): —

> The Dies Committee investigators and I found conditions very bad in the War Relocation Centers.
> Camp newspapers are virulently critical of anyone who opposes Japanese interests.
> Short wave radios are permitted, although even a Japanese subject may not own or use one in Japan.

At the time that these and many similar statements were released to the press, Representative Thomas had yet to visit a relocation center. On May 29, Mr. Stripling, an investigator for the committee, authorized a statement in the *Washington Star* that WRA was releasing "spies and saboteurs." Representative Thomas charged that "food and wine" were being served in relocation centers (the food allowance was 45 cents per person per day). On May 28, the staff of the committee released statements to the press that the evacuees were being so well fed that they were sending packages of "butter, coffee, and other rationed food to friends outside the centers." Again on May 28, the staff of the committee informed the press that 76 per cent of the Japanese in one camp had refused to profess their loyalty — a gross exaggeration. On June 4, the *Washington Times-Herald* carried a story to the effect that "evacuees at the centers are allowed five gallons of whiskey per person," and this statement was attributed to Acting Chairman Joe Starnes (who subsequently denied that he had made the statement). Needless to say, the statement was not true.

For at least a month before the committee had taken a single word of testimony these false, malicious, demagogic statements were fed to the press. As indicative of the perspicacity of the Dies Committee investigators, suffice it to say that on a flying visit to Los Angeles in 1941, they had wired Chairman Dies as follows: JAPANESE PREFECTURAL SOCIETIES ARE CALLED KENS STOP

SIXTEEN SHINTO TEMPLES IN LOS ANGELES STOP THIS IS NOT A RELIGION BUT WORSHIP OF THE JAPANESE RACE PERSONIFIED IN THE EMPEROR. This sensational bit of news is quoted by Mr. Alan Hynd in his book *Betrayal From the East* as proof of the investigatory talents of Messrs. Steedman and Stripling, who, apparently, have never had access to the *Encyclopedia Britannica*. The systematic dissemination of "vital lies" by the Nazis about the Jews should be compared with the systematic propagation of "vital lies" about the resident Japanese by the Dies Committee. Here, indeed, is real competition in falsehood.

When the Dies Committee finally got around to holding public hearings (they had really conducted their hearings in advance in the press), it developed that Mr. Dies had been pushed aside to make way for an ambitious junior colleague, Representative John Costello of California. Mr. Costello — a member in good standing of the Native Sons of the Golden West (decisively defeated for re-election to Congress in the May 16, 1944, primary election) — chaired the meetings on the West Coast; and, for his benefit, the press obligingly referred to the committee as the "Costello Committee." Hearings were held between June 8 and July 7, 1943. Following its familiar "smear" techniques, the committee always managed to call the so-called smear witnesses before it heard from WRA officials, thereby permitting the newspapers to carry sensational stories which the committee must have known were false and untrue. Prominently featured, for example, was the testimony of a discharged employee of WRA. An examination of his testimony later revealed some thirty-five separate and distinct falsehoods. While the committee was hearing from these disgruntled witnesses, WRA was not permitted to comment upon the evidence or to correct, at the time, obvious misstatements of fact. Despite the laudable efforts of Representative Herman P. Eberharter to be fair about the evidence, the acting chairman, Mr. Costello, conducted not a hearing, but an inquisition.

No effort whatever was made to get a really representative cross section of Southern California opinion. The committee permitted witnesses to tell "scare stories" about "dynamite caches" and such, which were known to be thoroughly "phony" stories and which were subsequently exposed as such. Witnesses were encouraged to threaten the Japanese with mob violence and actual threats of violence went unrebuked. While the committee was in session, the so-called "zoot-suit" race riots occurred in Los Angeles. There is no doubt whatever that the sensational racist propaganda released by the committee throughout May of 1943 contributed to kindling the fires of racial antagonism in the community and were in part responsible for the riots.

The Dies Committee never intended to make an investigation of the evacuation program. It was summoned to California to make newspaper headlines and to keep the "Japanese issue" alive, for political and other purposes. Considering its sensational pre-hearing publicity releases, the final report of the committee is laughably mild. For, after all this sound and fury, a majority of the committee recommended: that the segregation policy be pushed as rapidly as possible; that a board be established to investigate evacuees who applied for release; and that a program of Americanization be instituted (one was already in effect). The committee also intended to smear the WRA — which it did — and to interfere with the release program — which it did. But the effect of the committee's hearings was not precisely that which had been intended. Generally speaking, the committee was thoroughly denounced in the national press for its prejudiced attitude and its farcical procedures. In short, the hearings badly backfired and, as a consequence, were quickly dropped. The notable minority report of Representative Eberharter tells the story. "I cannot avoid the conclusion," he stated, "that the report of the majority is prejudiced, and that most of its statements are not proven."

6. Free Murder

Since the agitation conducted by both the Senate Subcommittee on Military Affairs and the Dies Committee had, in effect, backfired on the race baiters, it then became necessary to enlist the services of various committees of the state legislature, in order to keep the public properly excited about the Japanese question, so-called. California's "Little Dies Committee," headed by Senator

Jack Tenney, throughout 1943 was continually sniping at the relocation program. As a matter of fact, the American Legion had abandoned its plan for an investigation by announcing that Senator Tenney's committee would undertake the task for them. Following the Dies Committee fiasco, various state legislative committees, with roving assignments, began to fish in the troubled waters.

One of these committees was a State Senate Committee consisting of Senators Hatfield, Quinn, Slater, and Donnelly, which held hearings throughout the state in October, 1943. In Los Angeles, the committee was told by Mr. Fred Howser, District Attorney of Los Angeles County, that "we are going to have large scale massacres or we might say free murder or manslaughter" if any Japanese were permitted to return to the Coast. The usual parade of special-interest groups was in evidence: the agricultural section of the Los Angeles Chamber of Commerce; the floral industry; the nurserymen's industry — all merrily grinding the same axes. Representatives of the Native Sons of the Golden West volunteered the information that they opposed any modification of our immigration policy insofar as the Chinese were concerned. The Gold Star Mothers were represented as were the Navy Mothers. The following colloquy from the transcript is typical of the lush and emotional atmosphere that prevailed: —

> MRS. BENAPHFL, representing the Gold Star Mothers: We want to keep the Japs out of California.
> SENATOR SLATER: For the duration?
> A. No, for all times.
> SENATOR SLATER: That's the stuff! [19]

I testified at these hearings and was cross-examined at length about my views on "miscegenation," "racial purity," "mongrelization," and similar fancy topics. Watching the proceeding at close range, I was constantly impressed with the fact that this was not a hearing but rather the enactment of a native-son pageant or ritual. It had something of the character of an old-style morality

[19] Vol. II, Transcript, p. 171.

play. It provided a marvelous opportunity for those present to express long-pent-up emotions; to wallow in the corniest sentiments; to beat an invisible adversary; and to evidence an unspeakable self-righteousness. The hearings were conducted in the assembly chamber of the State Building in Los Angeles. On the walls of the chamber appear some handsome murals depicting the colorful background of the state and its varied population. I could imagine, at moments, that the Indians and Mexicans in these murals enjoyed the show as much as I did.

This particular "show," however, got badly sidetracked. For Miss Pearl Buck happened to be in Los Angeles and some of us prevailed upon her to appear before the committee. She testified for over an hour, during most of which time the members of the committee were consulting their watches and suggesting an adjournment. They had not planned on her appearance, which had the effect of disturbing the performance of a time-honored ritual. Naturally the committee members had to treat Miss Buck with a certain amount of courtesy and even a measure of respect (attitudes they never show when dealing with a local resident who commits the unpardonable heresy of advocating fair play). While one or two Los Angeles newspapers carried fairly complete stories on Miss Buck's appearance, the press of the state, as a whole, neglected so much as to mention the fact that she had appeared as a witness.

Following the appearance of the State Senate Committee came the so-called Gannon Committee (a committee of the state assembly presided over by Legislator Chester Gannon of Sacramento County). This particular committee had, as its avowed purpose, an examination of those individuals and organizations in the state who were advocating fair play. Its guns were particularly directed at the Committee on American Principles and Fair Play which includes among its members Dr. Robert Gordon Sproul of the University of California, Dr. Ray Lyman Wilbur of Stanford University, and Dr. Robert Millikan of the California Institute of Technology. Among the witnesses questioned at the Los Angeles hearings was Mrs. Maynard Thayer of Pasadena — a member of the D.A.R. and a sponsor of the Committee on

American Principles and Fair Play. As a sample of the hearings, I quote the following (Mr. Gannon is interrogating, or rather shouting at, Mrs. Thayer): —

GANNON: What do you know of the Bill of Rights? The Bill of Rights has no application to state legislation and we know you attacked the American Legion and the Native Sons. When was the Bill of Rights written? What is it?

MRS. THAYER: Of course, it's the first ten amendments of the Constitution.

GANNON: You're like all these people who prate about the Bill of Rights and don't know a thing about it. The Bill of Rights is not such a sacred thing after all. Don't you know at the time the Bill of Rights was written that we had 150,000 slaves in the U. S.? What did the Bill of Rights do about that — nothing. Slavery was accepted. And yet you talk about the rights of minorities being protected by the Bill of Rights.

MRS. THAYER: I think we've made some progress in our interpretation since then. Our committee will back any groups whose constitutional rights are threatened. It is of the greatest importance that in time of war we do not get off into race hatred.

GANNON: Are you a Communist? This sounds like Communist doctrine.

MRS. THAYER: I have been a registered Republican for thirty years and have been active in various things connected with good citizenship. This is a matter of American citizenship with which I am concerned, not with the Japanese as such.

GANNON: You don't have anyone near or dear to you fighting the Japs, do you, Mrs. Thayer? Don't you think if you had sons you would feel different at this time of the year?

MRS. THAYER: No, what does the war in the Pacific have to do with the rights of American citizens in California? I do not want the return of the Japanese to the Pacific Coast. It is a military matter for the War Department to decide. Our committee merely says that we must not do anything in time of war which threatens the principles of American citizenship.

259

GANNON: What do you know about the morals of the Japs in Santa Barbara County? Do you want your U. S. government to protect a people who farm their wives out to another man to procreate his name?

MRS. THAYER: We have no concern or knowledge of this.

GANNON: Do you want to champion the rights of a people where different sexes do nude bathing together? You don't know anything about the habits and morals of Japs in California. Mrs. Thayer, have you ever smelled the odor of a Jap home?

It is interesting to note how the whole tenor of the Japanese problem had changed since 1942 when, at the Tolan Committee hearings, all witnesses were treated with respect and when, so we were told, the evacuation of the Japanese was being ordered for their protection and as a matter of "military necessity." By December, 1943, witnesses were being browbeaten for defending the Bill of Rights and all Japanese were loathsome and immoral creatures whose homes "smelled" bad. The hearings were too much even for the *Los Angeles Times,* which has consistently supported the anti-Japanese forces. The day following the examination of Mrs. Thayer, the *Times* carried an editorial captioned: "Legislative Committees Should Not Be Bullies." Previously the *Times* had shown no such laudable concern for the rights of witnesses before legislative committees. But Mr. Gannon had committed the unpardonable sin of having insulted Mrs. Maynard Force Thayer, a stanch Republican, a member of the D.A.R. and a resident of Pasadena. So the *Times* was moved to characterize the whole proceeding as a "witch-burning" enterprise. Actually the Gannon hearings were no more unfair than the Dies Committee hearings or the hearings of the Little Dies Committee or the hearings of the State Senate Committee. The *Los Angeles Examiner,* on the other hand, devoted sixty-two inches of space in one issue to the Gannon Committee hearings. By and large, however, these particular hearings, like those which had preceded them, seriously backfired. *Time* magazine did an excellent piece on the hearings (December 20, 1943) and this, coupled with the *Times* editorial, served momentarily to silence the Cali-

fornia samurai, who, previously, had been figuratively waving
swords, making hideous grimaces, and shouting imprecations
from Eureka to San Diego.

7. The Tramp of Racial Hatred

The Great California Razzle-Dazzle Campaign continued
throughout 1943 without abatement. During the year two Congressional and three legislative investigations of the relocation
program were conducted. All of these investigations were inspired
by the anti-evacuee forces in California. Thus there was not a
month, and scarcely a week, throughout the entire year in which
the Japanese problem was not being publicly agitated. Throughout the year, groups were busily organizing, collecting resolutions, circulating petitions, bombarding Congress and the President with memorials. The seeds of suspicion were planted
throughout the Southwest, the Middle West, the East, and the
South. Libels that had been repeated for forty years in California
began to be echoed in Colorado and the Dakotas, in Arkansas
and Illinois. On December 5, 1943, 1500 Iowa, Missouri, and
Nebraska farmers held a protest meeting in Hamburg, Iowa,
objecting to the relocation of any evacuees in the area.[20] Similar
meetings were held in many areas in which, prior to this agitation,
excellent reception had been accorded the evacuees. All during
1943, as Mr. Dillon Myer has said, one could hear the "tramp,
tramp, tramp of racial antagonism."

In California itself hatred was constantly fomented and by
increasingly more unscrupulous means. The use made by the
newspapers of stories told by Americans who had been seized
in Shanghai, and other parts of the Far East, is a case in point.
Doubtless some of these individuals had received shocking and
inhuman treatment; but to direct the resentment which they felt,
and which their stories aroused, at the evacuees was not striking
at Japan: it was striking at American citizens. Dr. J. S. Pyne, a
California dentist, told, for example, of having had "his finger-

[20] *Los Angeles Times*, December 6, 1943.

nails pulled out by the roots"; [21] and Commander C. M. Wassell told the Los Angeles Rotary Club, "For God's sake keep the *Japs* behind barbed wire." [22] A Mrs. Garnett Gardiner, who spent seven months in a prison camp in Shanghai, addressed mass meetings in San Diego and Los Angeles. After her appearance in San Diego, 4000 residents signed a petition against the return of any evacuees to the Coast. "When I hear," she said, "of those Japs getting steaks and chocolate bars, which even American citizens can't always get, and being permitted to throw away meat, I can hardly believe my ears." [23] It needs to be emphasized, however, that Mrs. Gardiner *heard* only these things. While one can readily understand — even sympathize with — such expressions from persons who have suffered injury and mistreatment, it is not so easy to sympathize with other statements of the same character. For example, at one legislative hearing, Dr. Ralph L. Phillips, "for 26 years a missionary in China," told how Japanese soldiers had massacred 50,000 Chinese men on one occasion and "attacked thousands of girls and women." The story may have been perfectly true, but one would expect a representative of Christ on earth not to make use of such a story, before such a committee, for the obvious purpose of whipping up racial hatred against 70,000 American citizens of Japanese ancestry.[24] The contrast between the manner in which these stories were featured — always in connection with an appeal for petitions to be signed, and so on — and the treatment accorded the stories of repatriates on the *Gripsholm* who told of "fair enough treatment" in Japan could not have been greater.[25] It may well be that our repatriates were instructed to minimize the stories of their mistreatment; but it is worthy of note that a dozen or more American repatriates, who had been held in *civilian detention camps* in Japan, issued such statements.

During 1943, Governor Warren appointed a committee on

[21] *Ibid.*, October 6, 1943.

[22] *Los Angeles Herald-Express*, November 30, 1943; italics mine.

[23] *Los Angeles Times*, November 17, 1943.

[24] *Los Angeles Herald Express*, December 8, 1943.

[25] See *Los Angeles Daily News*, December 7, 1943.

race relations in Los Angeles. Mr. Leo Carrillo, a Native Son of Mexican descent, was appointed a member of this committee. Shortly after his appointment, Mr. Carrillo made a series of speeches throughout the state. Here is a sample: "When people in Washington say we must protect American-Japanese, they don't know what they're talking about — there's no such thing as an American-Japanese. If we ever permit those termites to stick their filthy fingers into the sacred soil of our state again, we don't deserve to live here ourselves." [26] The sheriff of Los Angeles County, another Native Son, made a series of similar speeches. At a meeting of the State Board of Agriculture in December, 1943, three members of the board (Dr. Paul S. Taylor, Mr. Stewart Meiggs, Mrs. Grace McDonald — all appointees of former Governor Culbert L. Olson) succeeded in passing a resolution in favor of the return of the evacuees to California and urging fair treatment. Governor Warren lost no time in making new appointments to the board so that this action might be reversed (which was done). Individuals who, in testifying before California legislative committees, had urged fair play were denounced over the radio as "Jap-Lovers" and the "Kiss-a-Jap-a-Day boys." Typical headlines from the *Los Angeles Times* were: "District Attorney Sees Bloodshed if Japs Return — Servicemen Vow to Kill Nips" (October 19, 1943) and "Rioting Predicted in Event Japs Return to California" (December 10, 1943). As during prior agitations, novelists began to write fancy tales about the Japanese invasion and conquest of Los Angeles.[27] In reviewing this record, one is reminded of the prediction made by Dr. Eric Bellquist of the University of California when he told the Tolan Committee in 1942 that California's attitude toward this problem "will blacken its record for years to come."

As a sample of the tactics employed in this campaign, reference must be made to a "survey of opinion" conducted by the *Los Angeles Times*. The questions and the answers received were as follows: —

[26] *Los Angeles Times*, October 6, 1943.
[27] See *Invasion!* by Whitman Chambers.

	Yes	No
1. Do you think the War Relocation Authority has capably handled the problem of Japanese in the United States?	639	10,773
2. Do you favor Army control of Japanese in this country for the duration?	11,203	372
3. Do you approve of the policy of freeing avowedly loyal Japanese to take jobs in the Midwest?	1,139	9,750
4. Would you favor "trading" Japanese now here for American war prisoners held in Japan, if it could be arranged?	11,249	256
5. Do you favor a constitutional amendment after the war for the deportation of all Japanese from this country, and forbidding further immigration?	10,598	732
6. Would you except American-born Japanese if such a plan as the above were adopted?	1,883	9,018
7. Would you permanently exclude all Japanese from the Pacific Coast states including California?	9,855	999

The results were published in the issue of December 6, 1943, accompanied by a page of comments from irate readers denouncing the evacuees, and with a pious editorial plea entitled: "Public Demands New Policy on Japs in U. S." On the same page was a cartoon in which the West Coast states were shown putting their thumb down on something labeled "Jap-Molly-Coddling." It is hardly necessary to point out that each and every one of these questions was leading, not to mention being misleading and loaded; and that the order of the questions represents a delicate but obvious fraud. Who would want to see *avowedly* loyal" evacuees released? As to question No. 5, all Japanese immigration has been prohibited since 1924 by statute, and since 1908 by agreement. To couple this phrase with the rest of the question betrays the venom of the entire questionnaire.

One incident occurring in 1943 serves to show, most effectively, how this attack on the relocation program was used for partisan political purposes. A well-meaning official of the employment office of WRA in Cleveland wrote an article in which he stated that relocatees might be able to teach Eastern and Middle Western farm hands the merits of a regular bath. This article was seized upon by the *Washington Times-Herald* and the fabulous "bath-tub" story hit the pages of nearly every newspaper in America. A studied attempt was made to use this story to alienate Middle Western farm sentiment from the administration. The Master of the National Grange promptly announced that the statement sounded like propaganda to him; Senator Taft and Congressman Costello made speeches in Congress; and the West Coast newspapers had a field day. "Jap Sanitation Claim Amazes Southlanders" reads a headline in the *Los Angeles Times* for Decmber 7, 1943; "Harby Says Japs Live With Pigs" is another headline from the same paper (December 8). The *Times* then proceeded to run a series of articles, with photographs, showing the "squalor" of Japanese communities in California. That the unfortunate author of this article was a professor in Ohio State University was cited as further proof of the "day-dreaming of New Deal professors." The professor happens to be a registered Republican.

As a matter of fact, there was some truth in the original story. Having been for four years Chief of the Division of Immigration and Housing, in California, I can state that Japanese labor camps were as good as the average and definitely better than some of the miserably squalid rural housing provided by some of the largest "farm factories" in the state. Early reports of the Division, prepared in 1918, complimented the Japanese on their efforts to provide good labor camps.[28] Another sample of the same type of propaganda story was one which appeared in the National press in October captioned: "Prison Camp Wooing Jails 5 Jap Girls." The purport of the story was that five girls in a relocation center had been arrested for "wooing" with German prisoners of war. While the story received considerable publicity, not a newspaper carried the indignant denial that appeared in the Granada Relocation Center *Pioneer*.

[28] *Rising Japan* by Jabez T. Sunderland, 1918, p. 152.

8. The Tule Lake Barrage

The selection of Tule Lake as the center to receive the segregants — the "disloyal" evacuees — was a serious error. For the Tule Lake center is located on the sacred soil of California: to house "disloyal Japs" on this soil was to invite disaster. WRA selected Tule Lake for three reasons: it is a large center; it has good farming lands and offers the best possibilities of becoming self-sufficient insofar as food is concerned; and it had the largest number of segregants. Even before Tule Lake had been designated as the camp for segregants, California elements began to protest the policy of segregation which, for over a year, they had been loudly advocating. These "anti" groups were quick to realize that segregation implied that the loyal elements would be released. Noting this possibility, the *Los Angeles Examiner* quickly reversed its stand in favor of segregation and reverted to its earlier position that it was impossible to segregate the loyal from the disloyal. Within a few weeks, the same newspaper was screaming that the real danger consisted not of the disloyal, but of the *loyal* elements. The only *honest* "Japs," it stated, were those in Tule Lake; the others "who are LOOSE in the country" were dishonest, disloyal, and subversive.[29]

The real "riot," in fact, did not occur at Tule Lake: it occurred in the California press. The moment the disturbances were reported, the *Los Angeles Examiner* got out a special "war extra"[30] with a two-inch banner headline across the front page: "14,000 Japs on Strike in State! Army Guarding Fenced-In Nips at Tule Lake." The *Los Angeles Times* on November 10 carried a lurid cartoon captioned "Hon. Dr. Jekyll and Mr. Hyde," showing the usual bucktoothed guerilla-like Jap lighting a bomb. For weeks on end, the Tule Lake "riots" pushed the war news from the front pages of the California newspapers. Nearly every public official from Governor Warren to the lowliest justice of the peace managed to make his particular two-bit contribution. Legislative committees converged on Tule Lake from north, south,

[29] Editorial, December 3, 1943.   [30] October 29, 1943.

east, and west. There had been "bombs, knives, guns, and various lethal weapons" at Tule Lake; a Japanese evacuee had "pushed his way into" the bedchamber of a "white woman" at the camp; the personnel of the center was "intermingling" with the evacuees; "sabotage" had been discovered; the staff was ridden with "Jap lovers"; the evacuees were being "coddled" and the staff was "pussyfooting"; and severe measures must be taken. Ray Richards implied that Mr. Dillon Myer had knowingly failed to confiscate "lethal weapons"; in fact, he implied that Mr. Myer had been a party to the "manufacture" of such weapons.[31]

A new West Coast Congressional committee was formed in Washington, as such California Congressmen as Poulson, Engle, Costello, Lea, and Phillips fought for the headlines "back home." At fairly regular intervals over a two-week period, Governor Warren kept announcing that he "would take action" and that "the menace must be removed" and that "California was threatened." The Dies Committee reopened its hearings in Washington and two California legislative committees began hearings at Tule Lake. The usual ex-employees of WRA were paraded before these committees and interviewed at length in the press. A spate of editorials appeared urging a bewildering and contradictory barrage of recommendations: Remove Dillon Myer! Stop the Segregation Program! Don't Stop the Segregation Program! Stop Releasing the Japs! Let the Army Take Over! Don't Bother the Army with the Problem! Deport Them All! Intern Them All! The prize discovery of these frenzied weeks was that made by Senator Jack Tenney: evacuees from the Poston center were violating the state laws of Arizona by "despoiling desert flora." The *Los Angeles Herald-Express* carried a headline reading: BARE DEADLY PERIL AS ARMED JAPANESE STREAM INTO CALIFORNIA. There was not one word of truth in the story. Congressman Costello announced on December 8 that "hundreds of Japanese-Americans and alien Japanese" were being permitted to return to California.[32] There was not one word of truth in this report. Even the emphatic denials issued by General Delos Emmons failed to

[31] See *Call-Bulletin*, December 21, 1943.
[32] *Los Angeles Times*, December 9, 1943.

quiet these rumors. Investigation revealed that there were exactly *twenty* American-born Japanese in Los Angeles County: all accounted for, all women married to Caucasian men, all mothers of minor children. Newspapers all over the nation carried echoes of the same stories.

Just to spice the campaign, the *Los Angeles Times* announced on December 4, 1943: "450 Cases of Whisky to Go to Tule Lake." A headline from the same newspaper on December 5 reads: "Whisky Flow to Tule Lake Under Inquiry." In an editorial of the same date the *Times* coyly inquired: "Is there perhaps some relation between rioting Japanese and a lot of whisky for Tule Lake?" Needless to say, whisky is not permitted at the Tule Lake center, nor at any other relocation center. The whisky in question had been consigned to the *town* of Tule Lake, California, not to the relocation center. "These Japs," wrote Ed Ainsworth in the *Los Angeles Times*, referring to the evacuees, "are a depraved breed who can't be dealt with like mischievous boys at a Sunday-school picnic . . . we should wake up to the fact that protection of Americans from these degraded Jap brutes is of more importance than the Little Tokyo Knitting and Brotherly Love Club." [33]

A number of very serious consequences flowed directly from the newspaper campaign precipitated in California by the Tule Lake incident. In the first place, the Japanese government broke off negotiations for the exchange of nationals pending an investigation to be made by the Spanish Embassy. There can be no doubt, as stated by Mr. R. B. Cozzens, Assistant Director of WRA, that "the interruption of negotiations . . . was caused by the malicious campaign which has been carried on by agitators of race hatred, including public as well as private organizations and individuals." [34] Despite clear warning from Mr. Myer that the Tule Lake situation was loaded with dynamite, and might involve the most serious complications, the newspapers in California refused to abandon their carefully planned campaign. They persisted in the campaign even after negotiations with Japan had

[33] November 11, 1943.
[34] UP dispatch, December 15, 1943.

been terminated. "Report that Tokyo Halting Exchange Pending Tule Lake Check Discounted," reads a headline in the *Los Angeles Times* for December 13, 1943.

In shouting for Army control of Tule Lake, despite repeated statements from the War Department that the Army did not want to assume this additional burden, the newspapers did so despite the warning that, if such a transfer of control were effected in this country, Japan would probably transfer control of its civilian camps to the Japanese Army. Not only did the press ignore these warnings, but it proceeded to castigate Mr. Myer for having attempted to impose a "censorship of the press." When it became apparent, however, that Japan really had broken off negotiations for the exchange of nationals, then and only then did the papers quiet down. The manner in which the California press handled this incident, in fact, seriously backfired. Earlier in November, Governor Warren had intimated that "anti-Japanese legislation" would be the principal subject matter of a special session of the California legislature called for January, 1944.[35] The various California legislative committees that had been holding hearings during 1943 were planning on filing elaborate reports upon the basis of which forty or fifty proposed "anti-Japanese" bills would be enacted. But after he had observed the manner in which the Tule Lake incident had backfired, the Governor suddenly decided to limit the legislature's attention to penal reform! American civilians in Japan will probably suffer additional hardships as a result of this campaign in California. On November 24, 1943, Radio Tokyo announced that the Japanese government "might reconsider its treatment of Americans because of the manner in which Japanese in the United States were being treated." For "the witch hunters," in Mr. Cozzens' phrase, "were not content with the facts. Distortions, half-truths and exaggerations were more in keeping with their desires. Official investigations and public hearings were used to dignify the most fantastic stories, thus giving them a semblance of truth."

Thoughtful Americans will do well to consider with care what Congressman Herman P. Eberharter has to say in his minor-

[35] See *Los Angeles Herald-Express*, November 26, 1943.

ity report on the Dies Committee investigation of the Tule Lake disturbances. Apropos of the majority report, he writes: —

> Groundless public fears and antagonisms have been stirred up at a time when national unity is more than ever needed, and widespread distrust has been engendered toward the operations of a hard-working and conscientious agency. Even more important, the investigation has encouraged the American public to confuse the people in relocation centers with our real enemies across the Pacific.
>
> Thus it [the investigation] has fostered a type of racial thinking which is already producing ugly manifestations and which seems to be growing in intensity. Unless this trend is checked, it may eventually lead to ill-advised actions which will constitute an everlastingly shameful blot on our national record.[36]

The Tule Lake incident also precipitated a grave constitutional problem. Taking advantage of the incident itself, certain groups in California began to renew their plan to strip the Nisei of American citizenship. On December 9, 1943, the Dies Committee forced Mr. Biddle to suggest, or rather to imply, that an act of Congress, along these lines, would be constitutional. He referred, of course, to the Kibei and to those Nisei who had given negative answers to questions No. 27 and No. 28 during the registration. The difficulty is that 50 per cent of the nearly 15,000 evacuees at the Tule Lake center are children under seventeen years of age. It will be recalled that the registration itself was restricted to evacuees over seventeen years of age. Any such legislation, therefore, is likely to divest thousands of American-born evacuees, under seventeen years of age, of their citizenship although they have never expressed themselves one way or another about their loyalty. At the present writing, it seems to be a foregone conclusion that the Nisei in Tule Lake will be stripped of their American citizenship (in the manner suggested by Mr. Biddle) and eventually deported to Japan.[37] Mr. Warren Atherton, National Commander of the American Legion, is now de-

[36] Quoted in *PM*, March 18, 1944.
[37] Statement of Mr. Cozzens, October 2, 1943.

manding the deportation of all aliens regardless of whether they are in Tule Lake or elsewhere.[38]

The "anti" groups in California will not rest until they have secured the deportation of all the evacuees — of every person of Japanese ancestry in the United States. Whether they will succeed in this campaign remains, of course, to be seen. But no one should be under any illusions about the real objective itself. The curiously belated "final report" of General J. L. De Witt on the evacuation program (released January 20, 1944) was skillfully used as still an additional step in the carefully planned propaganda campaign. Finally the release, on January 28, 1944, of the horrible and shocking story of the mistreatment of American prisoners of war aroused a wave of justifiable indignation throughout the nation. As might be expected, however, the West Coast press, which had been clamoring for five months for permission to break the story, managed to sandwich into the columns they devoted to it little items about the evacuees. Reading the editions of the West Coast papers that carried Captain Dyess' story, one got the unmistakable impression that it was being deliberately used, not for the purpose of whipping up hatred of Japan, not for the purpose of exposing the barbarous nature of the enemy, but as propaganda in support of the deportation campaign. The story was accompanied, at least in the West Coast press, by no official words of caution — no warning, for example, that American hatred should not be directed against the evacuees. It was not accompanied by an explanation of why fascists are fascists. It was immediately seized upon with great glee by the leaders of the Fight-Japan-First clique — the Hearsts and the McCormicks — eager to get possession of such an effective weapon on the eve of the opening of a great second front in Europe. When the story was released, police in such cities as Denver immediately went on the alert, fearing mob violence against the evacuees in those areas.

The effect of this agitation in California is clear: it leads directly to mob violence; it constitutes an incitement to racial hatred. In Martinez, California, Mrs. Horton Terry (who happens

[38] Boston, January 30, 1944.

to be of Japanese descent, married to a Caucasian defense worker, the mother of an American-born child) has been frequently intimidated and threatened by her neighbors. "No Japs Wanted Here" signs have been posted in view of the apartment house in which she resides. It is worthy of note, however, that when a mob threatened to drive her from the community, people from all over California wrote letters of protest. Mrs. Terry has a brother now serving with the American forces in Europe. Similar campaigns have been launched near Hayward, California. The Colorado legislature has now begun to investigate its local "Japanese problem." One witness testified: "I doubt that California could be entirely wrong in its stand against the Japanese. California is determined not to let the Jap return, even after the war." [39] At these hearings, nine Nisei soldiers appeared and asked to be heard. "We are going overseas. We're going to be hungry and wounded and we may not come back. But let us have this assurance — that our loved ones over here won't be discriminated against." It remains to be seen whether they will be given this assurance, even in Colorado, where there are some public officials who speak like Americans. "I hate the Japanese," said Senator Roy Chrysler of Denver, "God help me, with all the bitterness I possess. But never would I take out my personal revenge by voting for a law which violates the first principle which has made America great — justice for all." Senator Chrysler has a son in the Army and his grandson was killed at Pearl Harbor.

* * *

"I beg of you men and women of the most important part of our country," Pearl Buck told a Town Hall group in Los Angeles, November 1, 1943, "as I now believe California is, to keep your wits and common sense. For on your attitude toward Asia depends the attitude, I am convinced, of our whole country. In a curious fashion you are — or soon will be — the leader of the nation. The people in our Eastern states are already looking toward you as these great questions arise of how to deal with the people

[39] *Los Angeles Times*, February 6, 1943.

of Asia and South America. 'What does the West Coast say?' — I hear that question asked every day and wherever a policy is about to be shaped. The Eastern states are far more sensitive to your opinions today than they have ever been before. Imperceptibly the center of gravity in our country is moving westward. I say confidently that the future foreign policies of our government will be primarily decided by you, looking out over the Pacific, and not by those who face the Atlantic. The reason is that the center of the world has moved from Europe to Asia. . . . Once in an aeon a single people is given the opportunity to shape the world's direction. That opportunity is now ours. And because you in California face the Pacific and Asia, you among us have the crux in your hands. You can, by what you decide, be a barrier — or you can be a gateway to a new and better world, for us and for all peoples."

At the conclusion of this speech, Miss Buck was warmly applauded. A majority of the people of California are fair-minded; and many of them have the courage of their convictions. I could cite, if space permitted, a long list of distinguished citizens of California who have not hesitated to urge fair play for the evacuees; who have denounced proposals to strip the Nisei of their American citizenship; and who have called attention to the unfairness of the current attacks being leveled at the WRA. At every hearing in California, dozens of citizens have come forward to speak for fair treatment and to urge a respect for constitutional rights. The "anti" groups described in this chapter do not speak for a majority opinion in California; the newspapers quoted do not voice a majority sentiment. As a Californian, I take pride in the fact that, during a period of widespread hysteria and intense prejudice, there have been citizens like Dr. Robert Gordon Sproul, Mr. Chester Rowell, and Dr. Paul S. Taylor, and many others, who, by their courage, their intelligence, and their conspicuous fairness have upheld the rights of a luckless minority. It is my best judgment that these men speak for a majority of the residents of California.

CHAPTER VIII

Towards the Future

AT THE end of 1943, the Japanese-Americans were distributed somewhat as follows: between 8000 and 10,000 were in the United States Army; about 87,000 were in the relocation centers (including nearly 15,000 in the Tule Lake center); 8000 who had voluntarily moved from the West Coast and 20,000 who had never resided in the Western Defense Command were not involved in the relocation program. In addition, 19,000 evacuees had been released from the centers during the year. They were to be found primarily in the Middle West, the inter-mountain West, and the East: 3500 in Chicago; 1083 in Denver; 740 in Salt Lake City; 787 in Cleveland; 531 in Detroit; 464 in Minneapolis; 406 in New York City; around 350 in the District of Columbia and the rest in other areas. Several thousand evacuees were away from the centers on seasonal work permits. Immediately after Pearl Harbor, 5234 resident Japanese were arrested on Presidential warrants as "dangerous enemy aliens." Of this group, 40 per cent had been cleared by the authorities; around 1300 were paroled to WRA centers, and others were released. Of those originally arrested, 2079 were ordered interned for the duration (in special detention camps operated by the Department of Justice — not to be confused with WRA centers). By the end of 1943, 368 evacuees had been repatriated to Japan.

There are so many uncertain factors involved that it is impossible to chart the future course of WRA policy. Of the 19,000 evacuees who have been granted permanent leaves, 85 per cent are Nisei. Thus nearly 50 per cent of the Nisei eligible for release are already outside the centers. The general success of the individual relocation program will doubtless encourage others to

274

apply for release. As more and more Nisei become established outside the centers, they will send for their families and relatives. It is quite likely, also, that WRA will experiment in the future with "group relocation," so as to make it possible for small groups of families to relocate as units. Such a policy would assist in getting the Issei out of the centers. Now that the Nisei are being drafted, Selective Service will doubtless draw additional evacuees from the centers. Assuming that Congress does not reverse present WRA policies, it is possible that an additional 30,000 evacuees can be relocated by the end of 1944.

However this will leave a "residue" population — the lame, the halt, and the blind; old Issei bachelors; aged Issei couples; teen-age Nisei — who are likely to remain in the centers for the duration of the war. Resistance to relocation is still an important factor. Recently in one center 75 per cent of the Issei indicated that they intend to remain in the center for the duration and 28 per cent of the Nisei expressed a similar intention. While WRA is trying to minimize the number of residue cases — the future "reservation population" — still it is not reasonable to expect that all of the evacuees can be relocated before the war is over. As the center population declines, some of the centers will probably be closed. It is possible that one or two of them will be converted into genuine resettlement projects, of a co-operative character, and gradually turned over to the remaining evacuees. This would mean that, at the end of the war, there would be one or two small rural Japanese colonies left in the inter-mountain West. As to the Tule Lake segregants, some will doubtless apply for a review of their cases and a few will be released (the first couple was released on April 4, 1944). Of those remaining in Tule Lake, some will request repatriation, others will probably be deported to Japan at the end of the war.

The relocation centers could probably be emptied tomorrow, if the ban on return to the West Coast were lifted. When I visited the centers in the fall of 1943, I found many evacuees who were remaining in the centers primarily in the hope of eventually being able to return to the West Coast. California was a favorite topic of discussion. A survey in the Heart Mountain center revealed that nearly 50 per cent would return to California or the West Coast, if they were permitted to do so. People cannot live in a particular area for most of their lives without coming to regard it, however ironically, as "home." The hope of an eventual return to their homes is certainly one of the resistances militating against relocation at the present time.

I also talked with numerous Issei farmers who had investigated the possibilities of produce farming in other areas. The prospects, they reported, were not encouraging. The one type of farming they know — intensive produce farming — requires certain types of soil and certain climatic conditions. Many of them still retained interests in California: leases, machinery, equipment, property in storage. They felt that their best prospects of again becoming self-supporting were on the West Coast. Some of them would be willing to relocate elsewhere, if they could return to the Coast for the purpose of liquidating their holdings and arranging their affairs. As the Issei come to realize that there will not be a mass return, they will be more inclined to leave the centers. For, in the absence of a mass return, it would be impossible to reopen Japanese businesses which catered almost exclusively to a Japanese clientele.

Agitation against the return of the evacuees has served to direct many of them eastward. The Nisei, in particular, are very bitter on the subject of California. A recent article in the *Heart Mountain Sentinel* (September 8, 1943) indicates current Nisei thinking: —

> Californians need not exert themselves to prevent the return of evacuees. Evacuees know when they are not wanted. They are not looking back. Their eyes are projected eastward, where people are in control of their emotions, where greed, avarice and spite play minor roles in the drama of human relations. . . . California's pattern of living and thinking is designed to hate Japanese. It's a new and different California, in an ugly, unbelievable sort of way. . . . California is foreign, and will always be to the evacuees. In the seething cauldron that is California since Pearl Harbor, the scum has risen to the surface, overflowing and over-

running the Golden State, contaminating and putrefying, giving it a sour, diseased, unrecognizable complexion.

The trouble with California is that it doesn't do anything in half measures. It always goes for the jackpot. It builds the biggest race tracks, the roomiest stadium, the most sprawling estates. It grows the biggest oranges and grapefruits. And even if they aren't the biggest and the best, Californians really believe that they are. It's a complex. And so when they go in for race hatred, watch out; they really do it up brown.

Returning evacuees will find it will be only a matter of time before they will be booted out again. Evacuees will do well to forget California completely, to lock its memory in their chamber of horrors. They've just lost a friend who ran true to form in the pinch; they will find a better and true friend on the rockbound Atlantic, on the rolling plains of the expansive midwest, and on the hills and dales of the stretching Alleghenies.

Of the 93,717 persons evacuated from California, William Flynn of the *San Francisco Chronicle* estimates that 50,000 will never return. As a result of a survey which he conducted, Mr. Flynn came to the conclusion that 50 per cent of the evacuees are determined not to return to the West Coast; 40 per cent are undecided although they would "like to return"; and 10 per cent are fearful of the consequences if they do return. Many evacuees live for the day when they can return to their former home town — "just to see what would happen." Nisei soldiers, who have visited the West Coast on furloughs, went there primarily to see, as many of them have told me, how they would be received. Much to their surprise, they did not meet with unpleasant incidents. They were entertained in the canteens; welcomed by their former friends; and, in many cases, royally entertained. The predicted "violence" and "free murder" did not take place. In the files of WRA are perhaps 50,000 letters written by residents of California vouching for the character and patriotism of a particular evacuee — some person that the writer *knew*, as employee, friend, neighbor, or classmate.

While the Little Tokyos on the West Coast will probably

never exist again, Americans of Japanese ancestry have a place in California, Oregon, and Washington. Relocation is a backstream movement; it is an attempt to reverse the current of migration. Unquestionably some of the evacuees will return, not immediately but gradually, not en masse but individually. They will return perhaps the better for the experiences they have undergone. "Living away from the west coast," writes Larry Tajiri, "we felt more a part of the whole of America and less a member of a minority group. We liked New York because there we felt that we were losing our racial identity."

1. The Opportunity Is Ours

In considering the future of the Japanese-Americans, it is important to recognize that a unique opportunity now exists, not only to eradicate the dangerous tension zone of race feeling on the West Coast, but to change our racial ideologies in general. In the case of the Japanese-Americans, this opportunity arises by reason of the concurrence of a number of largely unforeseen factors which have tended to accelerate the process of cultural change. This process involves a change in the thinking and feeling of the minority group itself, as well as a change in the thinking and feeling of the dominant group. What is said in this section has, of course, particular reference to Japanese-Americans; but to some extent the same observations would apply to other racial minorities.

In the first place, the visible and invisible ties which existed between the Japanese settlements on the West Coast and Japan have been severed. This severance has occurred all the way from Alaska to Peru. The Japanese communities have been uprooted; the Little Tokyos have vanished. As long as Japanese were concentrated in relatively small areas on the Coast, there was always the possibility of friction and the manipulation of the resulting tensions by Japan or by Germany or by local race bigots. While this possibility still exists, the dangers have been minimized.

The relocation of the evacuees has taken the "Japanese issue" away from the West Coast bigots. The problem has now become part of a national minority question for the solution of which the federal government has begun to assume a measure of responsibility. While in the past the federal government has been powerless to cope with anti-Japanese agitation on the West Coast, it has been finally forced to assume exclusive jurisdiction. It was the federal government that ordered evacuation; it is the federal government that must assume responsibility for the direct and indirect consequences of mass evacuation. Evacuation has been but one of a number of wartime measures all of which have served to bring the whole question of race relations within the reach of the democratic process applied at the federal level. In other words, the management of race relations has become a function of the federal government.

Wide dispersal of the evacuees should reduce some of the prejudice against them. For race tensions do tend to abate in relation to the number of racially different persons in a particular area and to their general geographical distribution within that area. While I do not share the view that race prejudice is directly related to the size of a particular minority in a particular area, nevertheless Dr. David P. Barrows is probably right in urging that this relationship is an important factor in the problem.[1]

A factor of still greater importance, however, is that Japanese-Americans are now becoming known to Americans in the East and Middle West. The national press has already begun to refute some of the prejudicial nonsense that has so consistently issued from the West Coast newspapers. Other colored minorities, notably the Negro minority, have become interested in the Japanese-Americans.[2] Not only are the racial minority groups coming to recognize the similarity of their problems, but, as a nation, we are beginning to realize that we have *a race problem* in the United States and not a series of unrelated local issues. With this recognition comes a widespread realization that we can never "solve" any one minority problem until we undertake a solution of the race problem as such.

The kind of world that emerges from this war will have a

[1] See "Citizen and Alien," *California Monthly*, April, 1942.
[2] See *Common Ground*, Winter, 1944, p. 94.

great deal to do with the future of racial minorities in the United States. If it is a world that breeds fear and distrust between nations, then fear and distrust will continue to separate groups inside the nation. Not only will Germany and Japan be overwhelmingly defeated, but we are not likely to repeat our former errors in dealing with Germany; and I am sure that the Japanese will not be dealt with in a tender manner. In the past, both nations have manipulated the West Coast Japanese issue to their own advantage. Until both nations are liquidated as military powers, we can never hope for a solution of the resident Japanese issue. Long before Pearl Harbor even the Nisei had come to recognize that they were distrusted because Japan was distrusted.

In an article addressed to the Nisei, the *New Canadian* of December 25, 1940, had this comment to offer: —

> You are feared and disliked because the country of your father's origin, Japan, is in open alliance with Germany and Italy, two powers and two systems against which Canada is pledged to war to the death. This is no fault of any of you; but many Canadians, understandably, wonder if and how many of you rejoice at this alliance.
>
> You are feared and disliked because Japan seems very much akin in ideals and government to an authoritarian, undemocratic state. Again, no fault of yours; but, honestly, Nisei, you would be much more trusted and respected if you did not attempt to tell Occidental Canadians that Japan is a Japanese version of democracy. And there's no need to be apologetic; there is no scientific nor historic reason for supposing that a system devised and developed in one part of the earth is necessarily fitted for another part.
>
> You are feared and disliked because of what, for lack of a better term, may be called your "questionable relations" with Japan, — "dual citizenship" and the whole vague aspect of your allegiance. This is a cruel question to raise. It is natural and proper to love and value the country and culture of one's fathers; but these times are not natural and if you are not for this country you are against her.
>
> Finally, and as importantly, you are feared and disliked

because you do not do very much about clearing up the fear and dislike. Take the matter of friendship and getting together; there are many Occidental Canadians, with the kindliest and most interested intentions towards you and your possible human and cultural offerings, who simply do not know how to get to know you. It is up to you to break down your own barriers of conservatism and formality, not the Occidentals. Mention of shyness brings up a notable reason for calling you ostriches. You have worked yourselves into a resentment-complex because you are denied a few rights in this country. Admittedly it is not fair, but when weighed against the above mentioned causes of your un popularity, it is understandable.

The war is in process of removing "this whole vague aspect of allegiance" and of liquidating these external causes of fear and distrust. One factor in the distrust of the Nisei on the West Coast and in Hawaii was the doubt, in the minds of friends and enemies alike, of just how they would act in a crisis. It was assumed, by those who knew them, that they would be loyal; but no one could attest to their loyalty as an unequivocal fact since the test itself had not arisen. Not only has the test finally occurred, but, thanks to the good sense of an enlightened administration, the Nisei have finally been afforded a chance to demonstrate their loyalty. Loyalty does not exist in a vacuum. It grows or withers in response to external as well as subjective factors. It must be given a chance to express itself. As one observer has said of the Nisei: "You must give them something to be loyal to."

The Nisei have met the test of their loyalty in a magnificent manner under the most trying circumstances. The fact that they have done so will, in the long run, finally remove those longstanding doubts and misgivings. In this sense, one can even say that the war has been a war of liberation for the Nisei — liberation from doubt, suspicion, hatred, and distrust. As the American and Canadian evacuees move eastward and settle in communities in which there is no traditional prejudice against them, some of their sensitivity vanishes, some of their notorious reserve disappears, and the "oppression psychosis" is lifted. The circumstances of their new life are forcing them to make that initial first step toward the other person.

Another factor of great importance has been pointed out by Dr. Robert E. Park.[3] "Isolation," he writes, "as a geographical and geopolitical fact has ceased to exist and isolationism as a doctrine and policy has become obsolete." The isolationism that we practised in foreign affairs was related to the isolationism we practised toward racial minorities at home. Since a change in the one type of isolationism is likely to bring about a change in the other, the whole minorities question is inextricably interwoven with the outcome of the war and the nature of the peace. "In the prosecution of the war," writes Dr. Park, "and in the organization of the peace, racial diversities of the American population will be either a national handicap or a national asset, depending upon our ability to make our racial policies and our racial ideology conform to our national interests. We have not succeeded in doing that yet. A revolution in race relations in the United States may be impending, but it has not yet arrived. The war has changed the nature of the race problem, but it has not changed fundamentally the mind of the American people."

It should also be pointed out that the modern social sciences now have a good working knowledge of how to deal with the problem of cultural conflicts and how to assist in the process of acculturation (anthropology has recently become an "applied science"). In the past, the inadequate state of the social sciences was responsible for an enormous amount of misinformation on the subject of "race" and "racial conflicts." It was an American economist, Francis A. Walker, who first developed the fearful notion that "foreign immigrants" were driving Anglo-Saxon workers from their "rightful heritage" in America. It was an American sociologist, Dr. Edward Alsworth Ross, chief theoretician of the anti-Oriental forces in California, who gave wide popularity to the kindred notion that the Anglo-Saxons were committing "race suicide." Both notions have had a baneful influence on race relations in the United States.

The modern social sciences have also made some important

[3] *American Society in Wartime*, p. 180.

contributions to our understanding of immigration and migration movements. In prewar days, such publicists as K. K. Kawakami and the Reverend Sidney Gulick deeply impressed American church groups with the argument that Japan must solve its population problem by sending immigrants throughout the world. Japan itself made excellent use of the argument, thereby subtly cultivating the "yellow peril" myth. Not only did Japan sell its own people this particular bill of goods, but it consistently lied about its population problem, juggled its population statistics, and, at the time of the Washington Conference, spent a million dollars on publicity and propaganda which was largely predicated on this same argument. Immigration from Japan did not come from the areas where the pressure of population on resources was greatest; emigration never made a dent on Japan's so-called "population problem"; nor can what is termed a population problem be solved by emigration. To advance such an argument is usually to obscure the real causes of the problem, which are to be found, in most cases, in the social structure of the particular country. India has, perhaps, the most acute population problem in the world today. Yet, as H. N. Brailsford has so conclusively demonstrated, emigration is not the answer to the problem.

There is more interest in, and more intelligent discussion of, the race question today than at any time in our history. Over two hundred interracial committees have been established in American urban communities since the war. At a conference held in Chicago in March, 1944, a national "clearinghouse" committee was established to assist in co-ordinating the work of these committees. Not since the Civil War, writes Horace Cayton, has the Negro problem received the attention that it is receiving today. Negroes from the Deep South are moving north and west (500,-000 to the North, 170,000 to the West); Japanese-Americans are moving into the Middle West and East; "whites" from the Deep South have moved north and west by the thousands. Northern draftees have been trained in Southern army camps and Southern draftees have been trained outside the South. With increasing industrialization, trade-unionism is getting a real foothold in some

Southern areas. The militant fight waged by the CIO and numerous AFL unions against discrimination is a powerful leavening influence. All of these developments, and many others not mentioned, merely indicate that the rate of cultural change in America is being rapidly accelerated. In considering what can be done, as well as what should be done, about race relations in the United States, these factors must be kept in mind.

2. Change within the Minority Groups

One of the most hopeful aspects of the relocation program is that it now becomes possible for the Nisei to win full acceptance. By loosening the ties of the Japanese family system and by breaking the barriers of Little Tokyo, many formerly restricting influences have been removed. "The attack on Pearl Harbor," writes Yoshitaka Takagi, "ended the old traditional bondage to the established leadership, and Japanese-Americans were freed for the first time from the rigid political-social machinery which had so tightly held them, freed to express their own opinions and to act according to their individual consciences."

Great changes have come over the Nisei since December 7, 1941. They are asserting themselves today, not as Japanese-Americans or as American-Japanese, but as American citizens. They are using new techniques to win respect and acceptance. They are discovering the *real* American tradition — the tradition of Emerson, Thoreau, Whitman, and Lincoln — and they are no longer confused by its bogus counterpart. "New vistas," to quote from an editorial in the *Heart Mountain Sentinel* of May 22, 1943, "have been opened to the Nisei. Economic opportunities denied them by the west coast's deep-rooted prejudices are being made available to skilled and trained individuals in other sections of the land. Unions are being opened up, and evacuees are being accepted in literally hundreds of communities as social equals and fellow-Americans. The evacuees are re-discovering the real America, to their and America's advantage."

They are reaching out to identify themselves with other minority groups, such as Negroes, Chinese, and Filipinos. They are showing a very healthy interest in the Negro problem. They are subjecting their own experience, and the experience of their parents, to an extremely exacting scrutiny and criticism. Recognizing that there might be factors in their own background that contributed to the prejudice against them, they are seeking to discover and to isolate these factors. They are becoming increasingly interested in the play of social forces in American life. Their publications contain excellent editorials on the poll tax, on the Fair Employment Practice Committee, and on similar issues. The experience of relocation has aroused in them a new consciousness of the value of civil liberties and they are inclined, as one of them has said, "to start swinging back" at their detractors.

They are using the courts, with increasing frequency, as a means of winning recognition of their rights — a procedure thoroughly in keeping with the manner by which all minority groups, economic and political as well as racial, have traditionally functioned in America. They have borrowed the strike technique from the labor movement and used it to win acceptance of their rights. They have shown a real understanding of the labor movement and a growing political maturity. The Nisei leaders are constantly urging the Nisei to join American organizations, or rather to join with other Americans in mixed or interracial organizations. Realizing that the Japanese-American church had a tendency to set them apart, they have taken a strong stand against the segregated church and against all types of segregation. They are reaching out, in a variety of ways, to function as American citizens.

It should also be observed that evacuation has leveled off many social distinctions within the group. It has brought "to an unprecedented degree the majority of us into the ranks of the working proletariat." [4] Evacuees are tending to identify their views with those of the economic group to which they have become attached in the process of relocation, rather than to the ethnic group itself or the Japanese-American family or the

[4] *Pacific Citizen*, September 11, 1943.

Japanese-American community. Typical of these new-found attitudes are these words from an article by Tom Shibutani: "The only salvation for the Nisei or for anyone in a racial minority is to throw off the narrow personal interest in local and personal problems and to join in the larger battle for a better world. The Nisei must try to lose their identity and must take part in a united effort with people of other racial extractions to defeat fascism and to reconstruct the world along lines that are more conducive to peaceful and co-operative living. We should begin in our own backyards by getting rid of our own prejudices against peoples of other races and creeds. By being prejudiced against the Negroes, Jews, Chinese, and Filipinos, the Nisei are contributing to their own self-destruction." All over the country, racial minorities are showing a similar tendency to move out of their segregated worlds and to live in the full stream of American life. This tendency is in itself an indication of cultural change. In fact, there are observers who insist, and with much evidence to support their views, that the rate of cultural change within the minority groups is actually faster than in the nation as a whole.

3. The Nisei and the War

The California groups who opposed the induction of the Nisei into the armed services were, from their point of view, extremely farsighted. They realized that if the Nisei were given a chance to demonstrate their loyalty in this concrete fashion, the majority of Americans would admire their spirit and would want to accept them as fellow citizens. The opposition of Southern race bigots to the use of Negroes in combat units is premised upon a similar consideration. But this being a total war, it has become difficult to restrict the opportunities of the minority groups in the services. The hero of Pearl Harbor was Dorie Miller, a Negro; the hero of the Aleutian campaign was José Martinez, a Mexican sugar-beet worker from Colorado.

It is for this reason that the War Department's announcement of the formation of a special Japanese-American combat team was the boldest and most effective step taken by the administration to win for the Nisei a measure of acceptance in American life. While discrimination still exists in the sense that Nisei are not eligible for all branches of the service, still the discrimination against them in Selective Service has been removed. Today Japanese-Americans are serving with our armed forces all over the world. Over 200 of them are in the Merchant Marine. Between 8000 and 10,000 are in the Army.

They have given an excellent account of themselves. Some have served as intelligence officers in the Southwest Pacific with distinction and courage. A Japanese-American combat battalion was among the first units to land at Salerno. This particular battalion has suffered casualties amounting to more than 40 per cent of its entire personnel. One Distinguished Service Cross and thirteen Silver Stars have been bestowed on members of the unit for gallantry in action, and fifty-eight, or more, have been awarded the Purple Heart. Sergeant Kazuo Komoto and Sergeant Fred Nishitsujii have been cited for gallantry in dispatches from the Southwest Pacific. Several hundred Nisei are with the British and American forces in India as intelligence officers. Nisei have served in Africa, India, Italy, Attu, and in the European theater of the war. General Mark Clark has repeatedly praised the Nisei soldiers in his command. Lieutenant Colonel Karl Gould has described the Nisei as playing an "indispensable role in the war" as interpreters. Brigadier General R. E. Mittelstaedt and Colonel Farrant L. Turner have praised the Nisei in unstinted terms.

Sergeant Ben Kuroki, of Hershey, Nebraska, has taken part in twenty-nine combat flights over Hitler's Europe. He participated in the raid on the Ploesti oil fields. He wears the Air Medal with four Oak Leaf Clusters. He has been on bombing missions over Wilhelmshaven, Bordeaux, Danzig, Vegesack, Munster, La Pallice. When he was in Los Angeles recently a local radio station canceled a broadcast in which he was scheduled to take part on the ground that the appearance of a Japanese-American on a radio program in California would raise a "controversial issue"! When he spoke in San Francisco, however, before the Commonwealth Club, he received a ten-minute standing ovation. "I had

287

thought," he said, "that after Ploesti and twenty-nine other missions so rough it was just short of a miracle I got through them, I wouldn't have to fight for acceptance among my own people all over again. In most cases, I don't, and to those few who help breed fascism in America by spreading such prejudice, I can only reply in the words of the Japanese-American creed: 'Although some individuals may discriminate against me, I shall never become bitter or lose faith, for I know that such persons are not representative of the majority of the American people.' The people who wrote that creed are the thousands of Japanese-Americans whom certain groups want deported immediately. These Japanese-Americans have spent their lives proving their loyalty to the United States, as their sons and brothers are proving it now on the bloody battlefields of Italy. It is for them, in the solemn hope that they will be treated justly rather than with hysterical passion, that I speak today."

In literally hundreds of ways the Japanese-Americans, once provided with a chance to demonstrate their loyalty, have done so in the most conclusive manner. They have purchased war bonds in the relocation centers; organized volunteers for victory committees; made radio transcriptions for the OWI; and, within the limitations of their detention, have done everything in their power to aid in the war effort. At the time the Tokyo fliers were executed, the Nisei soldiers in training at Camp Shelby bought $100,000 in war bonds in a single day to demonstrate how they felt about this act of barbarism. Nisei girls are serving in the WAC. It is interesting to note, however, that, with rare exceptions, little news of their participation in the war effort has been carried in the West Coast newspapers.

The magnificent spirit shown by these people, both here and in Hawaii, cannot but win the admiration of the American people. Faced with such conclusive proof of loyalty, plans for the deportation of the parents of these soldiers become monstrously unfair. To turn from a dispatch from Italy listing the casualties of the Japanese-American combat unit to an item in which some demagogue is advocating a constitutional amendment to strip the Nisei of their citizenship is to experience a feeling of extreme nausea. I should like to see Pfc. Yoshinao Omiya, who lost the sight of both eyes from a land-mine explosion during the Italian campaign, attend the next annual convention of the Native Sons of the Golden West. In the days, weeks, and months to follow, the Nisei will be steadily building up an indefeasible title to fair treatment, to full citizenship, just as the loyal Issei will be establishing, by their excellent conduct under the most trying circumstances, an irrefutable claim to the chance to become American citizens. There are some facts which not even bigots can ignore. There are some facts which, unadorned and unelaborated, speak far more convincingly than the rantings of a Representative Rankin or an editorial in the *Los Angeles Examiner*.

4. Towards a Policy and Program

While an excellent opportunity exists today to liquidate the last vestiges of racism in America, this opportunity must be used in a dynamic fashion. Sensing the factors that I have outlined above, our domestic fascists are seeking a national alliance on the race question. Reaction against further changes in the racial status quo has already begun to crystallize on a national scale, with representatives from the Deep South extending the right hand of bigotry to their colleagues from the Far West and seeking support in Northern industrial communities. With the migration of racial groups, the issue has arisen in Detroit and Chicago, in Seattle and Los Angeles: "Are Southern patterns of racism to be implanted here?" "Is segregation the answer?" This much is to be said for the advocates of White Supremacy: they have *a policy* and *a program*. They know what they want. In the absence of a federal policy and program, these forces might win in America by default. They realize that their position has been seriously jeopardized, but they are resourceful and determined. When the Supreme Court handed down its decision in the Lonnie Smith case on April 4, 1944 (upsetting the Texas "white" primary), Southern spokesmen in Congress, with one accord, denounced the decision. They not only denounced the decision — they spewed contempt upon the Supreme Court, boasted that they would defy its mandate and evade the effect of the decision by trickery, and voiced their determination to uphold the White Supremacy doctrine by every means at their disposal. There is only one way to cope with these individuals and that is to mobilize majority American opinion behind a far-reaching federal policy and program. Without attempting to list the items of such a program in detail, the salient points can be briefly summarized.

The essence of the matter is that we have no federal policy on race relations. Prior to the issuance of President Roosevelt's Executive Order No. 8802, it could be said that the federal government had never taken a single affirmative step to discourage discrimination, much less to cultivate understanding and acceptance. This negative policy has been particularly striking in the field of education. We have thrown our schools open to minority groups and have instructed our children to believe that there should be complete equality before the law; that there should be no taxation without representation; that individual rights should be respected; and that all careers should be open to all citizens. But the content of our education has been largely barren of constructive and affirmative programs designed to combat prejudice, to explain cultural differences, to expose the myth of race. If the state of California had spent on an intelligent educational program one tenth of what groups in California have spent on anti-Oriental campaigns, there would be a much larger area of racial tolerance in the state today.

Here is what we need: (1) a declaration of federal policy in the form of a joint resolution of both houses of Congress to the effect that it is the declared public policy of the United States government that there shall be no discrimination based upon race, color, creed, or national origin. Once such a policy has been declared, it can be implemented in various ways: in the armed services; in government service; in every agency of the federal government; by utilizing the purchasing power of the federal government to force compliance with the policy itself. Our courts could rely upon such a declared public policy in striking down discriminatory statutes, state and federal, as being in violation of the Fourteenth Amendment. (2) In addition to eliminating the poll tax in federal elections and enacting an anti-lynching statute, we need to (adopt a new federal civil-rights statute in the form of a Fair Racial Practices Act, and to give the Fair Employment Practice Committee real legislative sanction.) We should enforce the second section of the Fourteenth Amendment, which provides for the reduction of the representation of any state in Congress when that state discriminates in the exercise of the franchise. What we tend to forget is that discrimination has been legislated into existence, as a glance at the statute books of almost every state in the Union will demonstrate. Since we have embalmed our prejudices in the form of discriminatory statutes, an obvious first step is to eliminate these statutes, or to nullify their effect, by federal action. It is *against the law* to be fair-minded on the race question in most Southern states today. If you practise racial equality in these states, you are likely to end up in jail. (3) Remove every vestige of racism from our immigration and naturalization codes. (4) Create a federal agency expressly authorized to deal with the problem and thereby recognize that the management of race relations has become a function of the federal government.

Since I made this last suggestion in *Brothers under the Skin*, it has begun to receive considerable consideration.[5] Mr. Ward Shepard has made some particularly important contributions to the proposal. He has suggested that such an agency should be assigned five major functions: research and education; the redefinition and enforcement of legal and constitutional rights; mediation; welfare planning; and the function of organization (that is, seeking to correlate the activities of existing groups and stimulating the expression of latent good will). Much of the work of such an agency could, as Mr. Shepard points out, be carried on through already existing local agencies. The proposal itself is premised upon a simple basic proposition: that it is the responsibility of the federal government to see to it that no citi-

[5] See "An Institute of Ethnic Democracy" by John Collier and Saul K. Padover, *Common Ground*, Autumn, 1943; "Are Race Relations the Business of the Federal Government?" *Common Ground*, Winter, 1944; and "The Tools for Ethnic Democracy" by Ward Shepard, *Common Ground*, Spring, 1944.

zen of the United States is discriminatorily denied, on the basis of race alone, access to those services and facilities which are a vital requisite of good citizenship. It does not contemplate an extension of the wardship principle or the creation of another Indian Bureau. The pattern for such an agency might well be found, for example, in the Children's Bureau of the Department of Labor.

Before rejecting this proposal, we should consider our experience in dealing with other disadvantaged groups in American life. At one time women occupied a position in our democracy which, in some respects, was not unlike that of certain racial minorities today. How did we proceed to remedy this situation? First, by removing the disabilities which handicapped women (giving them the franchise, making it possible for them to hold property in their own names, and so on); and, second, by recognizing certain special problems which they faced as women and by giving them additional, or, if you will, special protection in the form of legislation requiring rest periods, restrictions on hours of employment, and so forth. When we sought to improve the status of labor, we followed exactly the same procedure: we removed labor's disabilities by recognizing the principle of collective bargaining and by safeguarding the exercise of this right through special legislation.

The case for federal intervention is unanswerable. Recently Dr. L. D. Reddick listed the basic objectives of Northern Negroes as follows: equal access to employment; equal access to adequate housing; full civil liberty; an end to Jim Crow practices in the armed services; and an end to anti-Negro propaganda and ridicule. With the possible exception of the last item, each of these objectives presupposes federal action. The Northern Negro will never accept a solution of the problem which involves segregation; while the South insists, and will continue to insist, that segregation is not a debatable point but a major premise of any approach to the problem. In view of this continuing impasse, how can we even pretend that the Negro problem is the "peculiar problem" of the South? In the absence of federal intervention, the problem will become increasingly involved. Although the percentage of Negroes residing in the Deep South has been declining, the South still adheres to the doctrine of White Supremacy and Jim Crow regulations are more prolix today than they were twenty years ago. Do we want California to dictate our policy toward the peoples of the Far East? Shall we concede to the South the right to formulate our policy toward the peoples of Africa?

"Our edifice of racial inequality," as Dr. Earnest A. Hooton has so well said, "is a sepulchre, whitened without and full of festering corruption. It smells to high heavens and is an offense in the nostrils of all honest men. We have a Government Bureau of American Ethnology, restricted, however, to the study of dry bones, ruined dwellings, dying languages, and dead customs of the American Indian, — harmless but relatively futile pursuits. . . . Why do we not have a powerful, nonpolitical, honest government organization devoted to the study, protection, and improvement of our oppressed Negro minority, another for our large population of Mexican origin, and still others for various underprivileged racial and national elements which live in this land of freedom and equality without experiencing either? We could do a great deal better if in our government an effective Department of Race and Culture would bend its efforts to the scientific development of every racial and national stock in our country and to the task of co-ordinating the efforts of each to further its own happiness and the advance of American civilization."

When I am told that progress in racial understanding can only come about as the result of a millennial process of education, I am moved to suggest that *education is action*. Involve the important mass organizations of the nation in the struggle to achieve a program such as I have suggested, and, by this very process, you will educate the people on the issues involved. In fact, I can think of no more effective means of mass education. Powerful sources of organized support can be mobilized behind such a program, such as the trade-unions, the churches, the welfare organizations, the minorities themselves. A clear majority of the American people will support such a program. They have never been asked to join in a campaign of this kind. In organizing them behind such a program, we shall be building a powerful national wall against prejudice and intolerance in America. Adopt a policy of "nonintervention" and "appeasement" and bigotry will be left in possession of the field. We can end that curious schism in American life — the distinction between our overt morals and our covert mores — by evoking the real American tradition; by seeking to apply it in practice; and by appealing to a national public opinion on racial equality.

5. The West Coast and the Pacific

The federal government must also take official cognizance of the problems of cultural conflict in the world of the future. "In the new and more inclusive society which is emerging," writes Dr. Park, "we shall be living — particularly if it is to be a free and democratic society — in a new intimacy with all the peoples of the world, not only with our allies but with our enemies. . . . We shall need, as never before, to know human geography and, perhaps, geopolitics. We shall need to know — not all of us — but some of us — all the languages. We must have institutes, such as they have long had in Germany, France, and England, for the study of the languages and cultures of the peoples outside of Europe, in Asia and Africa. We must, in short, prepare ourselves as never before to live not merely in America, but in the world." [6]

This suggestion is particularly apposite in relation to the peoples, languages, and cultures of the Far East. As a nation, we knew little about Japan prior to Pearl Harbor. Not only was our knowledge of the most superficial variety, but we rationalized our ignorance by creating a myth of Oriental inscrutability. According to the *Washington Post* of December 12, 1943, there were only about 600 civilians in this country, aside from the evacuees, who were familiar with the Japanese language.

"The basic reason," writes Dr. Jesse F. Steiner, "for our misjudgment of the Japanese nation lies in our superficial knowledge

[6] *American Journal of Sociology*, May, 1943, p. 107.

of the history and culture of the Far East. The perpetuation of this myth of oriental incomprehensibility was made possible by our abysmal ignorance of the history of Japan and of the factors that have entered into the building of this nation. Our historical interest has been largely limited to the study of those countries and peoples to which our ancestral roots can be traced. However inadequate may be our knowledge of the history of western civilization, we at least are familiar with the names and exploits of its great leaders and feel that our present heritage is a product of their struggles and aspirations. But to most Americans Japan's past is a closed book. . . . The religions to which Japanese have given allegiance are looked down upon as pagan and therefore unworthy of serious study except by scholars. Their customs that come to our attention impress us as exotic and irrational and strengthen our convictions that the Japanese are a peculiar people whose behavior is difficult to forecast."[7]

Far Eastern studies, as Dr. Steiner notes, have never been popular in American colleges and universities. Even the universities on the Pacific Coast failed to devote much attention to Oriental cultures. A few West Coast colleges had a chair of Oriental Art and Philosophy which was usually occupied by a Chinese or a Japanese scholar. In more than one case, the Japanese "scholar" was an official apologist for Imperial Japan; and, in at least a few cases, his salary was in part paid by funds raised by the local Japanese associations![8]

The need for readily available bodies of organized information about the Far East will be magnified after the war. It requires no imagination to appreciate the problems of rehabilitation, of reconstruction, of relief, that will arise in the Far East; not to mention the problems arising by reason of the necessity of military occupation. We are woefully unprepared to assume these responsibilities. For not only has the field of Oriental studies been of limited interest in this country, but our few trained Orientalists have tended to become increasingly preoccupied with the more recondite subjects in their field. Only a small portion

[7] *Behind the Japanese Mask*, 1943, p. 7.
[8] See *Must We Fight Japan?* by Walter B. Pitkin, 1921, p. 452.

of the available information has undergone a process of vulgarization and percolated down to the people.[9]

This is not a matter of academic interest: it should be of vital concern to the people of the West Coast. For whether they realize it or not, the economic future of the area lies in the Pacific. The war has brought about an industrial revolution in California and, to a lesser extent perhaps, throughout the Pacific Coast. Heavy industry rather than agriculture is now the chief factor in the economy of California. The war has accelerated the industrial growth of the Far West by at least twenty years, and in some fields by fifty years, in advance of normal expectations. Nearly 1,500,000 people have flocked to the West Coast since 1940. For the first time, the region now has a steel industry; it has aluminum mills and magnesium plants. It has vast manpower and great resources in petroleum and wood chemistry, food processing, and the exploitation of minerals; and it has great untapped sources of hydroelectric power. The increasing utilization of light metals will afford West Coast industry an exceptional opportunity for expansion in the postwar period.

The major problem, of course, is markets. The Coast really has no hinterland. It is encased by the arid, sparsely settled intermountain West. This territory can never provide a market large enough to absorb the production of which Pacific Coast industry is now capable. Mr. Robert Elliott of the *San Francisco News* is obviously correct in stating that the future markets for the emerging industrial West are in the Orient. China, according to Mr. Elliott, will want to buy equipment for twenty thousand (eventually a hundred thousand) miles of railroads. China will want equipment for factories, for highways; it will need machinery, planes, petroleum products, railway equipment, raw cotton, automobiles and tires, tools and accessories. And China is but part of the Far East.

At the present time, however, the West Coast is entirely unprepared to take advantage of whatever economic opportunities may exist in the Far East. Language and cultural barriers exist

[9] See comments of Cyrus Adler, *Journal of the American Oriental Society*, September, 1924.

and fundamental information about the areas involved is lacking. The task of organizing such a body of information is far beyond the resources of the colleges and universities; and the necessary trained personnel is not presently available. Furthermore the continued existence of present West Coast anti-Oriental attitudes would jeopardize not merely a sound foreign policy in the Far East, but the development of a give-and-take policy in trade and commerce. Testifying before the House Committee on Immigration and Naturalization on May 27, 1943, Mr. J. J. Underwood of the Seattle Chamber of Commerce spoke out in support of the legislation lifting the ban on Chinese immigration. The measure involved, he testified, an estimated $5,000,000,000 in postwar trade with the Orient. The "irritants" in our relations with the Far East had to be removed. "We fear," he said, "that this all-Asia propaganda might be successful — if they Japanize the Chinese you gentlemen are going to think that the gates of hell have been left ajar — in the countries washed by the Pacific Ocean are two thirds of the raw material of the world and three fourths of the people who tread the earth."

Economic considerations such as these will, in the long run, bring about important changes in West Coast racial mores. But the process needs to be intelligently aided and, if possible, accelerated. There should be established, for example, a federally supported Institute of Pacific Affairs. It should be located in California — not in Boston or New York, New Orleans or Des Moines. It is worthy of mention, in passing, that the American Oriental Society was founded by John Pickering *in Boston* in 1842; the present headquarters of the Institute of Pacific Relations is *in New York City*. It should form a part of the institutional life of the peoples of the West Coast, so that they might come to look upon it with great pride and feel that it belonged to them. It should assemble a large staff of experts and correlate and organize, on an area basis, all the available information about the Far East. Through such media as lectures, exhibits, motion pictures, and publications it should seek to develop an intelligent public opinion on Far Eastern affairs.

To be effective such an institute would have to be publicly

financed. The people of the West Coast would be suspicious of any privately supported organization. Far too much special pleading has been involved in the past in cultivating an understanding of the Far East. Today all such special pleading in relation to the Orient is looked upon with profound distrust. Considering the background of such men as the Reverend Sidney Gulick and the Reverend Frank Heron Smith, who would blame the Californians for ignoring all that they had to say about Japan and the Japanese people? Missionary spokesmen of this type only arouse additional antagonism on the West Coast. I have before me, at the moment, a copy of a pamphlet by the Reverend Frank Heron Smith entitled *The China-Japan Imbroglio* which is certainly an unblushing defense of Japanese aggression in the Far East. No organization after the pattern of the Japan Society; no spokesman such as Hamilton Holt or Lindsay Russell; no committees such as those established by the Federal Council of Churches, can possibly bring about a change in racial attitudes on the West Coast. In fact, no individual or organization suspected of having even a remote interest or stake in amicable postwar relations with Japan can contribute toward a broader understanding of the problems of the Orient on the Pacific Coast.

6. Remove the Racial Wall

Lastly, we need to bring the relocation program to the speediest possible termination. If it can be successfully concluded at an early date, such a conclusion can be pointed to with justifiable pride as an example of how democracy corrects its own mistakes. It can be pointed to as an example of how democracy converts a harsh wartime measure into an instrumentality for strengthening democracy itself. We do not need to apologize for the program as a "detour from democracy," for it has a strong democratic potential.

The damage which the program has caused to the fabric of democracy can be repaired. During the postwar period, for example, a claims commission can be established to pass upon the claims of the evacuees for damages suffered. There is ample precedent for such a procedure. The federal government has, on occasion, assisted the victims of natural disasters, such as floods, earthquakes, and fires. The volume of claims alone will require some such procedure. In many cases, WRA already possesses the information upon the basis of which losses might be estimated with accuracy. Many citizens have suffered economic losses as a result of the war and certainly the Japanese-Americans should not be accorded favored treatment. But to the extent that they have suffered special losses directly caused by the action of the federal government, they should be compensated.

In view of the changed military situation, the time has arrived when the ban on the return of loyal evacuees to the West Coast should be lifted. The Little Tokyo settlements have been destroyed; the colonies located around strategic installations have been removed; the disloyal elements have been ferreted out and are now isolated. Virtually every person of Japanese descent in the United States has been thoroughly investigated by the authorities. There is no longer a danger of an actual military invasion of the West Coast (although, of course, there is always a possibility of token raids). The Japanese have been removed from the Aleutians; Japan itself is now on the defensive. On the West Coast itself, the dim-out restrictions have been removed and many of the emergency measures taken after Pearl Harbor have been modified. Even in Hawaii, the restrictions imposed under martial law have been relaxed.

The ban on the West Coast should be lifted gradually, not only for the protection of the evacuees, but to guard against a possible mass return. Nisei soldiers are now permitted to return on furloughs; and the wives of Caucasians have been permitted to join their families. New categories should gradually be added to the list. For example, the wives of Nisei soldiers might well form the next category permitted to return to the Coast. Any lifting of the ban should be accompanied by emphatic statements from the proper federal authorities that inciters to racial hatred will be dealt with in the most vigorous manner and that the government will intervene whenever necessary to protect the civil rights of American citizens. Proper measures should likewise be taken to insure that the West Coast public is fully advised of the valuable contributions of the Nisei and the Issei to the war effort. If these measures are taken, there will be no rioting on the West Coast; there will be no violence.

If the ban were lifted it would assist in emptying the relocation centers; it would improve the morale of the evacuees; it would remove the shadow of suspicion that now hangs over the entire group. It would demonstrate to the world that a measure dictated by "military necessity" was changed the moment the military situation improved. It would eliminate the inconsistency of our policy as between the West Coast and Hawaii. The longer the evacuees remain in the centers, the more difficult it will be to relocate them. Dependency within the centers is growing at an alarming rate. Those evacuees still remaining in the centers should be encouraged to minimize property losses either by liquidating their holdings on the West Coast or by resuming their former vocations now that the military situation has changed. The essence of the argument in favor of lifting the ban at the earliest possible date has been stated by *Fortune:* —

> The longer the Army permits California and the rest of the Pacific Coast to be closed to everyone of Japanese descent the more time is given the Hearst newspapers and their allies to convince Californians that they will indeed yield to lawlessness if the unwanted minority is permitted to return. By continuing to keep American citizens in "protective custody," the U. S. is holding to a policy as ominous as it is new. The American custom in the past has been to lock up the citizen who commits violence, not the victim of his threats and blows.[10]

"With the segregation of the disloyal evacuees in a separate center," President Roosevelt stated on September 14, 1943, "the War Relocation Authority proposes now to redouble its efforts to accomplish the relocation into normal homes and jobs in communities throughout the United States, but outside the evacuated area, of those Americans of Japanese ancestry whose loyalty to this country has remained unshaken through the hardships of

[10] April, 1944, p. 118.

the evacuation which military necessity made unavoidable. *We shall restore to the loyal evacuees the right to return to the evacuated areas as soon as the military situation will make such restoration feasible.*" Now that the military situation has changed, the time has arrived when this solemn pledge spoken by the President in the name of the American people should be redeemed.

7. The Next in Order

In considering the future of racial minorities in the United States, one or two simple propositions should be kept constantly in mind. "It seems to me," wrote Dr. Robert E. Park in a recent letter to Horace Cayton, "that the Negroes and Americans who seek to be intelligent on the race question should realize that the people who have kept democracy in America are just the immigrants who have had to fight for democracy from the time they landed in this country seeking to get themselves established. The Jew is fighting for democracy. Jews and other people in this country are beginning to recognize that our cause is bound up with that of the Jew. The same thing is true of the Negro. Democracy is not something that some people in the country can have and others can not have, not something to be shared and divided like a piece of pie — some getting a small piece and some getting a large piece. Democracy is an integral thing. If any part of the country has it they all have it, if any part of the country doesn't have it, the rest of the country doesn't have it."

Not only have immigrants kept democracy alive in America, but they have given our culture its "world potential," which is perhaps the most important asset that we possess as a people. "I believe," wrote William Dean Howells, "we have been the better, we have really been the more American for each successive assimilation in the past, and I believe we shall be the better, the more American for *that which seems the next in order*." The racial minorities are the next in order.

CHAPTER IX

Epilogue

COMMODORE PERRY, as Mr. Willard Price has reminded us, thought of his expedition to Japan as the completion of the voyage of Columbus. As a matter of fact, however, it really represented the resumption of an earlier relationship. As traders in the South Pacific, the Japanese had come in contact with the Spaniards from the New World in the latter part of the sixteenth century. In 1610 Japanese embassies had proceeded to Mexico to study the conditions of trade with New Spain. The *Mayflower* had not yet arrived — the back door to the North American Continent was wide open. But the Japanese failed to take advantage of their opportunity and withdrew into the seclusion that prevailed until 1854.[1]

With the opening of Japan to Occidental influences, the isolation of the Pacific ceased to exist. The staggering significance of the event itself has been frequently noted but usually in mystical terms. It has been heralded as ushering into existence "a new phase in world history"; as bridging the gap between East and West; as creating the circumstances out of which a "marriage of East and West" might be consummated and mankind, at long last, united. It has provided the stuff for magnificently sonorous sentences: "The Pacific Ocean," said Seward, "its shores, its islands, and the vast region beyond will become the chief theater of the world in the world's great hereafter." "The age of the Pacific begins," wrote Frederick Jackson Turner, "mysterious and unfathomable in its meaning for our future." Behind such rhetoric, however, were realities that we largely ignored.

Victimized by the illusions of time and space, we looked backward over our shoulders to Europe rather than forward across

[1] See article by George Kennard in the *Outlook*, June 27, 1914; and, also, *History of California* by Charles E. Chapman, 1921, Chapter IV.

he Pacific to the Orient. In our minds the Pacific — "that great
ocean of hopes and dangers" — separated not merely two con-
inents, but two worlds forever destined to remain separate and
part. We failed to recognize that, in one sense at least, the Pacific
unites rather than separates the peoples around its rim. It is a
highway as well as a barrier; a bridge as well as an abyss.

Long before the appearance of the airplane, modern technology had shattered the illusions of time and space. Fast steamers
were plowing their way from Seattle to Yokohama in less time
than it took a Roman captain to sail from Gibraltar to Phoenicia;
in one fourth the time it took to cross the Atlantic in 1776; in
ess time than it took to travel from New York to Washington
in colonial days. On occasion Japanese fishermen, in ordinary
fishing boats, have drifted across the Pacific and landed in Oregon.
The completion of the Panama Canal, described by geographers
as the most important political and economic event in the history
of the Pacific, profoundly changed our relation toward the Far
East.

With the discovery of gold in California, a great process of
change was set in motion around the Pacific Basin. It was the
discovery of gold in California that prompted Commodore
Perry's fateful mission to Japan in 1854. The letter that he carried from President Fillmore stated that "California produces
about sixty millions of dollars in gold every year, besides silver,
quicksilver, precious stones, and many other valuable articles" —
new wealth that we were anxious to use as the basis of trade.
The rapidly developing clipper trade between California and
China made it imperative that our ships put in at Japanese ports
for repairs and provisions — still another circumstance mentioned
by President Fillmore. The discovery of gold in California and
the opening of Japan to Occidental influences were, in fact, historically simultaneous and closely related events. "The extension
of California commerce, made suddenly important in consequence of the recent discovery of gold, was the chief argument
used with Japan in our successful effort to open the gates that
Iyeyasu had barred." [2]

[2] *The Japanese Crisis* by James A. B. Scherer, 1916.

It was the westward expansion of the American people that eventually initiated the significant movement of Japanese from their island empire. From 1683 to 1854, it had been an offense punishable by death for Japanese to emigrate. The building of all ocean-going boats had been prohibited by imperial decree to make certain that Japan would preserve its rigid policy of isolation. Even after the overthrow of the Tokugawa Shogunate in 1867, this policy was modified only to the extent of permitting students to go abroad. Although some two hundred Japanese students were enrolled in American schools, colleges, and universities in 1875, Japan still adhered to its policy of isolation.

With the conclusion of the Reciprocity Treaty of 1876 between Hawaii and the United States — which opened the islands for American capital — the sugar interests of Hawaii began to clamor for Japanese labor. As early as 1868 these interests had "piratically stolen" 147 Japanese for plantation labor in the islands. Most of these initial immigrants, however, were returned to Japan in response to a sharp note of protest. The execution of the Reciprocity Treaty was followed, in 1886, by the adoption of the Hawaiian-Japanese Labor Convention. It was this agreement that, for the first time, "officially opened the doors for the emigration of Japanese laborers to the outside world."[3] Under the terms of the agreement approximately 180,000 Japanese were sent to Hawaii — the largest single body of workers that Japan sent to any land. This development was a direct consequence of our westward expansion. When we annexed the Hawaiian Islands in 1898 and later acquired the Philippines, we pushed that much farther westward and came into still more intimate contact with the peoples of the Orient.

Just as it was the discovery of gold in California that started the first movement of Orientals — the Chinese — to the Western Hemisphere, so it was the annexation of Hawaii that launched the first major movement of Japanese to the mainland of the United States. Prior to the annexation of Hawaii, there were only 2039 Japanese on the mainland. The annexation of Hawaii had the effect of releasing thousands of Japanese contract laborers

[3] *An Island Community* by Andrew W. Lind, 1938.

from a kind of feudal bondage. For years prior to 1898, the breach of a labor contract had been a punishable offense in the islands. When this provision of the penal law was lifted after annexation, thousands of Japanese laborers began to escape to the mainland. By 1900 there were 24,235 Japanese in this country; by 1910, 72,157.[4]

As a nation we seemed incapable of grasping the fact that it was our westward expansion that had brought about this returning tide from the Orient. When the current of change which our appearance on the Pacific had set in motion reached the Orient and then reversed its direction, our amazement was complete and our resentment instantaneous. The Pacific Coast became our racial frontier. We proceeded to establish a racial picket line which was gradually extended from Alaska to Peru. Long after the physical isolation of the Pacific Basin had been broken, we insisted on the maintenance of a policy of cultural and racial isolation.

In much the same manner, we closed our eyes to the problem of cultural conflict which the opening of the Pacific had precipitated. For around the Pacific Basin were cultures in every imaginable stage of evolution. Long isolation had created the sharpest cultural differences. Increased travel, communication, and trade only aggravated the conflicts and tensions inherent in the disparity of these cultures, for, as so frequently happens, cultural change lagged behind technological advancement. Given the added fact of racial difference, it was inevitable that the ensuing cultural conflicts should have been rationalized, on both sides of the Pacific, as essentially racial in character. These conflicts still exist. They would continue to exist, in an aggravated form, even if we were to deport every man, woman, and child of Japanese ancestry in America. For the conflict precipitated by the appearance of Japanese immigrants on the West Coast is but one phase of a much larger pattern of adjustment and change taking place in the Pacific.

[4] On the effect of annexation on immigration to the mainland, see *Rising Japan* by Jabez T. Sunderland, 1918, pp. 142–143.

1. Japan and America

It would be difficult to imagine a more fundamental conflict of cultures than that which existed in the case of Japan and America. The highly homogeneous culture of Japan had been organized around the factors of a scarcity of resources and limitation of space; the heterogeneous culture of America upon an abundance of resources and unlimited space. The one culture was old, the other new; the one static, the other dynamic. From food habits to religious practices, from language systems to social customs, they were antipodal. Japan and America, wrote Carl Crow, are "two countries which in history, ideals, civilization, and culture have nothing in common." Neither country, he noted, could "without danger to itself, adopt the ideals and culture of the other."

Both the earliest and the latest American observers in Japan echo the same preoccupation with the utter contrast between the two cultures. From Percival Lowell to Helen Mears, from Lafcadio Hearn to Miriam Beard, the story is the same and the conclusion identical. "For to the mind's eye," wrote Percival Lowell in 1888, "their world is one huge, comical antithesis of our own. What we regard intuitively in one way from our standpoint, they as intuitively observe in a diametrically opposite manner from theirs. To speak backwards, write backwards, read backwards, is but the a, b, c, of their contrariety. The inversion extends deeper than mere modes of expression, down into the very matter of thought. Ideas of ours which we deemed innate find in them no home, while methods which strike us as preposterously unnatural appear to be their birthright." [5]

"One of the supreme contrasts to American civilization on the globe," wrote Miriam Beard, "is Japan. . . . She presents a powerful opposite to all we have seen or thought before. Her civilization rests on a foundation which is the antithesis of our own. The American way of living is a synthesis of European cultures, modified by vast natural resources and fabulously in

[5] *The Soul of the Far East.*

306

creasing wealth; it is the speediest, most flamboyant, most democratically comfortable. Japan's peculiar culture edifice, on the other hand, is a composite of Asiatic elements; it is supported by the most restricted natural resources behind any of the leading Powers . . . when the American returns from a sojourn in Japan he looks at his native land as if reborn. Everything from political conventions down to the custom of eating with knives and forks seems to require a revaluation." [6]

When Japan began to take over and readapt to her own uses some of the aspects of Western culture, the problem of cultural conflict in the Pacific was immediately magnified. It was this partial and one-sided fusion of cultures taking place in Japan that, some years before his death, began to alarm Lafcadio Hearn. During the fourteen years of his residence in Japan (1890–1904), he produced twelve books interpretative of Japanese life and custom. In the later chapters of this monumental record, he had occasion, again and again, to express his profound forebodings about what was likely to happen in Japan. [7]

The conflict precipitated by the immigration of Japanese to the western shore of the Pacific was but one phase of the deep-seated conflict which Hearn observed in Japan. The persistence of the struggle on the West Coast and the uses that were made of it — on both sides of the Pacific — should long ago have been recognized as an obvious warning of the vastly greater struggle in which we are now involved. When cultures so diverse are suddenly brought into intimate contact, and when the factor of racial difference also exists, hatred and hostility, fear and aversion, create a chasm which cannot be bridged by pious platitudes, missionary endeavors, or the exchange of products. "The day of the completed world is dawning," wrote Paul Valéry, "and henceforth there will be an ever more bitter conflict between the habits, emotions, and affections contracted in the course of anterior history and strengthened by immemorial heredity, by culture." The danger to the future peace of the Pacific

[6] *Realism in Romantic Japan*, 1930, p. 13.
[7] See *Japan: The Warnings and Prophecies of Lafcadio Hearn* by William V. Clary, April, 1943, No. 5, Claremont College Oriental Studies Series.

arises not by reason of the fact of cultural difference, but as a result of the tendency to rationalize this difference in terms of race.

2. Inside Japan

The story of Japan's remarkable transformation after 1854 has been frequently told. It was a favorite success story during the latter part of the nineteenth century. Taken at face value, it certainly demonstrated the ability of Eastern peoples to absorb and to master Western industrial technics in the span of a single generation. But of recent years, and particularly since December 7, 1941, it has become the fashion to rewrite this story. Today we are told, with increasing frequency and unanimity, that Japan took from the West only those phases of its culture which she needed in order to protect her own institutions and way of life from disintegration. So widely prevalent is this point of view at the moment that we run a distinct risk of overlooking our unique points of strength and Japan's peculiar weaknesses.

Shocked by the turn of events since December 7, 1941, we are belatedly searching the archives for a clue to the strength that Japan has shown. Our few Oriental scholars have been brought forth from their obscurity and assigned the task of deducing the character of "the Japanese mind" from the tenets of Japanese philosophy.[8] When these scholars report that Japanese philosophy is not based on logical concepts, as we understand them, and that they can throw but little light on the problem, we revive the myth of Oriental inscrutability and conclude that we can never understand the enemy. In much the same fashion, we conclude apropos of 70,000 American citizens of Japanese ancestry, that "a Jap's a Jap" and consign the entire lot to relocation centers. Both conclusions — the stated inability to understand the mind of the enemy or to distinguish one resident Japanese from another — indicate a definite weakness on our part and, at the same time, an ability to ignore realities that is truly alarming.

Years ago Thorstein Veblen provided us with the real clue to

[8] See "The Japanese Mind" by Karl Lowith, *Fortune*, December, 1943.

he strength (and weakness) of Japan as a nation. His attention
vas focused not on Japanese philosophy, but upon the cultural
onflict going on inside Japan. Writing in 1915, he predicted the
uture course of Japan with uncanny accuracy: —

It would of course be hazardous [he wrote], to guess how
long an interval must necessarily elapse between Japan's
acquirement of the western state of the industrial arts and
the consequent disintegration of that "Spirit of Old Japan"
that still is the chief asset of the state as a warlike power; but
it may be accepted without hazard that such must be the
event, sooner or later. And it is within this interval that
Japan's opportunity lies. The spiritual disintegration has already visibly set in, under all the several forms of moderniza-
tion, but it is presumably still safe to say that hitherto the
rate of gross gain in material efficiency due to the new scientific and technological knowledge is more than sufficient
to offset this incipient spiritual disintegration; so that, while
the climax of the nation's net efficiency as a political or warlike force lies yet in the future, it would seem at least to lie in
the calculable future.

. . . If this new-found efficiency is to serve the turn for
the dynastic aggrandisement of Japan, it must be turned to
account before the cumulatively accelerating rate of institutional deterioration overtakes and neutralizes the cumulatively declining rate of gain in material efficiency; which
should, humanly speaking, mean that *Japan must strike*, if at
all, *within the effective lifetime of the generation that is now
coming to maturity* . . . the imperial government must
throw all its available force, without reservation, into one
headlong rush; since in the nature of the case no second opportunity of the kind is to be looked for.

And here is what Veblen had to say, in this remarkably pro-
phetic essay, about the mysterious "Japanese mind": —

. . . As soon as her people shall have digested the western
state of science and technology and have assimilated its spiritual contents, the "Spirit of Old Japan" will, in effect, have
been dissipated. Ravelings of its genial tradition will still trail
at the skirts of the new era, but as an asset available for the

enterprise of dynastic politics the "Spirit of Old Japan" will have little more than the value of a tale that is told. There will doubtless continue to float through the adolescent brains of Young Japan some yellow vapor of truculence, such as would under other skies be called *el valor espanol*, and such as may give rise to occasional exploits of abandon, but the joy of living in obscure privation and contumely for the sake of the Emperor's politics and posthumous fame will be lost to the common man.[9]

"Life under the conditions imposed by the modern industrial system," wrote Veblen, "is in the long run incompatible with the prepossessions of mediaevalism." Japan, as he clearly demonstrate elsewhere in the essay, is no exception to this rule. The mere introduction of a competent system of internal and external communications had doomed "the isolation, parcelment, and consequent home-bred animus of its people." The introduction of popular education and of the workday habits of an industrial society comported ill, as he phrased it, "with those elusive putative verities of occult personal excellence in which the 'Spirit of Old Japan' is grounded." The spread of such matter-of-fact information would "unavoidably act to dissipate all substantial belief in the opera bouffe mythology that makes up the state religion and supplies the foundation of the Japanese faith in the Emperor's divine pedigree and occult verities; for these time-worn elements of Shinto are even less viable under the exacting mechanistic discipline of modern industry than are the frayed remnants of the faiths that conventionally serve as articles of belief among the Christian peoples."

A wealth of evidence has accumulated since 1915 to support this thesis. It was the "incipient spiritual disintegration" which Veblen noted that, in its more advanced stages, threw Japan in D. C. Holtom's phrase, "into an introverted psychosis of national proportions." After 1930 the rulers of Old Japan realized that they must act swiftly if they were to capitalize upon the op-

[9] From "The Opportunity of Japan" in *Essays in Our Changing Order* (copyright 1934 by The Viking Press, Inc.), pp. 255 and 265 (my emphasis) By permission of The Viking Press, Inc., New York.

portunity which Veblen granted that they possessed. They acted precisely as he predicted that they would act and within the time that he had estimated. A state of "crisis" was precipitated in Manchuria and continuously maintained; the whole apparatus of the state was utilized in an effort to stem the tide of Western influence. Demonic spirits were summoned from the murky past to stamp out the contaminating and infectious Western practices.

If additional proof of the accuracy of this thesis is required, it is available, in living form, in the ten relocation centers. For the cultural conflict that has raged in Japan for the last several decades has been resolved in America in a manner that can be appraised, examined, and documented. "Far from being impervious to educational processes," writes Miriam S. Farley, "the Japanese are one of the most teachable peoples on earth. The very thoroughness with which they have been indoctrinated with a false and vicious creed demonstrates their susceptibility to propaganda. The extreme type of chauvinistic nationalism which grips Japan today is, in fact, the recent product of one of the most comprehensive and efficient propaganda systems which the world has ever known. . . . Here in America we can see the results produced by another kind of training in the space of one generation. We have in this country several thousand persons of Japanese ancestry who were born and brought up in the United States. They attended American schools; they read American books, magazines, and newspapers. Their tastes, habits of thought and political ideas are the same as those of any other group of American citizens. They are good democrats and good Americans." [10]

If we fall into the trap of assuming that the Japanese are an incomprehensible people, we shall not be able to fight them intelligently, much less to live with them in a postwar world. If we continue to believe that a nonindustrial people can adopt Western industrial arts and techniques without, in the long run, also adopting the ideas that are inescapably a part of such a system, we shall have committed ourselves, in advance of peace, to a disastrous policy in the Far East. If such an assumption were cor-

[10] *Far Eastern Survey*, April 19, 1943.

rect, it could then be argued that it was our duty to prevent the spread of industrialism in the Orient.

The extent of American influence in Japan completely refute such an assumption. Japanese immigration to America was par alleled by the penetration of American influences in Japan. The rulers of Japan feared this "invasion of ideas" as much as our native sons feared the "Japanese invasion" of the West Coast In no small measure, Japanese immigration contributed to the spread of American ideas in Japan. The students who had stud ied in America, the Nisei who went to study in Japan, and the returning immigrants, all were carriers of American cultura influences. The thousands of Japanese who had relatives in America were at least emotionally involved in the same process. We had a remarkable influence in Japan — an influence that may ye prove to be a prime military asset.

The ordinary rank-and-file citizens that Carl Randau and Leane Zugsmith met in Japan, even during the height of the officially inspired anti-American campaign, were warm and friendly toward America. "They like American movies, American slang American baseball. *They like their American relatives.*" [11] "America," according to G. C. Allen, "has had a profound influence on the manners and general outlook of the younger people of the cities. . . . Many serious-minded young men with a libera political outlook are favourably disposed toward Americanization because it stands for individual freedom and is hostile to their oligarchial system of government. The films, the American magazines, American business men, tourists, missionaries and school teachers, Japanese business men who visit America and students who are trained there, and, finally, *the Japanese born in America* all help to spread the new way of life." [12] Jim Marshall, writing in *Collier's* for October 19, 1935, pointed out that there was a section of the younger generation in Japan that "speak American read and write American, laugh at Yankee jokes, love American movies, dote on cafeteria food, imitate Hollywood fashions dance to American jazz and trifle with Manhattan cocktails."

[11] See *The Setting Sun of Japan*, 1942, Chapter 9; italics mine.
[12] *Japan: The Hungry Guest*, 1938; italics mine.

While it is only a detail, still the fact that a thousand or more English words have been incorporated in the Japanese language is some measure of this influence. It would be extremely foolish, of course, to overestimate the extent of our influence in Japan; but it would be equally foolish to forget that it does exist.[13]

3. The Nisei in Japan

A few observers have long recognized the importance of the Nisei in America in terms of the future of Japan. Jim Marshall once wrote that the Nisei on the West Coast held the key to the future of Japan. In an editorial in June, 1941, *Common Sense* pointed out that they should be "feted and honored as living proofs of the universality of America rather than feared." What we tend to overlook is the curious "two-way passage" involved in the West Coast Nisei problem. The Nisei problem has existed, in fact, for the last two decades on *both* sides of the Pacific. If the Nisei constitute a problem for us, they constitute a similar problem for Japan. In this section I propose to tell something about the Nisei who went to live in Japan, reserving for the following section the story of those who went to Japan to study, or to live for a time, and then returned to America (the Kibei).

Because of the age level of the Nisei on the West Coast, only a few were living in Japan in 1922. The number steadily increased during the following years, reached a peak around 1935, and then began to decline. The bulk of the Nisei originally went there to study, usually at the insistence of their parents in America; but a few went to live in Japan as a matter of deliberate choice. Writing in the *Great Northern Daily News* of January 1, 1940, Edward Chishi voiced the sentiments of this latter group: —

There are two choices [he wrote]. One is living in America and own a small business, purchase a car, and live a comparatively easy life, besides benefiting from the abun-

[13] See comment by Carl J. Friedrich, in *American Journal of Sociology*, March 1944, p. 427: "Institutionally speaking, Japan is considered to have progressed farther toward democratization than China."

dance of food, clothing, and shelter. The other choice is to return to a country of poverty, of limited land, of over-population, and of a low standard of living. Here, the food prices are high, and the quality of the expensive clothing is poor. Lawns are seldom seen, as every inch of land is utilized for the production of food. Automobiles are a millionaire's luxury, and they don't fully enjoy this privilege, as car fuel is terribly expensive. After careful consideration, I am inclined to choose the latter choice. Why? Just for an equal opportunity for success if my ability warrants it. At least I will have a fighting chance for success, whereas in America it's like pounding one's head against a stone wall and expect the wall to break. Others possessing far superior ability than mine have tried to break the wall and have failed, and I feel that I would learn from their experience.

For years some variation of this debate echoed on the West Coast: were the chances better in Japan than in America? For what type of individual? With what training? All manner of advice was given the Nisei: by their parents; by the community elders; by Nisei already in Japan; by their American friends and sponsors. This debate was merely another phase of the conflict they faced in their homes and in the communities in which they lived. After 1937 the Japanese government began to encourage the Nisei to visit the homeland of their parents: by special propaganda; by offering cheap tourist rates; and by dangling various inducements before them. "We cannot urge too strongly," wrote Yuki Sato, a consular agent, "the advisability of as many as possible of the young people of the second generation crossing the Pacific to the shores of Nippon to study first-hand the Japanese conditions, traditions, culture and institutions." [14]

The number of Nisei in Japan, as might be expected, constantly fluctuated. From 1920 to 1940, movement back and forth across the Pacific was more or less continuous. At one time, however, it was estimated that there were 16,340 American-born Nisei in fourteen of the forty-six prefectures of Japan, with a total number in Japan probably in excess of 20,000.[15] An American Citizens

[14] *Great Northern Daily News*, January 1, 1940.
[15] *Rafu Shimpo*, December 12, 1929.

League had been formed in Wakayama, Japan; and there existed in Tokyo an organization known as the Ria Club (raised in America) made up of Nisei girls. Many of the Nisei in Tokyo lived in a section of the city that had come to be known as Little Tokyo, after the settlement in Los Angeles.

The Nisei have always been misfits in Japan. In a study of 1141 Nisei living in Tokyo and Yokohama,[16] it was found that most of the Nisei were antagonistic to the general scheme of things in Japan. They were critical of the school system; of the customs; of the dominant ideas; of the food; and of the mode of living. Many of them — particularly the Nisei girls — expressed a strong desire to return to America. For most of them, the language difficulty was as serious a problem as it had been for their parents in America. While stating that they had moved to Japan to escape the race prejudice that existed on the West Coast, they also stated that they had encountered a variation of the same prejudice in Japan. They were, for example, definitely set apart from the general population. The study refers to them as being "Japanese in features, American in ideas." Generally speaking, they were regarded as a dubious lot in Japan and were suspected by the authorities of harboring "dangerous thoughts."

While this study was prepared by Nisei in Japan, a wealth of testimony by disinterested observers confirms the same conclusions. Mr. Willard Price has reported that many Nisei discovered that they were out of place in Japan; that they were disliked because they were "different"; and that any number of them had returned to America "full of resentment toward their own people." John Patric met a young Nisei in Japan who complained to him that "the Japanese call us Americans, and the Americans call us Japs." He reported that he was constantly being spied upon in Japan and that his every movement was noted by the police. This particular Nisei disliked Japanese food; moaned over the absence of good coffee; and charged the Japanese with being "filthy" and "dirty" in their habits. "Which would you rather be?" Patric asked this Nisei. "American," was the reply; "you'll

[16] *The Nisei: A Study of Their Life in Japan*, published by the Nisei Survey Committee of Keisen School, Tokyo, 1939.

never find an American-born Japanese who, after he's seen the Japs, doesn't prefer the United States." [17]

"Most Nisei," report Carl Randau and Leane Zugsmith, "went to their parents' homeland in the period of 1935 to 1938. They went there to study Japanese culture and language or to find better jobs than they could get in prejudiced America. Some merely paid visits and some planned never to leave. At the end of 1938, there were about 1,500 Nisei in Tokyo and Yokohama, and they were not accepted as true Japanese." [18] "They're too individualistic," one Japanese manufacturer reported. "They can't *learn* filial piety and loyalty to the Emperor or, for that matter, our total-family system, no matter how hard they study. I do not hire Nisei. The food doesn't suit them, the winter doesn't suit them, they expect central heating. And they don't suit me. My employees must do only what they're literally told to do. Nisei want to learn everything that's going on and make suggestions about what they think they've learned in the United States. They may look Japanese to you. They don't to me."

Commenting on this statement, Randau and Zugsmith observe: "They did look Japanese to us, but they did not act Japanese. Their blood was pure Japanese; they were not Eurasians; their environment and, in many instances, their tastes were Western." In Japan they seemed to have improved their social, but not their economic, position. The Nisei girls, in particular, reported that they found it difficult to adjust themselves to "the debasing standards of etiquette for Japanese women." Many of them were preparing to return to America. As a group they are reported to have been critical of Japanese customs, Japanese living standards, and the censorious attitude of the Japanese. Only one small group among the Nisei in Japan were, in the judgment of these reporters, a danger to the United States: those employed in the Foreign Office.

As trade between the United States and Japan began to decline after 1940, many Nisei returned to this country and others were planning to do so when war broke out. Since December 7,

[17] See Chapter VII, *Why Japan Was Strong*, 1943.
[18] *Op. cit.*

316

1941, virtually no information has been available about the Nisei who were trapped in Japan. Max Hill has reported that they were being forced to relinquish their American citizenship and that many were being inducted into the Japanese army. Subsequent reports indicate that individual Nisei were putting up a courageous fight to retain their American citizenship.[19] Captain Paul Rusch, an American repatriated from Japan, reports that the Nisei "are being closely watched and checked almost daily by the government. Many have been placed in internment camps under conditions similar to those of the enemy nationals. The government will not allow the Nisei to leave Japan." [20]

As a group, the West Coast Nisei never had an active interest in Japan. Dr. Edward K. Strong, Jr., who made quite elaborate studies of the Nisei in California in 1934, concluded that "practically none expressed a desire to go to Japan." Even those who had visited in Japan were not enthusiastic about the land of their parents. "I felt out of place in Japan," one Nisei told Dr. Strong. "Everything seemed so strange to me. I was really afraid to go about alone because I could not read the signs and I was afraid I would get lost. The Japanese also made comments about me. They commented on my dress and my ways. . . . The modernness of the capitol surprised me, but like a true Angeleno, I compared everything I saw with some corresponding thing in Los Angeles and said to myself: 'We can beat that in Los Angeles.' "

Satoko Murakami, born in California, spent fifteen years in Japan. While there, she writes, "I felt a heavy fog in front of me. I began to wonder why the people had such a poor life in the darkness, burning their nails to live on. I could find no explanation in the Japanese school, where traces of feudalism still had a large influence. There was no relationship between school learning and the social life of man. The teachers did not dare explain, even if a student raised questions, which was seldom, for he knew his name would be put on the black-list." [21] "One has to go to some forsaken cluster of mud-houses like Bavabnusu

[19] See *Pacific Citizen*, January 28, 1943.
[20] *Gila News-Courier*, December 16, 1943.
[21] *Common Ground*, Spring, 1942, p. 15.

in North Manchuria," remarked Larry Tajiri, "before he realizes that a spot in the Lil' Tokyos of America looks pretty good — whether that spot is a two-bit job in a fruit stand, out in the hot fields, or behind the counter of a back street shop." [22]

The *Pacific Citizen* of June, 1938, contained the following quotation from an article which had originally appeared in the *Japan Chronicle* of Kobe: —

A Tokyo professor engaged in the education of American-born Japanese has made the discovery that the mental attitude of these pupils raised almost insuperable difficulties in the way of their proper instruction in the traditions of their forefathers. It is not, of course, a new discovery. It is made every now and then, in varying circumstances, but somehow never ceases to astonish. In the present case it is pointed out that American-born Japanese, unlike second or third generation Nisei in Hawaii, persist in looking at the Sino-Japanese crisis with American eyes. Even worse, many of them cannot think of the Far East except from the Chinese angle, and the professor has confessed himself at a loss as to how to bring his charges over to the Japanese way of thinking.

I know of no more graphic demonstration of the attitude of the Nisei toward Japan, in prewar days, than the following quotation from an article by Tani Koitabashi, which appeared in the *Pacific Citizen* for November, 1933. It was written in Tokyo on the eve of departure for America: —

Sailing time! The outward-bound *President Jackson* trembles impatiently at her moorings like a leashed greyhound eager for the chase. The cannonade rumbles of the winches are silenced and from the deck to shore is one colorful mass of serpentines. People making a last-minute rush for the gang planks, tear-blurred eyes, smiling faces. It is time to say goodbye.

From the inner bowels of the ship issues a deep-throated roar that scatters pell-mell the sea-gulls sunning themselves on the glistening white outer breakwater, and as the echoes

[22] *Pacific Citizen*, April, 1936.

roll and re-echo over the busy harbor and the green bluff, it seems joyously to say:

Sayonara, Japan, I am going home. Farewell, O nation of age-old traditions, of Bushido and the "way of the gods" — struggling with the perplexing inadequacies of modernism; where a coalition government fails to coalesce and politics is still in its rompers stage; where the uniform is a badge of superiority and gold-teeth a sign of affluence.

Good-bye Fujiyama, peerless of mountains, farewell, Biwako, lake of perfection. I am going to a land where the mountains are higher and the scenery more vast; where the lakes are bluer and the waters more serene, and not so over-emphasized. Good-bye Ginza, street of imposing exteriors and barrack-like interiors; where modern fronts hide shanty-town "back doors" and where "the great white way" is dark at eleven, avenue of much promise and little realization. Good-bye Tokyo, I am going home.

Good-bye to garret-like apartment houses and match-box homes, to high-walled gates and foot-square gardens. I am going to a land of spacious gardens. I am going to a land of spacious mansions and palacious pent-houses, where windows look far out over the city as from a mountain peak; where baths are taken individually and not collectively, and are a glory to the plumbers' art; where suburban gardens run into each other without hedge or fence, and are a thing to be seen, not hidden.

Gomen-nasai to bulky and unsatisfactory meals; and heaped-up rice bowl and the byproducts of the prodigal bean, the "tofu" the "shoyu," and the insipid, uninspiring "miso-shiru." Farewell, O anemic coffee, you deserve a better fate, and "ton-Katsu," half-brother to the pork cutlet. I am going to a land of sublimated viands, of thick-wedges of apple-pie and the juicy steaks on the plank; where asparagus is harvested from the field and not from a tin, and lettuce is a whole-meal instead of a garnish; of "scrunchy" celery and the melting melon; the five-layer cake with its inch-thick chocolate frosting.

Good-bye, Tempura.

Good-bye, O land of contradictions, where the soda bottles pop down instead of up; where theater box offices offer reductions at premiers instead of demanding a premium, and choice seats are in the balcony instead of the five-row aisle, where baggage cars usurp the section where fancy-priced "observation pullmans" should be; where self-deprecation is virtue and bluffing a sin. Good-bye, — Topsy-Turvy Land.

Farewell, to "salary men" whose sole incentive in life is semi-annual bonuses and a pension twenty years hence; whose pay day is pay-out day, leaving little or nothing. Good-bye to dimly-lit, grotesquely furnished, "joku" cluttered cafes where coffee is seldom served; where food is mostly liquid and the price is out of line; where noise is usually unconfined and joy is unrestrained; where "service" is a by-word but commensurate with the tip. Farewell, O Land of the Sun, I am going home.

I am leaving you for a far-off land where they believe all Japanese are inherently honest and always polite; to a place where all Japanese women are judged by Madame Butterfly standards and considered very cute; where it is smart to wear happy coats and artistic to clutter up mantel shelves with bric-a-brac of the "yomise" variety. Good-bye Nippon, and again, Good-bye.

I am going back to a people who are your best friends and yet who keep antagonizing you; who are always trying to understand your view-points and admire you. . . . Sayonara, gokigen — but who usually end up by misunderstanding you; who wish you well, yo. I long for America, Farewell!

Some of the Nisei in Japan have unquestionably gone over to the Japanese. A few of them hold responsible positions in the government and are taking a leading part in the war. The editor of a Japanese magazine published in China is a Nisei graduate of the University of Southern California. Herbert Erasmus Moy, a graduate of Columbia University, is reported to head Japanese radio propaganda. Some of them are serving in the Japanese armed forces. Clark Lee in *They Call it Pacific* has told of meeting a Sergeant Matsui who had been born in Southern California. "People would not accept me as an American," he told Lee; "because I look Japanese. So I went to Japan and they put me in uniform." Unquestionably Nisei are fighting under different flags in the Southwest Pacific today. The evidence would indicate, however, that the bulk of the Nisei who were trapped in Japan on December 7, 1941, are either in concentration camps or under close surveillance. When news stories mention Nisei serving in the Japanese armed forces or working in the government, they sometimes confuse Japanese who have studied in this country with Japanese born in this country; in many cases, the facts are not known.

4. The Kibei

There is still another level of cultural conflict involved in this weirdly complicated transpacific drama. If the Nisei are a problem in Japan, the Kibei are a special problem in America. The Nisei who have studied in Japan and then returned to America are known as Kibei (meaning, "returned to America"). There are about 9000 Nisei now in America who received part of their education in Japan. A sample study made in 1942 indicates that 72.7 per cent of the Nisei have never been in Japan. Of the 27.3 per cent who have been in Japan, 14.4 per cent received no schooling there, having gone merely as visitors; but 12.9 per cent received some education in Japan.

While the Nisei are distrusted in Japan, the Kibei are distrusted in both America and Japan. Not only are they especially distrusted here, but their own people view them with some suspicion. Kibei have been returning to this country, a few every year, for the last twenty-five years. Some Kibei served in the American Army in the First World War. Those who returned some years ago are, in general, quite well-adjusted. They are indistinguishable from the other Nisei. But those who have returned of recent years are, in many cases, products of a profound cultural confusion. The transition from America to Japan and from Japan to America has usually been effected during their most impressionable years. Many Kibei had no more than returned to America when they were interned in the relocation centers. They thus found themselves involved in a genuinely harrowing experience before they had had time to readjust themselves to American life. Many of the Kibei who have caused trouble in the relocation centers belong to this category.

In the history of American immigration there is no more complex story than that presented by the Kibei. With the sharp contrast between Japanese and American culture in mind, consider the anomalous position of the Kibei: raised by Japanese parents in America, partially educated in Japan (where they were ostracized and made conscious of a sense of difference), and then re-educated in America, where, in the eyes of many American-born Japanese as well as of most other Americans, they were regarded with suspicion and distrust. A recent report of the WRA on the Kibei appropriately refers to them as "a new immigrant group." Their return to America was an experience not altogether different from that of their parents who came to this country as an original immigrant group. The problem of the Kibei has endless complications. Often it was only the eldest child who was educated in Japan. Thus the Kibei, in most cases, is isolated from his own family by sharp cultural differences. Not only has he lived apart from his family during his most impressionable years, but he has been educated in a very different culture from his brothers and sisters. The Kibei have been aptly characterized as a minority within a minority.

The other side of the story — of the Japanese who have studied in America — cannot be documented. But thousands of Japanese have received a major part of their education in America. The Japanese-Student Christian Association, in its report for 1940–1941, indicated that there were 190 Japanese students enrolled in American colleges and universities in some twenty-six states. These students who have studied in America are a part of the "American problem" in Japan.[23]

5. The Jews of the Orient

One of the great risks that we run in this war is that the Pacific conflict may become, in Mr. Hearst's phrase, "a War of Oriental races against Occidental Races for the Domination of the

[23] See *Restless Wave* by Haru Matsui, 1940.

World." [24] It is not surprising to find that this view of the Pacific war so steadfastly advocated by Mr. Hearst and the Fight-Japan-First elements should be quoted with approval in Berlin and Tokyo.[25] For this is exactly the interpretation that Japan seeks to place upon the war in the Pacific.

Not only is the risk grave but its realization is dangerously possible. According to Mr. Menefee, only half of the American people feel that the Japanese government is our major enemy and not the people of Japan. In the case of Germany and Italy, three fourths of the American people hold the Nazi and Fascist governments, rather than the German and Italian people, responsible for the war. One third of us would oppose sending any food to Japan after the war, while only one sixth would take such a stand in the case of Germany. Only 39 per cent of the American people would allow Japan to join a postwar union of nations.

As Mr. Menefee points out, this feeling is primarily racial and it is strongest on the Pacific Coast. What is genuinely alarming is that this feeling may be gauged by the related feeling toward the evacuees. That people can confuse their hatred of Japan — even of the Japanese people in Japan — with their feeling toward 70,000 American citizens with Japanese faces indicates the dangerous extent to which race feeling has risen since the war.

So far as I know no one in America advocates a "soft" or a "negotiated" peace with Japan. But there are important segments of our population who feel that every liberalization of the WRA program represents "appeasement" of Japan. "As a native Californian born of native Californians," writes a woman in the *Los Angeles Times* on February 7, 1944, "I have felt keenly on this reprehensible subject, the liberation of the Japanese within the United States. Whoever started this vicious movement could not possibly have ever lived among the treacherous little grinning yellow beasts. Altruism cannot possibly be entertained toward these sons of hell. It is high time that the busybodies who prate about our 'Christian responsibilities' are silenced." I could match this quotation with nearly a hundred similar "letters to the

[24] *Los Angeles Examiner*, March 23, 1943.
[25] See *Assignment: U. S. A.* by Selden Menefee, 1943, p. 285.

editor" clipped from the West Coast press during the last year.

It would not take much, in the way of additional instigation and incitement, to unleash a furious popular hatred of the evacuees that would convert them into the most helpless and abject pariahs imaginable. They could easily become our modern "untouchables." Scattered over the country, lacking even the strength which internal solidarity gave their West Coast settlements, they could be singled out for attack, discrimination, and persecution. If the race bigots have their way, all the evacuees will be rounded up, before the war is terminated, relodged in concentration camps (not relocation centers), and deported to Japan at the end of the war. This possibility is closely related to a possible fate which may be in store for the Japanese people throughout the world.

On several occasions in the past the Japanese have been referred to as "the Jews of the Orient." Because anti-Semitism has become so closely identified with Nazism in the eyes of the American people, the Jew could scarcely be made the "ideal" scapegoat of a fascist movement in America. But the resident Japanese could be made the ideal "internal enemy," as, indeed, they already are on the West Coast. Substitute the "bucktoothed, slant-eyed, bow-legged Jap" for the "hook-nosed, grimy Jew," and you have created a symbol against which much of the accumulated hatreds (racial and otherwise), and all of the pent-up fury, of some sections of our population might easily be directed. Speaking in San Francisco recently, Sinclair Lewis shrewdly observed: "If fascism ever comes to California, its campaigns of racial hatred will be directed not at the Jews but at the Orientals."

The future peace of the Pacific unquestionably requires the destruction of Japanese militarism. The Japanese military machine must be completely destroyed and every vestige of fascism must be obliterated — at whatever cost, sacrifice, and suffering. But there is a difference between this type of defeat for Japan and the one recently conjured up by a well-known war correspondent when he said that Japan must be fought "until not alone the body but the soul is annihilated, until the land is plowed with salt, its men dead, and its women and children divided and lost among other people." If we permit the war in the Pacific to become a racial conflict then we may well have succeeded, better perhaps than we can now realize, in making the Japanese "the Jews of the Orient." For an undemocratic policy toward postwar Japan could make of the Japanese a nation of peddlers and hucksters and could result in a Far Eastern Diaspora that would make the wanderings of the Jew look like a minor pilgrimage in time and space. Today Japanese are already scattered over a fairly wide area: they are in South America, the United States, Canada, and throughout the Pacific. Like the Jews, the Japanese are a proud and gifted people; like the Jews they have shown a remarkable chameleon-like talent for adaptation; like Israel, Japan stands between two worlds.

The nation must realize that the foundations for the Second Pacific War are being systematically laid in California today. Recently a Los Angeles editor has been advising his public that we should take our time about defeating Japan. We shall need, he argues, a vast postwar military establishment. Popular sentiment will be against such an expensive undertaking. Therefore, we must keep the war going in the Pacific; and we must continue to harp upon "the grave national peril from the 1,000,000,000 people of the Orient." [26]

It is precisely this unreasoning, groundless, stupid fear of colored races that we must guard against. "When I consider," writes Mr. Ferner Nuhn, "the depths of fear out of which has come our action in the evacuation and detention of our people of Japanese descent, and the degree of unbelief it represents in our own ideas, I have forebodings not only as to our usefulness in the evolving of a world culture, but of our survival as a culture in the world. In numbers this group is one of the 'leasts' among us. In significance it is one of the most important. Our ability to be faithful in this 'least' is a test not only of sincerity but of fitness. How can we suppose ourselves ready to bring freedom and security to hundreds of millions of Asiatics when we have shown ourselves incapable of maintaining the minimum rights of a hundred thousand citizens of Oriental ancestry at home?"

[26] *Los Angeles Daily News*, October 14, 1943.

6. The Real Weakness of Japan

While it is the current fashion to scoff at the suggestion that we have any "liberal" allies inside Japan and to discount the belief that there ever existed in Japan a movement that might fairly be characterized as a liberal movement, nevertheless some of the outstanding experts on Japan have constantly reminded us not to forget the existence of these allies.[27] One may even share the current misgivings about liberalism in Japan, however, and still remain convinced that there is a distinct possibility of a social revolution in Japan.

The peculiar factors involved in the Japanese economy which point to the possibility of an internal upheaval were carefully analyzed by Freda Utley in 1937, and her analysis is more persuasive today than when it was written.[28] In 1937 Miss Utley was convinced that Japan was "as politically and socially unstable and as near to revolution as was the Old Russia." Within the last few months, reports reaching the United States from the Far East suggest at least the possibility that Japan is threatened with internal collapse.

In an interview with Walter Rundle of the United Press, March 24, 1944, General Ho Ying-Chin, China's War Minister, suggested the possibility of an early internal collapse and pointed out that the Japanese were, in his opinion, more vulnerable on this score than the Germans. One of the most significant news stories of 1944 — although it was generally ignored in the press — was the announcement of the formation of a Japanese People's Liberation Front in communist-occupied China and the issuance by Shushumu Okano, a Japanese communist, of a manifesto calling upon the Japanese people to revolt.

The recent dispatches of Israel Epstein, Chungking corre-

[27] See "Liberalism in Japan" by Sir George Sansom, *Foreign Affairs*, April, 1941; "Our Allies in Japan" by Harry Paxton Howard, *Commonweal*, October 9, 1942; and "Our Allies Inside of Japan" by William Henry Chamberlin, *Common Sense*, November, 1942.

[28] See the chapter entitled "The Imminence of Social Revolution" in *Japan's Feet of Clay*.

spondent for *Allied Labor News,* call attention to the fact that in 1941, Japan was shaken by a series of major strikes: at Kobe, in April, 1941 (a strike said to have involved 100,000 workers); at Nagoya in August; at Kokura in September; and in Taurumi in October.[29] In a dispatch from London dated March 24, Frederick Kuh pointed out that two of Japan's leading newspapers admitted the suppression of food riots in Kagoshima, the liquidation of the Japanese Farmers' Union, and the issuance of decrees disbanding the new Shakai or Workers' Party that had held a mass meeting in Ueno Park in Tokyo in 1942 attended by over 40,000 people. At this same meeting, some thirty-seven people were killed by the police. Among those arrested in the suppression of the food riots was one Mitsuhashi, a member of the Diet.[30]

Japan has long been overripe for a social revolution and now, with military defeat looming on the horizon, the likelihood of a revolutionary upheaval cannot be dismissed as unthinkable. Communist influence was widespread in Japan during the years from 1918 to 1930; and, as the Okano manifesto clearly shows, this influence has never been wholly extirpated. The narrow basis of the Japanese economy does not afford opportunities for the ruling class to make concessions of a reformist nature without jeopardizing their own position. Faced with a rising tide of unrest, these same classes plunged the nation into a state of crisis in 1932 in large part as a desperate attempt to avert an internal upheaval. The people of Japan will hold these classes responsible for the war. The prominence given the Okano manifesto in the communist press indicates that Soviet Russia is well aware of the revolutionary potential in Japan and that its policy in the Far East is governed, in large part, by the belief that, even before Japan suffers final military defeat, an internal collapse will occur.

* * *

The considerations briefly outlined in this epilogue have been advanced with one thought in mind: to place the relocation program in proper perspective; to suggest its relation to what has

[29] See *PM,* March 24, 1944.
[30] See summary of the Epstein stories, *PM,* February 6, 1944.

been going on in Japan and what is likely to happen in Japan; and to point out its relation to what is happening throughout the Pacific. We are in danger today, as in the past, of permitting a fog of prejudice to obscure our relationship to the momentous developments which now impend in the Pacific. A new world is coming into existence in the Pacific, a world of which our West Coast is an integral part; a world which we have ushered into being. The distant peoples and diverse cultures of the Pacific Basin have been brought into the closest possible intimacy. In the past, time and space have served to minimize some of the conflicts arising out of this new meeting of peoples and cultures in the Pacific. In the future, these conflicts are likely to increase in scope and in complexity. The first step toward a mastery of the conflicts involved is to understand their true character and this understanding we can never achieve so long as race prejudice is capable of blinding us to the most transparent realities.

Recently Donald Culross Peattie forwarded to *Time* (April 10, 1944) a letter which he had received from a captain in the Army Air Force who is now flying a Liberator in the Central Pacific and who wears the Air Medal with Oak Leaf Cluster. "I want to tell you," writes the captain, "what a group of us officers and enlisted men have been talking about tonight. Though we have done a good job of killing the enemy, I find no sign of an organized hate in any of our men. . . . Our men come closer to hating those at home who break faith with us at the fronts — the shirkers, the profiteers, those who bicker in Washington over our rights. . . . To the last man our group is not in accord with what some people in the states are trying to do with some American citizens, namely the Jap citizens. We say, if they step out of line of faithfulness to our country, punish them severely. But don't touch one of them just because he has Japanese blood. We are fighting for all American citizens, and when we die for them we don't stop to ask what kind of blood they have. We are fighting for the sacred rights of man; we don't want them toyed with behind our backs."

INDEX

Index

331

337